THE
EVERYTHING®
BREAD COOKBOOK

Dear Reader,

There is only one thing better than the smell of fresh-baked bread, and that's smelling it in your own kitchen.

Homemade bread is the most satisfying food a cook can create. The process is empowering, the method is stress relieving, and the result is the definition of comfort. But sadly, few people bake bread anymore. Why should they? With artisan bakeries on every Main Street, and a plethora of mediocre grocery store breads at the ready, there is really no need.

But if you're an adventurous cook, and you dare enter the realm of yeast bread, a multitude of glories await you. Bread bakers reap benefits, not only of a gastronomical nature, but of an intellectual and spiritual nature as well.

So if you're a lover of good food, and you enjoy cooking, you're in the right place. You will delight in this collection of recipes, which includes not only the classic staples, but a repertoire of artisan, off-beat traditional, and artfully unique recipes. The explanations are simple, and the results are impressive. But beware! Once you start baking bread, you'll be hooked.

Happy baking,

Leslie Bilderback, CMB

Welcome to the EVERYTHING® Series!

These handy, accessible books give you all you need to tackle a difficult project, gain a new hobby, comprehend a fascinating topic, prepare for an exam, or even brush up on something you learned back in school but have since forgotten.

You can choose to read an Everything® book from cover to cover or just pick out the information you want from our four useful boxes: e-questions, e-facts, e-alerts, and e-ssentials.

We give you everything you need to know on the subject, but throw in a lot of fun stuff along the way, too.

We now have more than 400 Everything® books in print, spanning such wide-ranging categories as weddings, pregnancy, cooking, music instruction, foreign language, crafts, pets, New Age, and so much more. When you're done reading them all, you can finally say you know Everything®!

QUESTION

Answers to common questions

FACT

Important snippets of information

ALERT

Urgent warnings

ESSENTIAL

Quick handy tips

PUBLISHER Karen Cooper

DIRECTOR OF ACQUISITIONS AND INNOVATION Paula Munier

MANAGING EDITOR, EVERYTHING® SERIES Lisa Laing

COPY CHIEF Casey Ebert

ACQUISITIONS EDITOR Katrina Schroeder

ASSOCIATE DEVELOPMENT EDITOR Hillary Thompson

EDITORIAL ASSISTANT Ross Weisman

EVERYTHING® SERIES COVER DESIGNER Erin Alexander

LAYOUT DESIGNERS Colleen Cunningham, Elisabeth Lariviere, Ashley Vierra, Denise Wallace

Visit the entire Everything® series at *www.everything.com*

THE EVERYTHING®

BREAD COOKBOOK

Leslie Bilderback, CMB

Avon, Massachusetts

mw

*This book is dedicated to Bill, Emma, and
Claire. Together, you are my bubbling yeast.
Without you, life would be flat and flavorless.*

Copyright © 2010 by F+W Media, Inc. All rights reserved.
This book, or parts thereof, may not be reproduced
in any form without permission from the publisher; exceptions
are made for brief excerpts used in published reviews.

An Everything® Series Book.
Everything® and everything.com® are registered trademarks of F+W Media, Inc.

Published by Adams Media, a division of F+W Media, Inc.
57 Littlefield Street, Avon, MA 02322 U.S.A.
www.adamsmedia.com

ISBN 10: 1-4405-0031-2
ISBN 13: 978-1-4405-0031-2
eISBN 10: 1-4405-0032-0
eISBN 13: 978-1-4405-0032-9

Printed in the United States of America.

10 9 8 7 6 5 4 3 2 1

Library of Congress Cataloging-in-Publication Data
Bilderback, Leslie.
The everything bread cookbook / Leslie Bilderback.
p. cm.
Includes bibliographical references and index.
ISBN 978-1-4405-0031-2 (alk. paper)
1. Cooking (Bread) 2. Bread. 3. Cookbooks. I. Title.
TX769.B55   2010
641.8'15—dc22   2010027240

*This book is available at quantity discounts for bulk purchases.
For information, please call 1-800-289-0963.*

Contents

Introduction

IN THE OLDEN DAYS, if you didn't know how to make bread, you went hungry. It was an essential element of life, like drawing water from a well. Although progress has advanced technologies in many wonderful ways, it has all but eliminated the need for many of the ancient household arts, including scratch baking.

Cooking in general has suffered in the age of fast food and TV dinners. Skills that were once passed on from mother to daughter must now be self-taught. But no cooking discipline has suffered quite like baking. The air of precision and aura of chemistry surrounding it has scared away even the most able professional chefs.

But there is a secret about baking: It's not that precise, and it's not that hard. In fact, it is no harder than making a sandwich, as long as you understand the process. But it is the process that scares people away. Consequently, bread bakers have become a rare breed. We feel, and are treated, like the medieval keepers of a sacred knowledge. But, as you are about to discover, the sacred knowledge is not complicated. In fact, bread-making techniques, so long shrouded in mystery and complexity, are actually super-easy. After reading this book, you should feel empowered to get back into your kitchen, break out the measuring cups, and create something delicious.

Creative and inquisitive people are rediscovering the joy of bread making at home. With motivating factors like this book, the Food Network, bread machines, and cooking classes, Americans are remembering their culinary roots. Kids are getting in on the act, too. Even though most schools have done away with the Home Economics class, instruction is frequently offered to them in community centers, youth groups, and afterschool programs. All hope is not lost!

This book has two distinct functions. First, in Chapter 1, it explains the process of making bread. Unless you already have some experience with bread making, do not skip that chapter. Learning about the basics first will clear up all your questions, and put you at ease with the entire process. Second, and perhaps more important, there are hundreds of recipes to try. Each one is different, but they are also the same. It is the similarities that bring appreciation. As soon as the baker identifies the common threads of each recipe, it is only a matter of time before his or her own ideas start springing forth.

So, welcome, fellow bakers, to the bread club. You'll definitely find your membership agreeable, if not downright inspiring.

CHAPTER 1

Bread Basics

Grain is the most important food a human can eat. It has the essential nutrients that keep the human body humming: carbohydrates, protein, and fiber. About 4,000 years ago, man came up with an ingenious way to consume grain. He made bread.

The Main Ingredients

There are not many ingredients in bread, but everything included has a vital importance. Understanding what works, and why, will help your creative juices flow and assist in troubleshooting if problems arise.

Flour

Flour is the most important ingredient in bread making. It provides the structure (or "crumb") of the bread, and most of the bread's nutritional value. The grain most commonly used is wheat. Although other grains are used, wheat alone contains enough essential gluten proteins to make bread production possible. Typical flour production involves cracking the grain and separating the different parts: bran, germ, and endosperm. The endosperm contains gluten.

Gluten proteins have unique properties that can change the consistency of a dough. When moistened and agitated through kneading, the gluten proteins tighten and elasticize. As a dough is kneaded it changes from a lumpy, goopy mess to a smooth, tight ball. The elasticity that develops allows the dough to rise. As the gasses build up during fermentation, the dough stretches, and because of the gluten, the dough is strong enough to trap the gasses inside.

Other grains, such as rye, millet, buckwheat, and oats, also contain gluten proteins, but not nearly enough to create such a strong elastic form. For this reason, breads made with these flours must contain at least 50 percent wheat flour.

Most flour today is made by finely grinding the endosperm, enriching it with nutrients, and bleaching it white. There are also many alternatives to standard white flour, including unbleached, whole grain, and organic flours.

Bread Flour

The most common flour for bread making is bread flour, also called high-gluten flour. The hard winter wheat in this flour is bred to have higher levels of gluten protein.

All-Purpose Flour

All-purpose is most commonly found in American kitchens. It works for bread too, but is not ideal. The protein content is lower than that of bread flour, balanced by an equal amount of starch. All-purpose is sometimes used in the beginning of bread recipes that require longer fermentation, taking advantage of its higher starch content as food for yeast.

QUESTION

Can bread be made without bread flour?
All-purpose flour works fine for bread, but it isn't perfect. You can approximate the gluten protein of bread flour by adding gluten flour or vital wheat gluten, at the rate of 1 teaspoon per cup of all-purpose flour.

Whole Wheat Flour

Another member of the wheat flour family is whole wheat. White flour production removes and discards the fibrous bran and nutrient-rich germ, leaving only the inner endosperm, which consists of starch and gluten proteins. Whole wheat flour retains the bran and germ and essential nutrients we need for good health. Most large flour production facilities make white flour first, then mix the bran and germ back in to create whole wheat. Stone-ground flours grind the whole grain and keep the flour parts together through the entire process. Wheat bran and wheat germ are also available separately to add into breads, enhancing flavor and nutrition. Graham is a similar whole grain wheat flour, with a slightly nuttier flavor. White whole wheat flour is made from a light-colored variety of wheat.

Specialty Wheat Flours

Wheat flours such as semolina, spelt, and kamut can be added to bread recipes to enhance flavor, texture, and nutritional value. However, these grains do not contain gluten in sufficient quantities for use as the sole grain, and must be combined with wheat flour (preferably bread flour) to make a proper loaf.

Cake, Instant, Self-Rising, and Gluten Flours

Cake flour, which has a high starch content and a very low amount of protein, is rarely used for bread. It is reserved for delicate pastry recipes that require a tender crumb.

Unless a recipe specifies their use, stay away from instant flour (Wondra), which is similar to cake flour in its high starch content, and self-rising flour, which has baking soda and salt added for leavening. Gluten flour, also known as vital wheat gluten, is an additive used to increase the protein content in recipes. A small amount can be added to bread machine recipes, or to all-purpose flour as a substitute for bread flour.

Yeast

Yeast is the one ingredient that makes bread taste like bread. That characteristic yeastiness is the fragrance we smell as we pull our loaves out of the oven. But more important, without yeast, our loaves would be less like bread and more like hockey pucks.

ALERT

Read the package! Most yeast can be stored at room temperature until it is opened, but once the vacuum seal is broken it needs refrigeration.

Yeast is a living organism that occurs naturally in the air all around us, and comes in different varieties. Yeast feeds on carbohydrates, and it prefers an environment that is warm and moist. When all the conditions are right, the yeast will feed and produce two byproducts, carbon dioxide and alcohol. Baker's yeast produces more carbon dioxide, while brewer's yeast produces more alcohol. The accumulating alcohol is harder to detect in baking, but the longer the fermentation, the more the alcohol accumulates.

Bubbling foam on the surface of the mixture shows that the yeast is working. As the carbon dioxide accumulates, the gluten proteins in the dough stretch, and the dough rises. The better the conditions, the more carbon dioxide is created, and the more the dough will rise. Easily absorbed carbohydrates, like sugar or honey, get to work quickly. Starches need more time to convert into sugar, so the process is slower.

Yeast Maintenance

Because yeast is alive, it can be killed. This happens eventually in the oven, but it can happen prematurely if care is not taken.

The first danger yeast encounters is water temperature. Warm water is recommended to get the yeast started, but anything over 110°F will kill it. Some bakers use a thermometer for precision, but a normal sense of touch works too. You should be able to easily hold your finger in the warm water. That will make it slightly above body temperature (98.6°F). If you can't handle it, the yeast can't either.

Salt can also kill yeast. Bread needs salt for flavor, and a touch of salt keeps the fermentation process in check. Bread with no salt will erupt in fermentation, as in Italy's Tuscan White Hearth Bread (page 34). But adding too much salt, or letting the salt come into direct contact with the yeast, will drastically retard the fermentation process to the point of stopping it.

Sugar can also have a slowing effect on yeast. Excessive sugar added directly to the yeast sends it into a feeding frenzy, and leaves little fuel for later in the fermentation process. When a dough is sweet, the increased amount of sugar must be added in stages, so as not to shock the yeast.

Choosing Yeast

The recipes in this book call for active dry yeast, which is the most readily available yeast in markets today. There are other options, however. Quick-rise yeast is fed large amounts of phosphorus and ammonia, which speeds its activity by 50 percent. Instant yeast is coated with ascorbic acid and sugar for immediate activation. Bread machine yeast is covered in ascorbic acid and flour for easy absorption, and can used interchangeably with active dry for most recipes.

Compressed yeast, also known as fresh cake yeast, is the yeast preferred by professionals. It is perishable, and if refrigerated, will hold for about a week. It may also be frozen for several months, although the consistency will change once defrosted.

Similar in constancy to a block of cheese, fresh yeast is more easily measured by weight, which is preferred by production bakers. But more important, fresh yeast has a superior flavor. It can be used instead of active dry (.06 ounces is equivalent to .25 ounces active dry) in the recipes in this book. Small cakes of yeast are available refrigerated in some markets, although they are often cut with cornstarch. The cornstarch accelerates fermentation, but results in a product with less flavor. If you are interested in baking with fresh yeast, try buying a 1-pound block from a local artisan baker. To store, cut it into sixteen cubes and freeze loose in a zip-top bag. Pull out ounce-sized blocks as needed.

Water

In order for the yeast to absorb nutrients, water must be present. Water can be straight from the tap, bottled, filtered, or purified. Milk, juice, tea, coffee, and eggs are commonly added in place of all or a portion of the water needed.

Many bakers insist on a certain type of water, based on taste and desired outcome. If your tap water tastes good, it is perfectly fine to use. If you are concerned about the mineral content, use a filter. Some bakers are known to import tap water from certain cities for authenticity.

Many recipes call for water to be at a certain temperature, the optimal temperature that promotes fermentation. However, fermentation takes place even when water is cold. Cool temperatures retard fermentation, but they do not halt it until a dough is frozen. For this reason, bakers can slow down production by making a dough in the evening, letting it rise slowly overnight in the fridge, and forming and baking it the following day. Bakers agree that if time allows, a longer rise is preferable, because more fermentation produces more flavorful bread.

Salt

The number one reason that salt is added to any type of recipe is flavor. Salt also plays a chemical role in baking yeast bread. Salt retards the process of yeast fermentation. This happens because salt attracts water. Remember that water is a necessary component of yeast fermentation. When water is attracted to the salt, there is less available for the yeast. Most dough can withstand salt up to about 2 percent before the effect becomes detrimental.

Salt also helps toughen gluten by helping bond protein molecules. Salt inhibits enzymes that soften protein, essentially protecting the gluten protein from destruction. Dough made without salt will be noticeably slack or mushy, and its fermentation will be rapid and unstable. Bread made without salt will have less structure, and a bland, overly yeasted, overly fermented flavor.

Too much salt will prevent the yeast from feeding, causing little rise, if any. The dough's texture will be tight, and flavor will be too salty to eat. The right amount of salt for optimal outcome is also the precise amount needed to make bread taste good.

ESSENTIAL

Most professional bakers use kosher salt for its superior flavor, which is less metallic and less "salty" than standard iodized table salt. Don't bother using fancy gourmet salts in dough recipes. Their subtle flavors will be lost in a sea of yeast. Save them for the top of breads, where they give a burst of flavor at first bite.

Sugar

Sugar makes five major contributions to bread dough. It is food for the yeast, flavor for us, and it promotes tenderness, preserves crumb, and gives the bread a nice color.

Sugar is the preferred source of food for yeast, because it is easiest for the yeast to consume. There are other sweeteners that contain glucose, and also work well as a sweetener and yeast food, including honey, date sugar, agave syrup, cane syrup, and maple syrup. Professional bakers use barley malt, a syrup (or powder) that has a unique flavor, and although it is half as sweet as sugar, the sprouted grain contains enzymes that convert the barley starch to sugar necessary for fermentation. Sugar is also converted from the starch in flour, which takes a little longer.

Sugar, like salt, attracts water. This effect is evident in the moistness of a sweet bread, and its shelf life. The ability to hold water keeps the bread moist days longer than a sugar-free bread. The effect of holding water also means that excessive amounts of sugar will inhibit fermentation by keeping the water away from where it needs to be. In bread recipes with a large amount of sugar, it must be added in stages to prevent disruption in fermentation.

When sugar is cooked, it caramelizes. This effect also occurs inside a dough, and is evidenced in the color of a crust. If two bread recipes are made identically, but one is made with sugar and one without, the crust of the sugar-free dough will be noticeably pale. It takes a surprisingly small amount of sugar to brown a crust, which is why most recipes contain at least a teaspoon or two. But sweet dough, with double or triple that amount, will be noticeably darker.

Sweeteners vary in their sweetening strength and caramelizing properties. Cane or beet sugars, which include granulated, brown, turbinado, and powdered, are half as sweet as honey. Date sugar, agave, and sugar substitutes don't caramelize in the oven. Substitutions may take a little experimentation for best results.

Fat

Fat moistens the bread, tenderizes the crumb, and prolongs the shelf life. A lean dough (fat-free dough), such as French bread, will begin to stale as soon as it cools, and will last less than a day before its drying texture becomes noticeable. Rich dough (dough with fat) remains soft and moist for twice as long.

Fat slows fermentation. Oily dough is heavier, which limits the stretch of the gluten and prevents large pockets of carbon dioxide from forming during fermentation. The absence of large bubbles of gas results in the absence of large holes in the finished bread crumb. Bread with a tight crumb is preferred for recipes such as sandwiches and canapés because it holds in the fillings.

Fat and oil are interchangeable; both produce the same effect on the crumb of the dough. The flavors, though, vary greatly. Neutral oils, like vegetable, salad, and canola, are good substitutes for butter. Olive oil has a strong, fruity flavor that is not always appropriate.

Fat is added into bread dough in several forms, including butter, milk, cream, sour cream, cheese, nut butters, and eggs. Recipes will specify how a fat is to be added, which is usually after the yeast is proofed, but before the main quantity of flour is added. It is not necessary to liquefy a solid fat before adding it. Mixing and kneading will add enough friction to warm the fats to liquid state, making them easily absorbed by the flour.

Techniques for Success

The ingredients are important, but if you don't know what to do with them, your chances of success are limited. One cannot simply throw everything listed together in a bowl. The proper order of mixing and kneading is key for professional outcomes.

Mixing

In this book, ingredients are always listed in the order they are to be used. One exception is when an ingredient is added in more than one stage. This usually occurs with sugar, as too much should not be added in the beginning, or it will retard fermentation. In those instances, such additions are clearly noted, ". . . add 1 tablespoon sugar," and later, ". . . add remaining sugar."

Mixing should be done in a large bowl, to prevent overflows. The initial mixing can be done with your tool of preference, but for ease of cleanup, a simple dinner fork is the best tool. Spoons do not incorporate ingredients enough, and a whisk only works well until flour is added, at which time the dough clumps into the center of the whisk. As soon as the dough holds together, the mass should be turned out onto a lightly floured work surface for kneading.

Kneading

Kneading is the most important step in bread making. This is the stage when the gluten is created, and the dough becomes capable of holding the carbon dioxide that is built up during fermentation. There are many ways to knead. The key is to keep the dough moving around the table. It must be well agitated. Some bakers fold and press; others lift and slap; others roll and drop. As long as it is kept moving for 8–10 minutes, any method will work. As the dough is kneaded, it may be necessary to add more flour.

Kneading with Electric Mixers

An electric standing mixer can do the work for you, but the best machines are those with a corkscrew-shaped hook. The angled screw shape encourages the dough to slide off and slap the edge of the bowl with each rotation. Machines with a fishhook-shaped attachment are more likely to grab the dough and hold on to it, spinning it around, but not actually agitating it. Regardless of the hook style, it is important to monitor the kneading periodically to be sure adequate agitation occurs. This may require stopping the machine and scraping the dough off the hook from time to time.

The Right Consistency

When dough is kneaded, it transforms from a slack, lumpy dough to a tight, smooth one. This transformation is key to the outcome of your bread. After 10 minutes the dough should be tight and elastic, and should spring back into shape when poked or stretched. If it does not, rest the dough for 5 minutes and check it again. It is possible to over-knead (although it is difficult to do by hand). The over-kneaded dough looks much like the under-kneaded dough, lumpy and rough. The difference is that the over-kneaded dough will feel tight, not slack.

Kneading and Flour

The yeast bread recipes in this book may list flour as the last ingredient, and most measurements are given as a range, such as 4–5 cups. This is because bread baking is an inexact science, and the amount of flour a particular recipe will require depends on several variables, including human error.

Air temperature, ingredient temperature, humidity, measurement accuracy, and the type of flour and its manufacturer contribute to the amount of flour a recipe will take on any given day. There is only one sure way to know how much is enough, and that is by looking and feeling. The dough should be smooth and soft, but not sticky, and not so tough that it's hard to knead.

To make a loaf of bread successfully, it is necessary to reserve the last cup of flour called for, and to add it slowly, a little at a time, as the dough is kneaded. Let each addition work in completely before determining if more is necessary. The dough should be moist and soft, but not sticky. Adding a little flour at a time prevents the over-addition of flour, which makes dough tough and hard to knead, and results in a dry finished product. Sometimes a recipe will require more than what is called for, sometimes less. That's what makes baking so exciting!

Fermentation

Once the dough is kneaded, it must be put up to rise, or double. This step is called fermentation, and it is when the yeast begins feeding and consequently releases carbon dioxide. If you've kneaded properly, that gas will be trapped within the dough, and the bread will rise.

QUESTION

What's the difference between proofing and fermenting?
They are the same thing. The dough is set aside to develop carbon dioxide gas through yeast feeding on carbohydrates. The terms are used interchangeably, but most professional bakers consider fermentation the main rise, when the bread doubles in volume. The proof is the final short rise just before baking.

Certain things control fermentation. Yeast likes warmth, so the more warmth you provide (up to about 100°F), the faster the yeast will create gas. Conversely, if you want to slow down the fermentation, you can remove warmth. Therefore, the placement of the rising dough has everything to do with controlling the speed of fermentation. Set in a sunny window or near a warm oven, and the dough will double in about an hour. Stored in the refrigerator, the dough will rise slowly, over a period of 8–10 hours. The slower, chilled method is ideal for busy cooks who may not have time to make a dough from start to finish in any one day. Fermentation stops completely below 32°F, which makes the freezer a great place to store dough for extended periods. Defrost frozen dough in the fridge for even results.

Forming

Before a loaf can be baked, it must first be formed. Each recipe in this book includes a suggestion for form, but most doughs can easily be made in a variety of shapes.

There are two key points to remember when forming a loaf. First, the dough should be tight, smooth, and free of air pockets. This is achieved by rolling, flattening, and folding as the dough is formed. The more a dough is worked, the tighter and more elastic the gluten will become. Second, the forming should be done fairly quickly, because as long as the dough is unbaked and unfrozen, fermentation will continue. As the dough sits, gasses build, gluten relaxes, and the loaf will lose its shape.

If the form is not to your liking, the process can easily be repeated, but the dough must rest for about 5 minutes first. Resting relaxes the gluten, allowing for more gas to build up, thus softening the dough and making it easy to form once again.

The Baking Processes

In the heat of the oven, several events take place. They do not happen simultaneously, but slowly, each peaking at certain temperatures.

Gas Expands

The first noticeable change is the expansion of gasses. A loaf will puff up quickly, within a few minutes. This effect is known as "oven spring." In yeast breads, carbon dioxide expands through the fermentation process. In quick breads, carbon dioxide expands too, but it is created by chemical leaveners (baking soda or baking powder). In soufflés and sponge cakes, air expands during the whipping of eggs. This expansion pushes the dough up and raises the bread until the proteins solidify and form a crust.

Proteins Solidify

When proteins solidify they react just like an egg in a hot frying pan, changing from something soft to something firm. This change creates the structure of bread as we know it. Heat causes the chains of amino acids to tighten, altering the overall structure of the protein. The most common proteins present in bread include gluten, egg, and dairy proteins.

Sugars Caramelize

Heat melts sugar and turns it brown in a process called caramelization. The higher the heat, the faster the caramelization takes place. This is not always a good thing, because the crust shouldn't brown before the interior is cooked. Therefore, oven temperature should be adjusted in accordance with the size of the loaf that is being baked. Rolls can be baked at high temperatures, because heat will penetrate quickly, usually before the crust caramelizes. In a large loaf, more time is required for the heat to penetrate to the center and cook. Unless the temperature is lowered, the crust will be well-browned long before the loaf is ready.

Fats Melt

Fats melt and liquefy in the oven, which allows them to be absorbed. If butter is not fully incorporated, either by accident or on purpose, it will melt away, leaving an air pocket.

Care should be taken when fermenting rich doughs. Fats start melting with very little heat, and if the dough gets too warm, the fat will run out of it, resulting in a greasy dough that is much harder to form into a loaf. Loss of fat also makes the bread less delicious.

Water Evaporates

Water evaporation in a loaf of bread is most easily observed by the weight of the finished product. A properly cooked loaf will be noticeably lighter in weight after baking because the water has evaporated. The hollow sound we listen for when determining whether a loaf is done is the echo from the hollow spaces that were once filled with water.

Water evaporation is also apparent in the making of biscuits and other recipes that use the cut-in method. Butter contains a large percentage of water. Because the butter in a cut-in dough is left in small chunks, the evaporation of its water creates steam that pushes up the dough, creating little pockets of air and a flaky texture. The same effect occurs in flaky pie dough and in puff pastry.

Starches Gelatinize

Oven heat causes starch to gelatinize. Just as cornstarch can thicken a sauce, natural starch in flour will thicken when moistened and heated. The starch is the part of flour that is not gluten protein, which means that there is abundant gelatinization in everything baked with grain. This thickening plays a major role in creating the texture of the finished crumb. Starch gives structure while remaining flexible and soft. Without starch, bread would be hard and tough.

Bread Production

The best made dough in the world is worthless if it isn't baked properly. Luckily, baking is the easy part. There are many different methods used to bake breads. Pans, temperatures, shapes, and oven moisture all affect the final outcome.

Crusty Breads

For crisp-crusted, artisan-style breads, there are two main factors: temperature and steam.

Temperature

The higher the temperature, the bigger the oven spring (initial expansion of gasses) will be. Standard home ovens heat to 500°F, but the impact of that heat can be increased with the use of tile. Tile and stone hold the heat, and, depending on the placement of the tile, focus that heat toward the loaf. A loaf is slid directly onto the tile surface, which has been preheated in the oven. The dough is formed and proofed on a wooden paddle, called a peel, which is first coated with cornmeal. When the dough is ready to bake, the loaf is slid off the peel onto the tile.

Some oven walls are completely surrounded with tile or stone, which is ideal. It is possible to purchase stone inserts for your oven that intensify the heat and focus it toward your loaf. But even a simple piece of terracotta tile from the hardware store will greatly improve your loaf over those cooked on a baking sheet.

Steam

Steam is the second element crucial to crusty bread production. It produces thinner, crispier crusts with a deeper golden brown coloration. The addition of steam to an oven softens the outer skin of a loaf, allowing it to stretch further during oven spring, thus producing a thinner crust. At the same time, the moisture liquefies the starch on the outer surface, allowing it to convert quickly to sugar. This additional sugar gets crispy, and is more evenly caramelized, creating a pleasing crust color.

Professional ovens have steam injection, which allows the baker to pump steam directly into the oven. This is a rare feature in home ovens, but there are several ways to simulate a steam injection. The dough can be misted with water as it goes into the oven, and again every 10 minutes, until coloration begins. This method works well, but the baker must be vigilant. Another option is to place a pan of water at the bottom of the oven, which slowly fills the oven cavity with steam. For quick burst of steam, toss ice onto a pan at the bottom of the oven.

Doneness

Recipes provide a cooking time, but the actual time it takes to completely bake a loaf can vary tremendously. The size of the oven, the size of the loaves, the thickness and material of the pans, recipe accuracy, ingredient variation, and the number of items in the oven at one time all affect the time required. The only sure way to judge doneness is by sight and feel.

ESSENTIAL

Knowing when a loaf of bread is ready to come out of the oven is made easier with the help of a thermometer. Choose an instant-read thermometer that can be calibrated by hand. Test its accuracy by measuring the temperature of boiling water, which should be 212°F, or 100°C (assuming you are at sea level). If the temperature is off, you can adjust the needle with the simple turn of a screw.

A finished loaf should be golden brown in color. It should also feel lighter coming out than it was going in, and make a hollow sound when thumped.

The internal temperature of a bread can be taken to determine doneness as well. Insert an instant-read thermometer into the thickest part of the loaf. The internal temperature should be in the range of 200–210°F when cooked through.

Tools of the Trade

Although it is possible to spend a fortune on fancy baking equipment, it is not necessary. There are only four pieces of essential equipment: a bowl, a fork, a pan, and an oven. However, there are hundreds of variations on those simple elements from which to choose.

Pans

Most breads can be baked on a simple baking sheet. In the professional kitchen these pans are called sheet pans. They are made of heavy aluminum, and have a ½" lip. These pans are indispensable to a baker, and are used for just about everything.

ALERT

Regardless of the type of pan chosen, the dough should always be placed into it seam-side down. This means that when the loaf is formed, the smooth, tight, seamless side of the dough should face up, and any rough, folded, or pleated skin should face down into the pan. The weight of the dough on these seams keeps them from opening up in an unattractive way.

Some breads require a loaf pan, and the market is flooded with a plethora of pans from which to choose. Heaviest is best, made from glass, ceramic, thick aluminum, or cast iron. These materials hold and spread heat evenly, and reduce the chance of a burned crust. Thin baking pans will cause bread to burn, especially when used for breads that require long baking times. The same criterion applies to muffin pans.

Professional bakers have several pans that are virtually unknown in the home kitchen, but are available to anyone through specialty purveyors (see Appendix B). The perforated baking sheet is made of aluminum and punched with several tiny holes. The holes let heat through the pan, allowing for more heat to surround the bread as it bakes. This is important in professional ovens that are stacked full, each rack holding a full pan of bread. When baking on solid baking sheets in a full oven, heat does not get to the center pan with equal measure. If a home baker plans to bake large quantities, perforated pans should be considered.

Some chefs use baguette pans, often perforated, which look something like a pleated or folded baking sheet, with a groove for each loaf. The shape is rounded to promote a rounded baguette. These pans are not necessary if the dough has undergone proper kneading and forming, but for large batches, it helps to ensure uniformly shaped loaves.

Parchment Paper

Parchment is an indispensable tool in any bake shop. It serves many purposes, including preventing baked goods from sticking to pans. Used as a pan liner, parchment not only eases removal of the finished product, but also promotes even browning and uniform texture of the crust. In addition, parchment extends the lifetime of bakeware. Lined with paper, the pans do not come in contact with ingredients. If they did, these ingredients would burn in the oven, leaving the pan with a coating of oil and carbon. These deposits weaken the pan, as does the excessive scrubbing needed to remove them. In addition, pans left with food deposits will warp, bend, and buckle in the oven where heat flow is interrupted.

Parchment is also useful for wrapping and storage. It is frequently used by professionals to hold ingredients, and can be formed into a cone for decorating.

Baskets

Europeans have long used cane baskets, called *banneton* or *brotformen*, to ferment bread. They promote an even, uniform shape, and encourage the loaf to grow in a bowl shape, which is higher and rounder than a loaf proofed flat on a baking sheet. Dusted with flour, the cane leaves a decorative impression on the proofing breads. Some of these baskets are lined with linen, which needs less flour to prevent sticking. Breads are turned out of the baskets onto a baking sheet or peel before going into the oven.

A proofing linen cloth, called a cloche, is sometimes used for baguettes for the same purpose. The cloth is a simple rectangle, pleated in between each loaf to shape the dough as it is proofed.

Racks

Cooling racks are an important last step in the production of bread. If bread is allowed to cool without a rack, condensation (also known as bread sweat) will form underneath, which results in a soggy bottom crust. A rack allows air to circulate underneath, releasing steam and evaporating any condensation for a dry, crisp crust.

Racks do not have to be fancy, or any particular shape, or made from any specific material. They do need to be large enough to support the loaf in question, and leave at least ¼" of space between the bread and the counter.

Convection Ovens

Any standard oven is suitable for baking bread, but the convection oven is a common appliance in many homes, and can be a little tricky for the new baker. Convection ovens were created to promote even browning of foods. They were not as successful at even browning as they were at increasing the speed of baking.

Convection ovens contain fans that move the air throughout the oven cavity, which results in an increased temperature. This is very convenient for small items, like cookies and muffins. But larger loaves of bread need more time for the heat to penetrate the dough, and convection baking usually results in a burnt crust and doughy center.

Some convection ovens have a switch that turns the fan on and off. For large items, the fan should be turned off, and the oven used in the conventional manner. If the oven does not have the on-off capability, consider baking smaller breads, such as rolls, or bake them in a high-sided pan that can be covered in foil to prevent the moving air from reaching the loaf.

CHAPTER 2

White Bread

Amish White Bread

*This easy recipe is a classic beginner's loaf. The large amount of sugar
gets the yeast going early, and the oil gives it a light, soft crumb.*

INGREDIENTS | YIELDS 1 LOAF

1 cup warm water

⅓ cup granulated sugar

1¾ teaspoons active dry yeast
(1 package)

2 tablespoons canola oil, plus more as
needed

3 cups bread flour

¾ teaspoon plus 1 pinch kosher salt

1 egg

1 tablespoon water

1. In a large bowl, combine the water, sugar, and yeast. Stir to dissolve and let stand until foamy, about 10 minutes.

2. Add 2 tablespoons oil and 1 cup flour; stir to combine. Add ¾ teaspoon salt and remaining flour. Stir to combine. Turn out onto a floured surface and knead 8–10 minutes. Return to bowl, oil the top, and cover with a damp cloth or plastic wrap. Rise at room temperature until doubled in volume, about 1 hour.

3. Coat a 9" × 5" loaf pan with pan spray, and line the bottom and short sides with a strip of parchment. Turn risen dough onto a floured surface and shape into an oblong loaf. Place into the prepared pan and set aside to proof for 30 minutes. Preheat oven to 350°F.

4. Whisk egg with 1 tablespoon water and a pinch of salt, and brush lightly onto the surface of the risen loaf. Bake until golden brown and hollow sounding, about 30–40 minutes. Cool 10 minutes, remove from pan, and cool completely on a rack.

Basic White Bread

This recipe uses ingredients similar to the Amish White, but it employs the sponge method, which adds complexity to the bread's final flavor.

INGREDIENTS | YIELDS 1 LOAF

1½ cups warm water

1¾ teaspoons active dry yeast (1 package)

1 cup all-purpose flour

1½ teaspoons plus 1 pinch kosher salt

2 tablespoons unsalted butter, room temperature

3–4 cups bread flour

1 egg

The Sponge Method

The sponge method extends the fermentation time, which creates a more complex flavor in the finished bread. Any recipe can be made into a sponge recipe, simply by pre-fermenting part of the ingredients. A small amount of water, yeast, and flour is all it takes, plus 8–12 hours for the sponge to sit and bubble.

1. Combine 1 cup water and yeast. Stir to dissolve and let stand 5 minutes. Add all-purpose flour and beat 1 minute. Cover and let stand at room temperature for 8–12 hours.

2. Add to the sponge ½ cup water, 1½ teaspoons salt, butter, and enough bread flour to make a soft dough. Turn out onto a floured work surface and knead 8–10 minutes. Add flour only to reduce stickiness. Return to bowl, dust with flour, cover with plastic, and rise at room temperature until doubled in volume, about 1 hour.

3. Coat a 9" × 5" loaf pan with pan spray, and line its length with a strip of parchment. Turn risen dough onto a lightly floured work surface, and shape into an oblong loaf. Place in prepared pan, seam-side down. Dust lightly with flour, cover loosely with plastic wrap, and proof until doubled in volume, about 1 hour.

4. Preheat oven to 350°F. Whisk egg with a pinch of salt, then brush lightly and evenly over the surface of the loaf. Using a serrated knife, slash down the center length of the loaf, about 1" deep. Bake 40–50 minutes, until golden brown. The loaf should sound hollow when tapped from the bottom. (Pop the loaf out of the pan into an oven mitt and tap the bottom. It will not sound hollow in the pan.) Cool 10 minutes, remove from pan, and cool completely on a rack.

Butter-Top Bread

No need to butter your toast with this bread, and the added richness makes leftovers from this loaf the perfect candidate for French toast and bread pudding.

INGREDIENTS | YIELDS 1 LOAF

¾ cup warm water

¾ cup milk

2 tablespoons granulated sugar

2½ teaspoons active dry yeast (about a package and a half)

1 egg

1 teaspoon kosher salt

2 tablespoons unsalted butter, softened

4–5 cups bread flour

¼ cup (½ stick) unsalted butter, melted

1. In a large bowl, combine the water, milk, sugar, and yeast. Stir to dissolve and let stand until foamy, about 10 minutes.

2. Add the egg, salt, softened butter, and 1 cup flour. Stir to combine. Add enough remaining flour to create a firm dough. Turn out onto a floured surface and knead 8–10 minutes. Return to bowl, dust the top lightly with flour, and cover with a damp cloth or plastic wrap. Rise at room temperature until doubled in volume, about 1½ hours.

3. Coat a 9" × 5" loaf pan with pan spray, and line the bottom and short sides with a strip of parchment. Turn risen dough onto a floured surface and shape into an oblong loaf. Place into prepared pan, seam-side down. Cover lightly with a damp cloth and set aside to proof for 30 minutes. Preheat oven to 350°F.

4. Using a serrated knife, slice risen loaf lengthwise, and brush with 2 tablespoons melted butter. Bake until golden brown and hollow sounding, about 30–40 minutes. Remove finished bread from the oven and immediately brush remaining melted butter on top of loaf. Cool 10 minutes, remove from pan, and cool completely on a rack.

Buttermilk Loaf

Because buttermilk adds a slight tang, recipes such as this are often used to mimic sourdough.

INGREDIENTS | YIELDS 1 LOAF

¼ cup warm water

2 tablespoons granulated sugar

1¾ teaspoons active dry yeast
(1 package)

2 cups buttermilk

1½ teaspoons plus 1 pinch kosher salt

6 tablespoons (¾ stick) unsalted butter,
room temperature

4–6 cups bread flour

1 egg

1 tablespoon water

1. In a large bowl, combine the water, sugar, and yeast. Stir to dissolve and let stand until foamy, about 10 minutes.

2. Add buttermilk, 1½ teaspoons salt, butter, and 1 cup flour; stir to combine. Add enough remaining flour to create a firm dough. Turn out onto a floured surface and knead 8–10 minutes. Return to bowl, dust the top lightly with flour, and cover with a damp cloth or plastic wrap. Rise at room temperature until doubled in volume, about 1 hour.

3. Coat a 9" × 5" loaf pan with pan spray, and line the bottom and short sides with a strip of parchment. Turn risen dough onto a floured surface and shape into an oblong loaf. Place into prepared pan, seam-side down. Set aside to proof for 30 minutes. Preheat oven to 350°F.

4. Whisk egg with a tablespoon of water and pinch of salt, and brush lightly over risen loaf. Bake until golden brown and hollow sounding, about 30–40 minutes. Cool 10 minutes, remove from pan, and cool completely on a rack.

Buttermilk Potato Bread

Consider making this bread with your next surplus of leftover mashed potatoes.

INGREDIENTS | **YIELDS 1 LOAF**

1 medium russet (baking) potato (about ⅓ pound)

Cold water, as needed, plus 1 tablespoon

1 tablespoon granulated sugar

1¾ teaspoons active dry yeast (1 package)

¾ cup buttermilk

1½ teaspoons plus 1 pinch kosher salt

1 tablespoon unsalted butter, room temperature

3–5 cups bread flour

1 egg

1. Peel and quarter potato, place in a small saucepan, cover with cold water, and bring to a boil. Cook until tender, drain, and reserve liquid. Mash with a fork and set aside.

2. In a large bowl, combine ½ cup potato water, sugar, and yeast. Stir to dissolve and let stand until foamy, about 10 minutes.

3. Add potato, buttermilk, 1½ teaspoons salt, butter, and 1 cup flour. Stir to combine. Add enough remaining flour to create a firm dough. Turn out onto a floured surface and knead 8–10 minutes. Return to bowl, dust the top lightly with flour, and cover with a damp cloth or plastic wrap. Rise at room temperature until doubled in volume, about 1 hour.

4. Coat a 9" × 5" loaf pan with pan spray, and line the bottom and short sides with a strip of parchment. Turn risen dough onto a floured surface and shape into an oblong loaf. Place into prepared pan, seam-side down. Set aside to proof for 30 minutes. Preheat oven to 350°F.

5. Whisk egg with a tablespoon of water and pinch of salt, and brush lightly over the risen loaf. Bake until golden brown and hollow sounding, about 30–40 minutes. Cool 10 minutes, remove from pan, and cool completely on a rack.

Farmhouse White

When using cool liquid, bread dough will require a longer fermentation. The outcome is a heartier flavor, commonly referred to as "country-style."

INGREDIENTS | YIELDS 1 LOAF

1 cup cold buttermilk

2 tablespoons honey

1¾ teaspoons active dry yeast
(1 package)

1 egg

2 tablespoons canola oil

1½ teaspoons kosher salt

3–4 cups bread flour

1 tablespoon cornmeal

2 tablespoons cream

Hearth Baking

Few home cooks bake on the hearth these days, but the traditional brick-oven look and feel can be easily re-created in a modern oven. Cornmeal is used on a traditional peel, the wooden paddle used to bring bread in and out of the hearth. Using cornmeal on your baking sheet will make it look like you've wielded a peel.

1. In a large bowl, combine buttermilk, honey, and yeast. Stir to dissolve and let stand until foamy, about 30 minutes.

2. Add egg, oil, salt, and 1 cup of flour; stir to combine. Add enough remaining flour to create a firm dough. Turn out onto a floured surface and knead 8–10 minutes. Return to bowl, dust the top lightly with flour, and cover with a damp cloth or plastic wrap. Rise at room temperature until doubled in volume, about 3 hours.

3. Line a baking sheet with parchment; dust with cornmeal. Turn risen dough onto a floured surface and shape into a smooth, round ball. Place onto prepared 9" × 5" pan seam-side down. Cover loosely with plastic and set aside to proof for 30 minutes. Preheat oven to 375°F.

4. Brush cream lightly over risen loaf. Using a serrated knife, slash a crosshatch design into the top of the dough, about 1" deep. Place a pan of cold water at the bottom of the oven to create steam. Bake until golden brown and hollow sounding, about 30–40 minutes. Remove to a rack and cool completely.

French Baguette

*The classic French baguette can be found just about everywhere,
but nothing compares to the one that comes out of your oven.*

INGREDIENTS | **YIELDS 3 18" LOAVES**

2 cups warm water

1 tablespoon granulated sugar

3½ teaspoons active dry yeast
(2 packages)

4–5 cups bread flour

1 tablespoon kosher salt

¼ cup cornmeal

1. In a large bowl, combine water, sugar, and yeast. Stir to dissolve and let stand until foamy, about 10 minutes.

2. Add 1 cup flour and salt. Stir to combine. Add enough remaining flour to create a firm dough. Turn out onto a floured surface and knead 8–10 minutes. Return to bowl, dust the top lightly with flour, and cover with a damp cloth or plastic wrap. Rise at room temperature until doubled in volume, about 2 hours.

3. Line a baking sheet with parchment; dust with cornmeal. Turn risen dough onto a floured surface and divide into 3 equal portions. Roll each piece into a tight rope, and taper the ends slightly. Place loaves on prepared pan, dust with flour, cover with plastic wrap, and rise another 30 minutes. Preheat oven to 400°F.

4. Using a serrated knife, make five or six angled slashes into the top of each loaf, about ½" deep. Place a pan of cold water at the bottom of the oven to create steam. Bake until golden brown and firm, about 15–20 minutes. Remove to a rack and cool completely before slicing.

French Epi

This recipe is similar to the Baguette, but it uses the sponge method, which enhances the flavor. The shape represents a shaft of wheat.

INGREDIENTS | YIELDS 3 18" LOAVES

2 cups warm water

1 tablespoon granulated sugar

2½ teaspoons active dry yeast (2 packages)

4–5 cups bread flour

1 tablespoon kosher salt

¼ cup cornmeal

Pain Epi

Epi is the French name for the flower of wheat, which is where the wheat kernels are found. *Pain* (French for "bread") *epi* is sliced before baking so that it opens up in the oven and resembles a shaft of wheat. It is a popular bread because it is both beautiful and useful. Rolls can be pulled off easily and shared, making a knife unnecessary and providing convenience when eating on the go.

1. Combine 1 cup water, sugar, and yeast. Stir to dissolve and let stand 5 minutes. Add 1 cup flour and beat 1 minute. Cover and let stand at room temperature 8–12 hours.

2. Add to the sponge 1 cup water, salt, and enough flour to make a soft dough. Turn out onto a floured work surface and knead 8–10 minutes. Add flour only to reduce stickiness. Return to bowl, dust with flour, cover with plastic, and rise at room temperature until doubled in volume, about 1 hour.

3. Line a baking sheet with parchment; dust with cornmeal. Turn risen dough onto a floured surface and divide into 3 equal portions. Roll each piece into a tight rope, and taper the ends slightly. Place loaves on pan, dust with flour, cover with plastic wrap, and rise another 30 minutes. Preheat oven to 400°F.

4. Coming in at a 45° angle, slice into each rope, alternating from side to side, every 3 inches all the way up. Dust with flour. Place a pan of cold water at the bottom of the oven to create steam. Bake until golden brown and firm, about 15–20 minutes. Remove to a rack and cool completely before slicing.

Hawaiian Bread

This sweet white bread is as popular on the mainland as it is in Hawaii.

INGREDIENTS | YIELDS 2 LOAVES

1 cup warm milk

⅓ cup granulated sugar

1¾ teaspoons active dry yeast
(1 package)

¾ cup pineapple juice

1 egg

1 teaspoon kosher salt

6 tablespoons (¾ stick) unsalted butter, melted

¼ teaspoon ground ginger

3–4 cups bread flour

King's Hawaiian Bread

Hawaiian history is rich with the cultures and cuisines of many immigrant groups, including the Portuguese, who were the first to bring sweet bread, called *Pão Doce*, to the islands. In the 1950s, a baker named Robert Taira began mass producing a popular Hawaiian version of this bread, and his success eventually led to the production of this bread on the mainland, too.

1. In a large bowl, combine the milk, sugar, and yeast. Stir to dissolve and let stand until foamy, about 10 minutes.

2. Add pineapple juice, egg, salt, 4 tablespoons butter, ginger, and 1 cup flour. Stir to combine. Add enough remaining flour to create a firm dough, and turn out onto a floured surface. Knead 8–10 minutes. Return to bowl, dust with flour, and cover with a damp cloth or plastic wrap. Rise at room temperature until doubled in volume, about 1 hour.

3. Coat two 9" × 5" loaf pans with pan spray, and line the bottoms and short sides of each with a strip of parchment. Turn risen dough onto a floured surface, divide into 2 equal pieces, and shape each into an oblong loaf. Place into prepared pans, and set aside to proof for 30 minutes. Preheat oven to 350°F.

4. Brush remaining butter over the surface of the risen dough. Bake until golden brown and hollow sounding, about 30–40 minutes. Cool 10 minutes, remove from pans, and cool completely on a rack.

Honey White

This easy loaf has the subtle tang of honey, making it the perfect slice for your morning toast.

INGREDIENTS | YIELDS 1 LOAF

1¼ cups warm milk

3 tablespoons unsalted butter

5 tablespoons honey

1¾ teaspoons active dry yeast
(1 package)

3 cups bread flour

¾ teaspoon kosher salt

1 teaspoon warm water

1. In a large bowl, combine milk, butter, 1 tablespoon honey, and yeast. Stir to dissolve and let stand until foamy, about 10 minutes.

2. Add another 3 tablespoons honey and 1 cup flour. Stir to combine. Add salt and enough remaining flour to create a firm dough. Turn out onto a floured surface and knead 8–10 minutes. Return to bowl, dust with flour, and cover loosely with a damp cloth or plastic wrap. Rise at room temperature until doubled in volume, about 1 hour.

3. Coat a 9" × 5" loaf pan with pan spray, and line the bottom and short sides with a strip of parchment. Turn risen dough onto a floured surface and shape into an oblong loaf. Place into prepared pan; set aside to proof for 30 minutes. Preheat oven to 350°F.

4. Combine remaining tablespoon of honey with a teaspoon of warm water, and brush gently over the surface of the risen dough. Bake until golden brown and hollow sounding, about 30–40 minutes. Cool 10 minutes, remove from pan, and cool completely on a rack.

Italian Batard

The olive oil and sponge method create a chewy crust and complex flavor that makes this white dough uniquely Italian.

INGREDIENTS | **YIELDS 2 LOAVES**

½ cup warm water

1 tablespoon granulated sugar

1¾ teaspoons active dry yeast (1 package)

1 cup all-purpose flour

1 cup warm milk

2 tablespoons olive oil

½ teaspoon kosher salt

3–4 cups bread flour

¼ cup cornmeal

Bread Shapes of Italy

Italy encompasses many regions, and each has its own specialty breads. Often, the name of the dough is reflective of its shape. The same dough recipe can be formed into a number of different shapes, including rolls (panini), flatbreads (focaccia, fougasse, or ciabatta), breadsticks (grissino), or crackers (salatini).

1. Combine water, sugar, and yeast. Stir to dissolve and let stand 5 minutes. Add all-purpose flour and beat 1 minute. Cover and let stand at room temperature 8–12 hours.

2. Add to the sponge milk, oil, salt, and enough bread flour to make a soft dough. Turn out onto a floured work surface and knead 8–10 minutes. Add flour only to reduce stickiness. Return to bowl, dust with flour, cover with plastic, and rise at room temperature until doubled in volume, about 1 hour.

3. Line a baking sheet with parchment and dust with cornmeal. Turn dough onto a floured surface and divide into 2 equal portions. Roll each piece into a football shape, no longer than the width of the baking sheet. Taper the ends slightly. Place loaves on the pan, dust with flour, cover with plastic wrap, and rise another 30 minutes. Preheat oven to 400°F.

4. Using a serrated knife, score ¼"-deep angled cuts into the top of each loaf. Place a pan of cold water at the bottom of the oven to create steam. Bake until golden brown and firm, about 20–30 minutes. Remove to a rack and cool completely before slicing.

Seeded Honey White

*This loaf does double duty, complementing both salty sandwiches, like
ham and cheese, as well as your best peanut butter and jelly.*

INGREDIENTS | YIELDS 1 LOAF

1¼ cups warm milk

3 tablespoons unsalted butter

3 tablespoons honey

1¾ teaspoons active dry yeast
(1 package)

1 teaspoon poppy seeds

1 teaspoon sesame seeds

1 teaspoon sunflower seeds

1 teaspoon millet

¾ teaspoon plus 1 pinch kosher salt

3–4 cups bread flour

1 egg

1 teaspoon water

1. In a large bowl, combine milk, butter, 1 tablespoon honey, and yeast. Stir to dissolve and let stand until foamy, about 10 minutes.

2. Add remaining honey and 1 cup flour. Stir to combine. Add seeds, millet, ¾ teaspoon salt, and enough remaining flour to create a firm dough. Turn out onto a floured surface and knead 8–10 minutes. Return to bowl, dust with flour, and cover loosely with a damp cloth or plastic wrap. Rise at room temperature until doubled in volume, about 1 hour.

3. Coat a 9" × 5" loaf pan with pan spray, and line the bottom and short sides with a strip of parchment. Turn risen dough onto a floured surface and shape into an oblong loaf. Place into prepared pan; set aside to proof for 30 minutes. Preheat oven to 350°F.

4. Whisk egg with a teaspoon of water and a pinch of salt, and brush gently over the surface of the risen dough. Bake until golden brown and hollow sounding, about 30–40 minutes. Cool 10 minutes, remove from pan, and cool completely on a rack.

Seeded Sandwich Loaf

This lovely loaf makes every sandwich a healthy sandwich.

INGREDIENTS | YIELDS 1 LOAF

1¼ cups warm milk

2 tablespoons honey

1¾ teaspoons active dry yeast
(1 package)

3–4 cups bread flour

¼ cup (½ stick) unsalted butter, melted

1 egg

½ teaspoon kosher salt

1 tablespoon milk

½ teaspoon sesame seeds

½ teaspoon sunflower seeds

½ teaspoon poppy seeds

½ teaspoon fennel seeds

1. In a large bowl, combine milk, honey, and yeast. Stir to dissolve and let stand until foamy, about 10 minutes.

2. Add 1 cup flour and stir to combine. Add butter, egg, salt, and enough remaining flour to create a firm dough. Turn out onto a floured surface and knead 8–10 minutes. Return to bowl, dust with flour, and cover loosely with a damp cloth or plastic wrap. Rise at room temperature until doubled in volume, about 1 hour.

3. Coat a 9" × 5" loaf pan with pan spray, and line the bottom and short sides with a strip of parchment. Turn risen dough onto a floured surface and shape into an oblong loaf. Place into prepared pan, seam-side down, and set aside to rise again for 30 minutes. Preheat oven to 350°F.

4. Gently coat the surface of the risen dough with milk. Mix the seeds together and sprinkle generously onto the surface. Bake until golden brown and hollow sounding, about 30–40 minutes. Cool 10 minutes, remove from pan, and cool completely on a rack.

Texas Toasting Bread

This loaf is a standard size. It's the slices that are remarkably huge.
Cut pieces 1½"–2" thick for Texas-sized toast.

INGREDIENTS | YIELDS 1 LOAF

1 cup warm water

1 teaspoon granulated sugar

1 tablespoon active dry yeast (about 2 packages)

1 cup evaporated milk

2 tablespoons canola oil

4–5 cups bread flour

½ teaspoon kosher salt

Pig Stand Toast

Texas toast is the creation of Pig Stand restaurants, a Texas institution. This mighty chain, first opened in 1921, is thought to be the first drive-in restaurant, offering curbside service to Model T Fords. Pig Stand is also said to have created the onion ring and the chicken fried steak, and was the first drive-in to use neon lighting.

1. In a large bowl, combine water, sugar, and yeast. Stir to dissolve and let stand until foamy, about 10 minutes.

2. Add evaporated milk, oil, and 1 cup flour. Stir to combine. Add salt and enough remaining flour to create a firm dough. Turn out onto a floured surface and knead 8–10 minutes. Place in an extra-large mixing bowl, dust with flour, and cover loosely with a damp cloth or plastic wrap. Rise at room temperature until tripled in volume, about 1 hour.

3. Coat a 9" × 5" loaf pan with pan spray, and line the bottom and short sides with a strip of parchment. Turn risen dough onto a floured surface, shape into an oblong loaf, and place into prepared pan, seam-side down. Set aside to proof for 30 minutes. Preheat oven to 350°F.

4. Dust the top of the risen dough lightly with flour, then bake until golden brown and hollow sounding, about 30–40 minutes. Cool 10 minutes, remove from pan, and cool completely on a rack. When completely cool, cut into 2" slices.

Tuscan White Hearth Bread

This unsalted bread is a staple of Tuscany. Use it to sop up flavorful soups and sauces.

INGREDIENTS | YIELDS 1 LOAF

1¼ cups warm water

1¾ teaspoons active dry yeast
(1 package)

¼ cup whole wheat flour

2–3 cups bread flour

¼ cup cornmeal

1. In a large bowl, combine water and yeast. Stir to dissolve and let stand until foamy, about 10 minutes.

2. Add whole wheat flour, and enough bread flour to create a firm dough. Turn out onto a floured surface and knead 8–10 minutes. Return to bowl, dust the top with flour, and cover loosely with a damp cloth or plastic wrap. Rise at room temperature until doubled in volume, about 2 hours.

3. Line a baking sheet with parchment; dust with cornmeal. Turn risen dough onto a floured surface and form into a large, round loaf. Place loaf on baking sheet, seam-side down. Dust with flour, cover loosely with plastic wrap, and rise another 30 minutes. Preheat oven to 400°F.

4. Dust the top of the risen dough generously with flour, and using a serrated knife, slice a crosshatch into the surface of the bread, 1" deep. Place a pan of cold water at the bottom of the oven to create steam. Bake until golden brown and hollow sounding, about 40–50 minutes. Remove to a rack and cool completely on a rack before slicing.

Friendship Bread Starter

This starter takes about 2 weeks to create, but will then last a lifetime! Share it with your friends, as the title suggests.

INGREDIENTS | YIELDS 9 CUPS STARTER

3 cups milk

3 cups granulated sugar

3 cups all-purpose flour

1. **Day 1:** Combine 1 cup milk, 1 cup sugar, and 1 cup flour in a ceramic or glass bowl. Stir to combine, cover loosely with a damp cheesecloth or towel, and set aside at room temperature. Stir once a day for the next 4 days.

2. **Day 5:** Add 1 cup milk, 1 cup sugar, and 1 cup flour. Stir well, cover again, and set aside at room temperature for another 5 days, stirring once a day, as before.

3. **Day 10:** Again, add 1 cup milk, 1 cup sugar, and 1 cup flour. Mix thoroughly. Starter is now ready to use. To keep your starter alive, replace the quantity used for bread making with an equal amount of milk, flour, and sugar. Stir it every day, and feed it every 5 days by removing some starter and replacing it with an equal amount of milk, sugar, and flour (for every 1 cup used, replace with ⅓ cup milk, ⅓ cup sugar, and ⅓ cup flour). If you do not wish to feed it, but want to keep it, refrigerate it indefinitely, taking it out and repeating the process for 10 days before using it again.

Friendship Bread

This sweet bread is meant to be shared. It freezes well, which makes it easy to keep one or two on hand, just in case you need to brighten someone's day.

INGREDIENTS | YIELDS 2 LOAVES

1 cup Friendship Bread Starter (page 35)

3 tablespoons canola oil, plus more as needed

1 egg

⅓ cup granulated sugar, plus more as needed

½ teaspoon kosher salt

½ teaspoon baking soda

½ teaspoon cinnamon

3–4 cups bread flour

Friendship Bread

Many recipes mistakenly refer to this recipe as Amish, but there is little evidence to suggest that origin. Sourdough, however, is a common starter made by the Amish. Before yeast was readily available, the creation of a starter was the only way bread could be made. The connection was probably made because starters are often shared with friends, and sharing is an Amish trait.

1. In a large bowl, combine the starter, 3 tablespoons oil, egg, and ⅓ cup sugar. Stir to combine. Add salt, baking soda, cinnamon, and enough flour to create a firm dough. Turn out onto a floured surface and knead 8–10 minutes. Add flour only to reduce stickiness. Return to bowl, oil the top, and cover with a damp cloth or plastic wrap. Rise at room temperature until doubled in volume, about 1 hour.

3. Coat two 9" × 5" loaf pans with pan spray, and line the bottom and short sides of each pan with a strip of parchment. Turn risen dough onto a floured surface, divide into 2 equal portions, and shape each into an oblong loaf. Place into the prepared pans seam-side down. Dust with flour, cover loosely with plastic wrap, and set aside to proof for 30 minutes. Preheat oven to 350°F.

4. Dust the risen loaves with sugar and bake until golden brown and hollow sounding, about 35–50 minutes. Cool 10 minutes, remove from pans, and cool completely on a rack.

CHAPTER 3

Hearty Whole Grain Bread

Cracked Wheat and Honey Bread

The hearty flavor of cracked wheat and the tang of sweet natural honey are a perfect pair. Try forming this dough into dinner rolls as well as standard loaves.

INGREDIENTS | **YIELDS 2 LOAVES**

1½ cups boiling water

½ cup cracked wheat

1⅓ cups warm milk

¼ cup honey

1¾ teaspoons active dry yeast (1 package)

¼ cup (½ stick) unsalted butter

1 cup whole wheat flour

¾ teaspoon kosher salt

3–4 cups bread flour

Cracked Wheat

Cracked wheat is crushed wheat kernels with the bran intact. It is similar to bulgur, which is also crushed wheat kernels, but par-cooked, or steamed. The result is a grain that cooks a bit faster. In a pinch, cracked wheat can be replaced with bulgur in this recipe.

1. In a medium bowl, combine boiling water and cracked wheat. Set aside for 10 minutes, stirring occasionally, until the cracked wheat has absorbed the water and has softened.

2. In a large bowl, combine milk, 1 tablespoon honey, and yeast. Stir to dissolve and let stand until foamy, about 10 minutes.

3. Add remaining honey, butter, and whole wheat flour; stir to combine. Add softened cracked wheat (drain off excess liquid if necessary), salt, and enough bread flour to create a firm dough. Add flour only to reduce stickiness. Turn out onto a floured surface and knead 8–10 minutes. Return to bowl, dust the top with flour, and cover with a damp cloth or plastic wrap. Rise at room temperature until doubled in volume, about 2 hours.

4. Coat two 9" × 5" loaf pans with pan spray, and line the bottom and short sides of each pan with a strip of parchment. Turn risen dough onto a floured surface, divide into 2 equal portions, and shape each into an oblong loaf. Place into prepared pans seam-side down, cover loosely with plastic wrap, and set aside to proof for 30 minutes, or until dough rises above the pan. Preheat oven to 375°F.

5. Dust risen loaves with whole wheat flour, and bake until golden brown and hollow sounding, about 30–40 minutes. Cool 10 minutes, remove from pans, and cool completely on a rack.

Dark Pumpernickel Rye

This dough is commonly baked in loaf pans that are short in height and long in length. This creates what is often called "cocktail loaves." Slices of these mini loaves make the perfect base for canapés and hors d'oeuvres.

INGREDIENTS | YIELDS 1 LOAF

⅔ cup warm water

1¾ teaspoons active dry yeast (1 package)

3 tablespoons molasses

2 teaspoons canola oil

1 cup medium rye flour

1 teaspoon kosher salt

1 tablespoon caraway seeds, toasted and ground

2–3 cups bread flour

1 tablespoon honey

1 tablespoon strong coffee

1. In a large bowl, combine water, yeast, and 1 tablespoon molasses. Stir to dissolve and let stand until foamy, about 10 minutes.

2. Add remaining molasses, oil, and rye flour; stir to combine. Add salt, caraway, and enough bread flour to create a firm dough. Add flour only to reduce stickiness. Turn out onto a floured surface and knead 5–8 minutes. Return to bowl, dust the top with flour, and cover with a damp cloth or plastic wrap. Rise at room temperature until doubled in volume, about 2 hours.

3. Coat a 9" × 5" loaf pan with pan spray and line the bottom and short sides with a strip of parchment. Turn risen dough onto a floured surface and shape into an oblong loaf. Place into prepared pan and set aside to proof for 30 minutes, or until dough rises above the pan. Preheat oven to 350°F.

4. Combine honey and coffee; brush gently onto the surface of risen dough. Bake until golden brown and hollow sounding, about 30–40 minutes. Cool 10 minutes, remove from pan, and cool completely on a rack.

Egyptian Kamut Bread

Kamut is an early form of wheat known to have been consumed by the ancient Egyptians. You can find it today in stores that specialize in healthy and organic foods.

INGREDIENTS | YIELDS 2 LOAVES

1½ cups warm water

¼ cup honey

1¾ teaspoons active dry yeast
(1 package)

3 tablespoons olive oil

2 cups kamut flour

1 teaspoon kosher salt

2–3 cups bread flour

2 tablespoons cornmeal

Homemade Flour

Flour made from specialty grains may be harder to find than the grains in whole form. If you own a food processor, you can make your own flour from whole grains. Fill the processor halfway to be sure the grains are getting to the blade. Process, pulsing occasionally, until the desired texture is reached. You can also intensify the flavor by toasting the grains before grinding.

1. In a large bowl, combine water, 1 tablespoon honey, and yeast. Stir to dissolve and let stand until foamy, about 10 minutes.

2. Add remaining honey, oil, kamut flour, salt, and enough bread flour to create a firm dough. Add flour only to reduce stickiness. Turn out onto a floured surface and knead 8–10 minutes. Return to bowl, dust the top with flour, and cover with a damp cloth or plastic wrap. Rise at room temperature until doubled in volume, about 2 hours.

3. Line a baking sheet with parchment, and sprinkle with cornmeal. Turn risen dough onto a floured surface, divide into 2 equal portions, and shape into round loaves. Place on prepared pan, at least 2" apart. Cover loosely with plastic and set aside to proof for 30 minutes. Preheat oven to 375°F.

4. Dust risen bread generously with kamut flour. Using a serrated knife, make two or three decorative slashes into the dough, about ½" deep. Place a pan of cold water at the bottom of the oven to create steam. Bake until golden brown and hollow sounding, about 30–40 minutes. Remove to a rack and cool completely.

Ezekiel's Bread

This is Biblical recipe is based on instructions found in the fourth chapter of Ezekiel. It has been modernized into a delectably hearty loaf.

INGREDIENTS | YIELDS 3 LOAVES

1 cup wheat berries
½ cup spelt groats
¼ cup barley groats
2 tablespoons whole millet
2 tablespoons dried green lentils
1 tablespoon dried white beans
1 tablespoon dried red beans
1 tablespoon dried black beans
½ cup cracked wheat
1½ cups boiling water
2 cups warm water
½ cup honey
1¾ teaspoons active dry yeast
(1 package)
¼ cup olive oil
1 teaspoon kosher salt

1. In a large bowl, stir together the whole grains and beans (first 9 ingredients), then grind to a fine powder, using a flour mill, coffee grinder, or food processor. Cover with boiling water and set aside for 30 minutes to soften.

2. In another large bowl, combine warm water, 1 tablespoon honey, and yeast. Stir to dissolve and let stand until foamy, about 10 minutes.

3. Add to the yeast mixture the remaining honey, oil, ground grain mixture, and salt. Stir to combine, and beat 8–10 minutes. The finished batter will be lumpier and thinner than traditional bread dough. Dust the top with flour, cover with a damp cloth or plastic wrap, and rise at room temperature until doubled in volume, about 2 hours.

4. Coat three 9" × 5" loaf pans with pan spray, and line the bottom and short sides of each pan with a strip of parchment. Stir risen batter and divide evenly among prepared pans. Cover and set aside to proof for 30 minutes, or until dough rises to the top of the pans. Preheat oven to 350°F.

5. Bake risen loaves until golden brown and hollow sounding, about 45–50 minutes. Cool 10 minutes, remove from pans, and cool completely on a rack.

Graham Bread

The flavor of this finished bread will remind you of Mr. Graham's crackers.

INGREDIENTS | YIELDS 2 LOAVES

1¼ cups warm milk

¼ cup brown sugar, packed

1¾ teaspoons active dry yeast (1 package)

2 tablespoons unsalted butter

4–6 cups graham flour

¾ teaspoon kosher salt

1. In a large bowl, combine milk, 1 tablespoon brown sugar, and yeast. Stir to dissolve and let stand until foamy, about 10 minutes.

2. Add remaining brown sugar, butter, and 1 cup graham flour; stir to combine. Add salt and enough remaining graham flour to create a firm dough. Add flour only to reduce stickiness. Turn out onto a floured surface and knead 8–10 minutes. Return to bowl, dust the top with flour, and cover with a damp cloth or plastic wrap. Rise at room temperature until doubled in volume, about 2 hours.

3. Coat two 9" × 5" loaf pans with pan spray, and line the bottom and short sides of each pan with a strip of parchment. Turn risen dough onto a floured surface, divide into 2 equal portions, and shape into oblong loaves. Place into prepared pans seam-side down, and set aside to proof for 30 minutes. Preheat oven to 375°F.

4. Dust risen loaves with graham flour, and make a ½" deep slash down the center. Bake until golden brown and hollow sounding, about 30–40 minutes. Cool 10 minutes, remove from pans, and cool completely on a rack.

Sourdough Rye Starter

This starter is easy to make and can be used for years.

INGREDIENTS	YIELDS APPROXIMATELY 1 QUART OF STARTER

6 cups water
1¾ teaspoons active dry yeast (1 package)
4½ cups rye flour
1 cup bread flour

1. **Day 1:** In a glass or ceramic bowl, combine 2½ cups water, yeast, 1 cup rye flour, and bread flour. Stir to combine, cover with cheesecloth, and set aside at room temperature for 7 days. Stir the starter once a day.

2. **Days 8–14:** Remove 1 cup of starter; replace it with ½ cup rye flour and ½ cup water. (Removed starter can be used instead of water to make pancakes, biscuits, or muffins.) Stir to combine, then set aside at room temperature for 24 hours. Repeat each day for the next 6 days.

3. The starter is now ready to use. Always replace what you use with an equal amount of rye flour and water, in the same proportions as in Step 2. Refrigerate when not in use, and repeat the process for 5–8 days before using again.

Light Caraway Rye

This delicious bread makes perfect pastrami sandwiches. Or, use it to sop up your favorite beefy stew.

INGREDIENTS | YIELDS 2 LOAVES

1 cup warm water

1 tablespoon granulated sugar

1¾ teaspoons active dry yeast
(1 package)

1 cup Sourdough Rye Starter (page 43)

1½ cups light rye flour

1 teaspoon kosher salt

1 tablespoon caraway seeds, toasted
and ground

3–4 cups bread flour

¼ cup cornmeal

Rye Flour

Rye is a grain related to wheat and barley,
but with much less gluten protein. Consequently, wheat flour must be combined
with rye flour to create a soft, airy crumb.

1. In a large bowl, combine water, sugar, and yeast. Stir to dissolve and let stand until foamy, about 10 minutes.

2. Add starter and rye flour; stir to combine. Add salt, caraway seeds, and enough bread flour to create a firm dough. Add flour only to reduce stickiness. Turn out onto a floured surface and knead 8–10 minutes. Return to bowl, dust the top with flour, and cover with a damp cloth or plastic wrap. Rise at room temperature until doubled in volume, about 2 hours.

3. Line a baking sheet with parchment, and sprinkle with cornmeal. Turn risen dough onto a floured surface, divide into 2 equal portions, and shape into round loaves. Place onto prepared pan, seam-side down. Dust with flour, cover loosely with plastic wrap, and set aside to proof for 30 minutes. Preheat oven to 375°F.

4. Using a serrated knife, slash two or three diagonal lines into the surface of the risen loaves, about ½" deep. Place a pan of cold water at the bottom of the oven to create steam. Bake loaves until golden brown and hollow sounding, about 30–40 minutes. Remove to a rack and cool completely.

Marble Rye

This beautiful loaf makes even an ordinary egg salad sandwich fancy!

INGREDIENTS | **YIELDS 4 LOAVES**

1 batch Dark Pumpernickel Rye dough (page 39)

1 batch Light Caraway Rye dough (page 44)

1 tablespoon molasses

1 tablespoon hot water

1. Make both doughs, and allow both to double in volume, about 1½–2 hours.

2. Coat four 9" × 5" loaf pans with pan spray, and line the bottom and short sides of each pan with a strip of parchment. Turn risen dough onto a floured surface, and divide each batch of dough into 4 equal portions. Using a rolling pin, roll each of the 8 pieces into a rectangle 8" wide by 10" long. Make 4 pairs of rectangles, stacking the pumpernickel on top of the light rye for each. Roll up each stack jellyroll-style, from one short end to the other. Place each roll into a prepared pan, seam-side down. Cover loosely with plastic wrap and set aside to proof for 30 minutes, or until dough rises above the pan. Preheat oven to 375°F.

3. Combine molasses and hot water, and brush gently onto the risen dough. Bake risen loaves until golden brown and hollow sounding, about 30–40 minutes. Cool 10 minutes, remove from pans, and cool completely on a rack before slicing.

Mediterranean Quinoa and Herb Bread

Quinoa is a tiny grain that is extremely high in protein. Consumed by the Incas and Aztecs, it now is gaining popularity as an interesting alternative to rice.

INGREDIENTS | YIELDS 2 LOAVES

½ cup quinoa

1 cup water

1 cup warm milk

2 tablespoons honey

1¾ teaspoons active dry yeast
(1 package)

2 tablespoons olive oil

1 cup whole wheat flour

¾ teaspoon kosher salt

1 tablespoon fresh thyme,
finely chopped

1 tablespoon fresh basil, finely chopped

1 tablespoon fresh tarragon,
finely chopped

1 tablespoon fresh sage, finely chopped

1 teaspoon fresh rosemary,
finely chopped

2–3 cups bread flour

2 tablespoons cornmeal

Herbs

Fresh and dried herbs can be used interchangeably, but they have very different characteristics. The fragrant oils in fresh herbs have a brighter flavor. However, the potency is greater in dried herbs, mostly because the water of the plant has evaporated. For this reason, use about a third as much dried herb as fresh.

1. In a medium saucepan combine quinoa and water. Bring to a boil over medium heat. At the boil, cover and remove from heat and rest for 10 minutes. Drain out excess water, then set aside.

2. In a large bowl, combine milk, honey, and yeast. Stir to dissolve and let stand until foamy, about 10 minutes.

3. Add cooled quinoa, oil, and whole wheat flour; stir to combine. Add salt, herbs, and enough bread flour to create a firm dough. Add flour only to reduce stickiness. Turn out onto a floured surface and knead 8–10 minutes. Return to bowl, dust the top with flour, and cover with a damp cloth or plastic wrap. Rise at room temperature until doubled in volume, about 2 hours.

4. Line a baking sheet with parchment and sprinkle it with cornmeal. Turn risen dough onto a floured surface, divide into 2 equal portions, and shape into 2 rounds. Place onto prepared pan and flatten into disks, 2"–3" thick. Set aside to proof for 30 minutes. Preheat oven to 375°F.

5. Dust risen dough with flour. Using a serrated knife, slash a crosshatch pattern into the surface of the risen dough, about ½" deep. Place a pan of cold water at the bottom of the oven to create steam. Bake until golden brown and hollow sounding, about 30–40 minutes. Remove to a rack and cool completely.

Peasant Bread

This rustic loaf, like many peasant dishes of old, is hardly the food of country bumpkins. It is bread fit for a king.

INGREDIENTS | YIELDS 2 LOAVES

1½ cups warm water

1 tablespoon honey

1¾ teaspoons active dry yeast (1 package)

¼ cup rye flour

¼ cup whole wheat flour

¾ teaspoon kosher salt

3–4 cups bread flour

¼ cup cornmeal

1. In a large bowl, combine water, honey, and yeast. Stir to dissolve and let stand until foamy, about 10 minutes.

2. Add rye flour and whole wheat flour; stir to combine. Add salt and enough bread flour to create a firm dough. Add flour only to reduce stickiness. Turn out onto a floured surface and knead 8–10 minutes. Return to bowl, dust the top with flour, and cover with a damp cloth or plastic wrap. Rise at room temperature until doubled in volume, about 2 hours.

3. Line a baking sheet with parchment, and sprinkle with cornmeal. Turn risen dough onto a floured surface, divide into 2 equal portions, and shape into round loaves. Place onto prepared pan and set aside to proof for 30 minutes. Preheat oven to 375°F.

4. Dust the top of the risen loaves with flour. Using a serrated knife, slash a crosshatch pattern into the surface of the risen dough, about ½" deep. Place a pan of cold water at the bottom of the oven to create steam. Bake until golden brown and hollow sounding, about 30–40 minutes. Cool completely on a rack before serving.

Peruvian Amaranth Loaf

Amaranth is a tiny grain, grown originally at high altitude, found both in the Andes and the Himalayas. Its high protein content has made it popular with vegetarians.

INGREDIENTS | YIELDS 2 LOAVES

1½ cups warm milk

2 teaspoons honey

1¾ teaspoons active dry yeast (1 package)

3 tablespoons unsalted butter

1 cup amaranth flour

½ teaspoon kosher salt

3–4 cups bread flour

1 tablespoon molasses

1 tablespoon hot water

Finding Specialty Grains

Specialty grains are becoming more and more available, as Americans discover the benefits of diets rich in whole grains. If your local market doesn't stock what you're looking for, try health-food stores, or head to the Internet.

1. In a large bowl, combine milk, honey, and yeast. Stir to dissolve and let stand until foamy, about 10 minutes.

2. Add butter and amaranth flour; stir to combine. Add salt and enough bread flour to create a firm dough. Add flour only to reduce stickiness. Turn out onto a floured surface and knead 8–10 minutes. Return to bowl, dust the top with flour, and cover with a damp cloth or plastic wrap. Rise at room temperature until doubled in volume, about 2 hours.

3. Coat two 9" × 5" loaf pans with pan spray, and line the bottom and short sides of each pan with a strip of parchment. Turn risen dough onto a floured surface, divide into 2 equal portions, and shape each into an oblong loaf. Place into prepared pans and set aside to proof for 30 minutes, or until dough rises above the pans. Preheat oven to 375°F.

4. Combine molasses and hot water, and brush gently onto the risen dough. Bake risen loaf until golden brown and hollow sounding, about 30–40 minutes. Cool 10 minutes, remove from pans, and cool completely on a rack.

Potato-Oat Bread

This stick-to-your-ribs bread is perfect with thick, meaty stews and creamy soups.

INGREDIENTS | YIELDS 2 LOAVES

1 medium russet (baking) potato (about ½ pound)

Water, as needed

1 tablespoon granulated sugar

1¾ teaspoons active dry yeast (1 package)

1½ cups milk

1½ teaspoons plus 1 pinch kosher salt

2 tablespoons unsalted butter, room temperature

1½ cups plus 1 handful rolled oats (not quick cooking)

5–7 cups bread flour

1 egg

1. Peel and quarter potato, place in a small saucepan, cover with cold water, and bring to a boil. Cook until tender; drain, and reserve liquid. Mash with a fork and set aside.

2. In a large bowl, combine ½ cup reserved potato water, sugar, and yeast. Stir to dissolve and let stand until foamy, about 10 minutes.

3. Add milk, 1½ teaspoons salt, butter, 1½ cups oats, and 1 cup flour. Stir to combine. Add enough remaining flour to create a firm dough. Turn out onto a floured surface and knead 8–10 minutes. Return to bowl, dust the top lightly with flour, and cover with a damp cloth or plastic wrap. Rise at room temperature until doubled in volume, about 1 hour.

4. Coat two 9" x 5" loaf pans with pan spray, and line the bottom and short sides with parchment. Turn risen dough onto a floured surface, divide into 2 equal portions, and shape into oblong loaves. Place into prepared pans, seam-side down. Set aside to proof for 30 minutes. Preheat oven to 350°F.

5. Whisk egg with a tablespoon of water and pinch of salt, and brush lightly over risen loaf. Sprinkle with a handful of oats, then bake until golden brown and hollow sounding, about 30–40 minutes. Cool 10 minutes, remove from pans, and cool completely on a rack.

Semolina Bread with Mushrooms and Shallots

This recipe is great as written, or you can substitute a more exotic variety of mushroom. Try shiitake, morels, chanterelles, or any dried and reconstituted mushrooms, which usually have a deeper, woodier flavor than the fresh variety.

INGREDIENTS | YIELDS 1 LOAF

2 tablespoons olive oil

2 shallots, chopped

2 cups sliced mushrooms

¾ teaspoon kosher salt

1 tablespoon fresh sage, finely chopped (or 1 teaspoon dried or rubbed sage)

2 cups warm water

1 tablespoon honey

1¾ teaspoons active dry yeast (1 package)

1 cup semolina flour

3–4 cups bread flour

2 tablespoons cornmeal

1. Heat oil in a large sauté pan over high heat. Add shallots and cook until translucent. Add mushrooms, ½ teaspoon salt, and sage. Reduce heat to medium and cook until mushrooms are tender and their liquid has evaporated, about 10 minutes. Remove from heat and set aside to cool.

2. In a large bowl, combine water, honey, and yeast. Stir to dissolve and let stand until foamy, about 10 minutes.

3. Add semolina and mushroom mixture; stir to combine. Add remaining ¼ teaspoon salt and enough bread flour to create a firm dough. Add flour only to reduce stickiness. Turn out onto a floured surface and knead 8–10 minutes. Return to bowl, dust the top with flour, and cover with a damp cloth or plastic wrap. Rise at room temperature until doubled in volume, about 2 hours.

4. Line a baking sheet with parchment, and sprinkle with cornmeal. Turn risen dough onto a floured surface, divide into 2 equal portions, and shape into round loaves. Place onto prepared pan, cover loosely with plastic wrap, and set aside to proof for 30 minutes. Preheat oven to 375°F.

5. Dust the top of the risen loaves with semolina. Using a serrated knife, slash three diagonal lines into the surface of the risen dough, about ½" deep. Place a pan of cold water at the bottom of the oven to create steam. Bake until golden brown and hollow sounding, about 30–40 minutes. Cool completely on a rack before serving.

Sprouted Grain Sandwich Loaf

You can buy sprouts or grow your own for this crunchy, fresh sandwich loaf.

INGREDIENTS | YIELDS 1 LOAF

¾ cup plus 1 tablespoon water

1 teaspoon granulated sugar

1¾ teaspoons active dry yeast
(1 package)

1 cup sprouted grains, chopped

½ cup whole wheat flour

2 teaspoons plus 1 pinch kosher salt

3–5 cups bread flour

1 egg

Super Sprouts

It's easy to grow sprouts yourself using wheat, barley, spelt, kamut, quinoa, and just about any other seed, bean, or grain. Place ¼ cup seeds or grains in a glass or plastic jar. Cover with cheesecloth or a clean nylon stocking and secure with a rubber band. Fill jar with lukewarm water and leave at room temperature for 2 hours. Turn jar upside down to drain, then set in indirect sunlight. Rinse and drain twice a day for 4–5 days. When sprouts are 1" tall, they are ready to use.

1. In a large bowl, combine ¾ cup water, sugar, and yeast. Stir to dissolve and let stand until foamy, about 10 minutes.

2. Add sprouts, whole wheat flour, and 2 teaspoons salt; stir to combine. Add enough bread flour to create a firm dough. Add flour only to reduce stickiness. Turn out onto a floured surface and knead 8–10 minutes. Return to bowl, dust the top with flour, and cover with a damp cloth or plastic wrap. Rise at room temperature until doubled in volume, about 1½ hours.

3. Coat a 9" × 5" loaf pan with pan spray and line the bottom and short sides with a strip of parchment. Turn risen dough onto a floured surface and shape into an oblong loaf. Place into prepared pan seam-side down, and set aside to proof for 30 minutes, or until dough rises above the pan. Preheat oven to 350°F.

4. Whisk egg with a pinch of salt and a tablespoon of water, and lightly brush it over the risen dough. Bake until golden brown and hollow sounding, about 30–40 minutes. Cool 10 minutes, remove from pan, and cool completely on a rack.

Stone-Ground Corn and Wheat Bread

Cornmeal gives this bread a lovely, sweet flavor and a hearty texture. Any type of cornmeal will do here, including yellow, white, blue, or red. Be adventurous!

INGREDIENTS | YIELDS 2 LOAVES

1 cup warm water

3 tablespoons honey

1¾ teaspoons active dry yeast (1 package)

3 eggs

¼ cup olive oil, plus more as needed

2 cups fresh or frozen and thawed corn kernels

1 cup scallions, finely chopped

1½ cups cornmeal

½ cup whole wheat flour

¾ teaspoon kosher salt

3–4 cups bread flour

¼ cup cornmeal

1. In a large bowl, combine water, honey, and yeast. Stir to dissolve and let stand until foamy, about 10 minutes.

2. Add eggs, ¼ cup oil, corn, scallions, cornmeal, and whole wheat flour; stir to combine. Add salt and enough bread flour to create a firm dough. Add flour only to reduce stickiness. Turn out onto a floured surface and knead 8–10 minutes. Return to bowl, dust the top with flour, and cover with a damp cloth or plastic wrap. Rise at room temperature until doubled in volume, about 2 hours.

3. Coat two 9" × 5" loaf pans with pan spray, and dust thoroughly with cornmeal. Turn risen dough onto a floured surface, divide into 2 equal portions, and shape into oblong loaves. Place into prepared pans seam-side down. Cover loosely with plastic wrap and set aside to proof for 30 minutes, or until dough rises above the pans. Preheat oven to 375°F.

4. Brush olive oil gently onto the surface of the risen dough and sprinkle lightly with cornmeal. Bake until golden brown and hollow sounding, about 30–40 minutes. Cool 10 minutes, remove from pans, and cool completely on a rack.

Whole Wheat Sandwich Bread

This recipe employs the sponge method, which gives this simple bread a more complex flavor.

INGREDIENTS | YIELDS 1 LOAF

1 cup buttermilk

1¾ teaspoons active dry yeast
(1 package)

4–5 cups whole wheat flour

½ cup water

2 tablespoons unsalted butter

2 tablespoons honey

¾ teaspoon plus 1 pinch kosher salt

1 egg

The Whole Wheat Feel

If this is your first whole wheat recipe, you may be surprised at the feel of the dough. Whole wheat flour is more coarse, and because it has less gluten than bread flour overall, the dough is stickier and less elastic. Never fear! Different is not necessarily bad!

1. For the sponge: Combine buttermilk and yeast. Stir to dissolve and let stand until foamy, about 5 minutes. Add 1 cup whole wheat flour and beat for 1 minute. Cover and let stand at room temperature 8–12 hours.

2. Add to the sponge the water, butter, honey, ¾ teaspoon salt, and enough of the remaining whole wheat flour to make a soft dough. Turn out onto a floured work surface and knead 8–10 minutes. Add flour only to reduce stickiness. Return to bowl, dust with flour, cover with plastic, and rise at room temperature until doubled in volume, about 1 hour.

3. Coat a 9" × 5" loaf pan with pan spray, and line its length with a strip of parchment. Turn risen dough onto a lightly floured work surface, and shape into a loaf. Place in prepared pan, seam-side down. Dust lightly with flour, cover loosely with plastic wrap, and proof until doubled in volume, about 1 hour.

4. Preheat oven to 350°F. Beat egg with a pinch of salt, then brush lightly and evenly over the surface of the loaf. Bake 40–50 minutes, until golden brown and hollow-sounding when tapped from the bottom. Cool 10 minutes, remove from pan, and cool completely on a rack.

Wild Rice Loaf

Wild rice gives this rustic loaf a chewy texture and hearty flavor.

INGREDIENTS | YIELDS 2 LOAVES

1½ cups water

¾ cup wild rice

1⅓ cups warm milk

¼ cup honey

1¾ teaspoons active dry yeast (1 package)

¼ cup (½ stick) unsalted butter

1 cup whole wheat flour

¾ teaspoon kosher salt

3–4 cups bread flour

1. Bring water to a boil in a small saucepan over high heat. Add wild rice and stir. When the water returns to boil, reduce heat to low, cover tightly, and cook for 50 minutes, or until rice is tender and water is absorbed. Remove from heat and spread rice onto a baking sheet to cool.

2. In a large bowl, combine milk, 1 tablespoon honey, and yeast. Stir to dissolve and let stand until foamy, about 10 minutes.

3. Add remaining honey, butter, and whole wheat flour; stir to combine. Add salt, and enough bread flour to create a firm dough. Add flour only to reduce stickiness. Turn out onto a floured surface and knead 8–10 minutes. Return to bowl, dust the top with flour, and cover with a damp cloth or plastic wrap. Rise at room temperature until doubled in volume, about 2 hours.

4. Coat two 9" × 5" loaf pans with pan spray, and line the bottom and short sides of each pan with a strip of parchment. Turn risen dough onto a floured surface, divide into 2 equal portions, and shape each into an oblong loaf. Place into prepared pans seam-side down, cover loosely with plastic wrap, and set aside to proof for 30 minutes, or until dough rises above the pans. Preheat oven to 375°F.

5. Dust risen loaves with whole wheat flour, and bake until golden brown and hollow sounding, about 30–40 minutes. Cool 10 minutes, remove from pans, and cool completely on a rack.

3-Grain Brown Loaf

This dough makes a satisfying dark loaf perfect for sandwiches. It makes great rolls, too.

INGREDIENTS | YIELDS 2 LOAVES

1¾ cups warm milk

¼ cup plus 1 tablespoon molasses

1¾ teaspoons active dry yeast (1 package)

2 tablespoons canola oil

1 tablespoon cocoa powder

1 cup whole wheat flour

1 cup rye flour

1 cup rolled oats (not quick cooking)

1½ teaspoons kosher salt

3–4 cups bread flour

1 tablespoon hot water

1. In a large bowl, combine milk, ¼ cup molasses, and yeast. Stir to dissolve and let stand until foamy, about 10 minutes.

2. Add oil, cocoa, whole wheat flour, rye flour, and oats; stir to combine. Add salt and enough bread flour to create a firm dough. Add flour only to reduce stickiness. Turn out onto a floured surface and knead 8–10 minutes. Return to bowl, dust the top with flour, and cover with a damp cloth or plastic wrap. Rise at room temperature until doubled in volume, about 2 hours.

3. Coat two 9" × 5" loaf pans with pan spray, and line the bottom and short sides with a strip of parchment. Turn risen dough onto a floured surface, divide into 2 equal portions, and shape into oblong loaves. Place into prepared pans seam-side down, cover loosely with plastic wrap, and set aside to proof for 30 minutes, or until dough rises above the pans. Preheat oven to 375°F.

4. Combine 1 tablespoon molasses with 1 tablespoon hot water, and brush gently onto the risen dough. Bake until golden brown and hollow sounding, about 30–40 minutes. Cool 10 minutes, remove loaves from pans, and cool completely on a rack.

7-Grain Hearth Bread

Seven grains may seem like overkill, but this wholesome loaf is loaded with flavor and nutrition.

INGREDIENTS | YIELDS 2 LOAVES

1 cup warm water

1 tablespoon honey

1¾ teaspoons active dry yeast (1 package)

½ cup buttermilk

2 eggs

1 cup 7-grain cereal

1 cup whole wheat flour

1½ teaspoons kosher salt

2–3 cups bread flour

2 tablespoons cornmeal

1 tablespoon olive oil

7-Grain Cereal

Many supermarkets and health-food stores now carry a 7-grain mixture. If you can't find one in your area, make your own. Combine 2 tablespoons each of rolled oats, brown rice, rye groats, cracked wheat, buckwheat, barley, and spelt. Add 1 tablespoon each of flax and sesame seeds for good measure, then grind the whole mixture coarsely in a food processor or coffee grinder.

1. In a large bowl, combine water, honey, and yeast. Stir to dissolve and let stand until foamy, about 10 minutes.

2. Add buttermilk, eggs, 7-grain cereal, and whole wheat flour; stir to combine. Add salt and enough bread flour to create a firm dough. Add flour only to reduce stickiness. Turn out onto a floured surface and knead 8–10 minutes. Return to bowl, dust the top with flour, and cover with a damp cloth or plastic wrap. Rise at room temperature until doubled in volume, about 2 hours.

3. Line a baking sheet with parchment, and sprinkle with cornmeal. Turn risen dough onto a floured surface, divide into 2 equal portions, and shape into round loaves. Place onto prepared pan and set aside to proof for 30 minutes. Preheat oven to 375°F.

4. Brush the top of the risen loaves with olive oil. Using a serrated knife, slice a few lines into the surface of the dough, about ½" deep. Place a pan of cold water at the bottom of the oven to create steam. Bake until golden brown and hollow sounding, about 30–40 minutes. Cool completely on a rack before serving.

CHAPTER 4

Artisan Loaves

Caramelized Onion and Asiago Bread

Sweet caramelized onions and salty Asiago cheese combine for a burst of flavor in every bite.

INGREDIENTS | YIELDS 2 LOAVES

2 tablespoons olive oil

2 medium yellow onions, diced

1 cup warm water

2 tablespoons granulated sugar

1¾ teaspoons active dry yeast
(1 package)

1 egg yolk

1½ cups grated Asiago cheese

¾ teaspoon kosher salt

3–4 cups bread flour

2 tablespoons cornmeal

Caramelizing Onions

When raw, onions are very pungent. But cooking releases their natural sugars and mellows their harsh flavor. The key to successful caramelization is patience. If heated too fast, the sugars will burn and become bitter. Allow enough time for slow, gentle heat to produce even colorization.

1. Heat olive oil in a large sauté pan over high heat. Add onions and stir to coat. Reduce heat to medium and cook, stirring frequently, until onions are golden and caramelized, about 30 minutes. Set aside to cool.

2. In a large bowl combine water, 1 tablespoon sugar, and yeast. Stir to dissolve and let stand until foamy, about 10 minutes.

3. Stir in remaining sugar, yolk, cheese, and cooled onions. Add salt and enough bread flour to create a firm dough. Add flour only to reduce stickiness. Turn out onto a floured surface and knead 8–10 minutes. Return to bowl, dust the top with flour, and cover with a damp cloth or plastic wrap. Rise at room temperature until doubled in volume, about 1½ hours.

4. Line a baking sheet with parchment, and sprinkle with cornmeal. Turn risen dough onto a floured surface, divide into 2 equal portions, and shape into round loaves. Place onto prepared pan and set aside to proof for 30 minutes. Preheat oven to 375°F.

5. Dust the top of the risen loaves with flour, and using a serrated knife, cut an "X" into the surface of the dough, about ½" deep. Place a pan of cold water at the bottom of the oven to create steam. Bake until golden brown and hollow sounding, about 30–40 minutes. Cool completely on a rack before serving.

Fuchsia Beet Bread with Horseradish

If you fancy a colorful table, try making a second batch of this dough with another purée, such as carrot or spinach, then swirl them together jellyroll-style for a Technicolor marble bread.

INGREDIENTS | YIELDS 2 LOAVES

3 large beets, scrubbed clean, with stems removed

⅔ cup warm water

1¾ teaspoons active dry yeast (1 package)

2 eggs

⅓ cup prepared horseradish

1 teaspoon kosher salt

2–3 cups bread flour

2 tablespoons olive oil

1. Preheat oven to 500°F. Wrap beets together in foil and bake until tender, about 1 hour. Cool completely. Peel off skin and purée beets in a food processor or blender. Set aside.

2. In a large bowl, combine water, beets, and yeast. Stir to dissolve and let stand until foamy, about 10 minutes.

3. Add eggs, horseradish, and salt; stir to combine. Add enough bread flour to create a firm dough. Add flour only to reduce stickiness. Turn out onto a floured surface and knead 8–10 minutes. Return to bowl, dust the top with flour, and cover with a damp cloth or plastic wrap. Rise at room temperature until doubled in volume, about 2 hours.

4. Coat two 9" × 5" loaf pan with pan spray and line the bottom and short sides of each pan with a strip of parchment. Turn risen dough onto a floured surface, divide into 2 equal portions, and shape into oblong loaves. Place into prepared pans seam-side down, and set aside to proof for 30 minutes, or until dough rises above the pans. Preheat oven to 350°F.

5. Brush the risen dough gently with olive oil, and bake until golden brown and hollow sounding, about 30–40 minutes. Cool 10 minutes, remove from pans, and cool completely on a rack.

Italian Altamura

Olive oil, semolina, and a prolonged fermentation give this crusty loaf a distinctively Italian taste.

INGREDIENTS | **YIELDS 2 LOAVES**

2 cups cold water

1¾ teaspoons active dry yeast
(1 package)

1 cup all-purpose flour

1 tablespoon olive oil

1 cup semolina flour

1 teaspoon kosher salt

2–3 cups bread flour

2 tablespoons cornmeal

About Altamura

Altamura, known throughout Italy as the city of bread, lies in Puglia, the region occupying the heel of Italy's boot. In Altamura, bread is made with as much reverence, history, and craftsmanship as any wine. Made from natural yeast starters and shaped into big wheels, this bread is so revered that if a loaf drops to the floor, it is picked up, kissed, and eaten.

1. To create the sponge, combine 1 cup water and yeast, stir to dissolve, and let stand 5 minutes. Add all-purpose flour and beat for 1 minute. Cover and let stand at room temperature 8–12 hours.

2. Add to the sponge 1 cup water, olive oil, semolina, salt, and enough bread flour to make a soft dough. Turn out onto a floured work surface and knead 8–10 minutes. Add flour only to reduce stickiness. Return to bowl, dust with flour, cover with plastic, and rise at room temperature until doubled in volume, about 1 hour. Punch dough down, fold it in half, and let it rise again, until doubled, about 45 minutes.

3. Line a baking sheet with parchment, and sprinkle with cornmeal. Turn risen dough onto a floured surface, and divide into 2 equal portions. Shape into round loaves, place onto prepared pan, cover loosely with plastic wrap, and set aside to proof for 30 minutes. Preheat oven to 375°F.

4. Dust the top of the risen loaves generously with flour. Using a serrated knife, cut decorative slash marks into the surface of the dough, about ½" deep. Place a pan of cold water at the bottom of the oven to create steam. Bake until golden brown and hollow sounding, about 30–40 minutes. Cool completely on a rack before serving.

Italian Ciabatta

Ciabatta *means "slipper," and this loaf is shaped like one. This shape, along with the airy crumb and crisp crust, are a direct result of this dough's high moisture content. It's a wet one!*

INGREDIENTS | YIELDS 1 LOAF

1 cup warm water
1¾ teaspoons active dry yeast
(1 package)
1 cup whole wheat flour
¼ cup milk
¼ cup olive oil, plus more as needed
1 teaspoon plus 1 pinch kosher salt
2¼ cups bread flour
¼ cup cornmeal

Docking

"Docking" is the method used to help flat-breads keep their flat shape. By marking the surface with holes or indentations, the gasses are prevented from accumulating in the center of the bread and inflating it into a mound.

1. To create the sponge, combine water and yeast. Stir to dissolve and let stand 5 minutes. Add whole wheat flour and beat for 1 minute. Cover and let stand at room temperature 8–12 hours.

2. Add to the sponge the milk, ¼ cup olive oil, 1 teaspoon salt, and bread flour. Beat by hand or electric mixer for 5–6 minutes, until elastic. The dough will be very loose. Cover with plastic, and leave at room temperature until doubled in volume, about 1 hour.

3. Line a baking sheet with parchment, brush with olive oil, and sprinkle with cornmeal. Turn risen dough gently onto a floured surface and divide into 2 equal portions. Transfer to prepared pan and shape each into a flat oval, using oiled hands. Press fingertips into dough to create dimples. Cover again with plastic and rise until doubled, another 1½ hours. Preheat oven to 475°F.

4. Brush the top of the risen loaves with olive oil and a pinch of salt, and bake until golden brown and hollow sounding, about 20–30 minutes. Cool completely on a rack.

Kalamata Olive Bread

Salty olives add a mouth-watering element to this artisan bread, perfect for pre-dinner nibbling.

INGREDIENTS | YIELDS 2 LOAVES

1 cup warm water

1 tablespoon honey

1¾ teaspoons active dry yeast
(1 package)

1 cup all-purpose flour

2¼ cups milk

1 cup kalamata olives, pitted
and chopped

¼ teaspoon kosher salt

3–4 cups bread flour

2 tablespoons cornmeal

1. To create the sponge, combine water, honey, and yeast. Stir to dissolve and let stand 5 minutes. Add all-purpose flour and beat for 1 minute. Cover and let stand at room temperature 8–12 hours.

2. Add to the sponge the milk, olives, salt, and enough flour to make a soft dough. Turn out onto a floured work surface and knead 8–10 minutes. Add flour only to reduce stickiness. Return to bowl, dust with flour, cover with plastic, and rise at room temperature until doubled in volume, about 2 hours.

3. Line a baking sheet with parchment and sprinkle with cornmeal. Turn risen dough onto a floured surface, divide into 2 equal portions, and shape into 2 oblong loaves. Place onto prepared pan seam-side down, cover loosely with plastic wrap, and set aside to proof for 30 minutes. Preheat oven to 375°F.

4. Dust the top of the risen loaves generously with flour. Using a serrated knife, cut decorative slash marks into the surface of the dough, about ½" deep. Place a pan of cold water at the bottom of the oven to create steam. Bake until golden brown and hollow sounding, about 30–40 minutes. Cool completely on a rack before serving.

Oatmeal Raisin Hearth Bread

Brown sugar and oats are a sweet and comforting pair. Their combination here makes a fantastic breakfast bread, especially when smeared generously with homemade jam.

INGREDIENTS | YIELDS 2 LOAVES

2½ cups boiling water

1¾ cups steel-cut oats

1 cup raisins

1 tablespoon plus 1 pinch kosher salt

3 tablespoons butter

½ cup warm milk

3 tablespoons brown sugar

1¾ teaspoons active dry yeast
(1 package)

1 cup whole wheat flour

4–6 cups bread flour

¼ cup cornmeal

1 large egg

1 cup rolled oats (not quick cooking)

All about Oats

Oats are one of the most nutritious grains on the planet. Oat protein is similar to that of a legume, and thought to be nutritionally comparable to soy. Consumption of the outer bran is thought to lower LDL cholesterol and reduce the risk of heart disease. Oats come in a variety of forms, including groats, steel-cut, rolled, or quick cooking.

1. In a large bowl, combine water, steel-cut oats, raisins, 1 tablespoon salt, and butter. Stir together, then let stand 30–45 minutes, until oats have softened. Set aside.

2. In another large bowl, combine milk, brown sugar, and yeast. Stir to dissolve and let stand until foamy, about 10 minutes.

3. Add whole wheat flour and oat mixture; and stir to combine. Add enough bread flour to create a firm dough. Add flour only to reduce stickiness. Turn out onto a floured surface and knead 8–10 minutes. Return to bowl, dust the top with flour, and cover with a damp cloth or plastic wrap. Rise at room temperature until doubled in volume, about 1 hour.

4. Line a baking sheet with parchment, and sprinkle with cornmeal. Turn risen dough onto a floured surface, divide into 2 equal portions, and shape into oblong loaves. Place onto prepared pan, seam-side down. Dust with flour, cover loosely with plastic wrap, and set aside to proof for 30 minutes. Preheat oven to 375°F.

5. Whisk egg with a pinch of salt and brush across the surface of risen loaves. Sprinkle liberally with rolled oats, and using a serrated knife, cut decorative slash marks into the surface of the dough, about ½" deep. Place a pan of cold water at the bottom of the oven to create steam, and bake until golden brown and hollow sounding, about 30–40 minutes. Cool completely on a rack before serving.

Potato Crunch Bread

With tangy sour cream and chives, this bread is reminiscent of your favorite side dish.

INGREDIENTS | YIELDS 2 LOAVES

1 large russet (baking) potato (about 1 pound)

½ cup water

2 tablespoons granulated sugar

3½ teaspoons active dry yeast (2 packages)

1 cup sour cream

1½ teaspoons plus 1 pinch kosher salt

2 tablespoons unsalted butter, room temperature

¼ cup fresh chives, minced

5–7 cups bread flour

½ cup warm water

1 tablespoon olive oil

¾ cup rice flour

1. Preheat oven to 450°F. Place potato on oven rack and bake until soft, about 30 minutes. Cool completely. Cut in half, scoop out all potato from skin, mash with a fork, and set aside.

2. In a large bowl, combine ½ cup water, 1 tablespoon sugar, and 1 package yeast. Stir to dissolve and let stand until foamy, about 10 minutes.

3. Add potato, sour cream, 1½ teaspoons salt, butter, chives, and 1 cup flour; stir to combine. Add enough remaining flour to create a firm dough. Turn out onto a floured surface and knead 8–10 minutes. Return to bowl, dust the top lightly with flour, and cover with a damp cloth or plastic wrap. Rise at room temperature until doubled in volume, about 1 hour.

4. While the dough is rising, make the crunch batter. Combine remaining yeast with warm water, remaining tablespoon sugar, olive oil, rice flour, and a pinch of salt. Beat until smooth, then set aside to rest until dough is doubled (at least 15 minutes).

5. Coat two 9" × 5" loaf pans with pan spray, and line the bottoms and short sides of each with a strip of parchment. Turn risen dough onto a floured surface, divide into 2 equal portions, and shape into oblong loaves. Place into prepared pans, seam-side down. Brush loaves with a thick layer of crunch batter and set aside to proof for 30 minutes. Preheat oven to 350°F.

6. Bake until golden brown and hollow sounding, about 30–40 minutes. Cool 10 minutes, remove from pans, and cool completely on a rack.

Pugliese

This beautiful loaf comes from the same region as the Italian Altamura (page 60). Its big, airy crumb is a result of prolonged fermentation. Don't rush it. It's worth the wait.

INGREDIENTS | YIELDS 2 LOAVES

2 cups water

1¼ cups all-purpose flour

1¾ teaspoons active dry yeast (1 package)

3–4 cups bread flour

2 teaspoons kosher salt

2 tablespoons cornmeal

1 tablespoon olive oil

1. To make the sponge, combine ½ cup water, all-purpose flour, and a pinch of the yeast. Stir to dissolve, cover with a towel or cheesecloth, and let stand at room temperature 12–16 hours.

2. Add to the sponge 1½ cups water, remaining yeast, bread flour, and salt. Beat by hand or electric mixer 5–6 minutes until elastic. Dough will be very loose and wet. Cover with plastic, and leave at room temperature for 3 hours, stirring briefly every hour to deflate.

3. Coat a baking sheet with olive oil and sprinkle with cornmeal. Divide dough into 2 equal portions. Transfer to prepared pan and, using oiled hands, shape each into a flat oval. Oil the top surface of dough and cover tightly with plastic wrap. Allow to rise 1½ hours more. The dough will spread.

4. Preheat oven to 475°F. Spray the surface of the risen dough with warm water, then bake until golden brown and hollow sounding, about 20–30 minutes. Cool completely on a rack before serving.

Rosemary Raisin Bread

This uniquely Italian pairing of fruit and herbs has both sweet and savory highlights. For best results, be sure to use fresh rosemary.

INGREDIENTS | YIELDS 2 LOAVES

1 cup warm water

1 tablespoon granulated sugar

1¾ teaspoons active dry yeast (1 package)

1 cup all-purpose flour

1 cup golden raisins

¼ cup fresh rosemary, finely chopped

2¼ cups milk

¼ teaspoon kosher salt

3–4 cups bread flour

2 tablespoons cornmeal

1. To make the sponge, combine water, sugar, and yeast, stir to dissolve, and let stand 5 minutes. Add all-purpose flour and beat for 1 minute. Cover and let stand at room temperature 8–12 hours.

2. Add to the sponge the raisins, rosemary, milk, salt, and enough bread flour to make a soft dough. Turn out onto a floured work surface and knead 8–10 minutes. Add flour only to reduce stickiness. Return to bowl, dust with flour, cover with plastic, and rise at room temperature until doubled in volume, about 2 hours.

3. Line a baking sheet with parchment and sprinkle with cornmeal. Turn risen dough onto a floured surface, divide into 2 equal portions, and shape into round loaves. Place onto prepared pan, seam-side down, cover loosely with plastic wrap, and set aside to proof for 30 minutes. Preheat oven to 375°F.

4. Dust the top of the risen loaves generously with flour, and using a serrated knife, cut a decorative crosshatch into the surface of the dough, about ½" deep. Place a pan of cold water at the bottom of the oven to create steam. Bake until golden brown and hollow sounding, about 30–40 minutes. Cool completely on a rack before serving.

Saffron Date Bread

The color of this bread is amazing, and the dates add a touch of sweetness.
Use good-quality dates, not the dried-up, pre-chopped kind.

INGREDIENTS | **YIELDS 2 LOAVES**

1 pinch saffron threads (about
⅛ teaspoon)

1½ cups warm water

1 tablespoon honey

1¾ teaspoons active dry yeast
(1 package)

1½ cups dates, pitted and chopped

½ cup whole wheat flour

¾ teaspoon kosher salt

3–4 cups bread flour

¼ cup cornmeal

Precious Saffron

Saffron, the most cherished of all spices, can be found in the center of a low-growing purple crocus. The exorbitant price of those three orange stigmata is justified when you consider that each stigma must be picked by hand. It takes approximately 75,000 stigmata to make 1 pound of saffron. Luckily, it doesn't take much saffron to color and flavor food. But be careful! Too much of this good thing can become unpleasantly bitter.

1. Heat a small, dry skillet over high heat, and add saffron threads. Immediately remove from heat and shake the pan for 20–30 seconds to evenly toast threads. Pour out of pan immediately and set aside to cool.

2. In a large bowl, combine water, toasted saffron threads (rub gently to crush), honey, and yeast. Stir to dissolve and let stand until foamy, about 10 minutes.

3. Add dates, and whole wheat flour; stir to combine. Add salt and enough bread flour to create a firm dough. Add flour only to reduce stickiness. Turn out onto a floured surface and knead 8–10 minutes. Return to bowl, dust the top with flour, and cover with a damp cloth or plastic wrap. Rise at room temperature until doubled in volume, about 2 hours.

4. Line a baking sheet with parchment and sprinkle with cornmeal. Turn risen dough onto a floured surface, divide into 2 equal portions, and shape into round loaves. Place onto prepared pan, seam-side down, cover loosely with plastic wrap, and set aside to proof for 30 minutes. Preheat oven to 375°F.

5. Dust the top of the risen loaves generously with flour, and using a serrated knife, cut decorative slash marks into the surface of the dough, about ½" deep. Place a pan of cold water at the bottom of the oven to create steam. Bake until golden brown and hollow sounding, about 30–40 minutes. Cool completely on a rack before serving.

Sea Salt and Herb Fougasse

This beautiful bread is often considered Italian, but is really from the Provence region of France. The shape, which is often representative of palm leaves, a stalk of wheat, or a ladder, is meant to have as many cuts and holes as possible, to produce as much crust as possible.

INGREDIENTS | YIELDS 1 LOAF

1¾ cups warm water

1¾ teaspoons active dry yeast
(1 package)

1 cup all-purpose flour

2 tablespoons granulated sugar

½ cup olive oil, plus more as needed

1 teaspoon kosher salt

3–4 cups bread flour

2 tablespoons cornmeal

2 tablespoons herbes de Provence

2 tablespoons coarse sea salt

Herbes de Provence

This classic French blend of herbs can be found in most supermarkets, or you can make your own, using either fresh or dried versions of these herbs. In a large bowl, combine equal parts of chervil, marjoram, tarragon, and basil, and half as much thyme and lavender. If fresh, mince all ingredients together. If dry, simply stir.

1. To make the sponge, combine water and yeast, stir to dissolve, and let stand 5 minutes. Add all-purpose flour and beat for 1 minute. Cover and let stand at room temperature 8–12 hours.

2. Add to the sponge the sugar, ½ cup oil, kosher salt, and enough bread flour to make a soft dough. Turn out onto a floured work surface and knead 8–10 minutes. Add flour only to reduce stickiness. Return to bowl, dust with flour, cover with plastic, and rise at room temperature until doubled in volume, about 2 hours.

3. Coat a baking sheet with pan spray and sprinkle with cornmeal. Turn risen dough onto prepared pan and, using oiled fingertips, flatten into a large oval, about 2" thick. Press fingertips into dough all across the surface to create dimples. Cover again with plastic and rise until doubled, about 30 minutes. Preheat oven to 475°F.

4. Brush the top of the risen loaf with olive oil. Using a knife, cut slits in the oval-shaped dough to resemble the rungs of a ladder. With oiled fingers, gently pull openings apart to create wide holes in the dough. Cover and rise another 15 minutes. Sprinkle loaf liberally with herbs and sea salt. Place a pan of cold water at the bottom of the oven to create steam, and bake until golden brown and hollow sounding, about 20–30 minutes. Cool completely on a rack.

Sourdough Starter

This starter takes about 2 weeks to create, but the longer you keep it going, the better it will be.

INGREDIENTS | YIELDS 9 CUPS STARTER

3 cups water
⅛ teaspoon active dry yeast
3 cups all-purpose flour

Ancient Sourdough

Bread is an ancient food. Bakeries have been unearthed in Giza dating to 2600 B.C., and loaves, grains, drawings of bakeries, and carvings of people kneading dough have been found in Egyptian tombs. The only way bread could have been made in the ancient world was by utilizing the long process of harnessing naturally occurring yeast, the same way we do it today. Sourdough is the delicious dough of antiquity.

1. **Day 1:** Combine 1 cup water, yeast, and 1 cup flour in a ceramic or glass bowl. Stir to combine, cover loosely with damp cheesecloth or towel, and set aside at room temperature. Stir this mixture once a day for the next 3 days.

2. **Day 5:** Add to the starter 1 cup water and 1 cup flour. Stir well, cover again, and set aside at room temperature for another 4 days, stirring once a day, as before.

3. **Day 10:** Again, add 1 cup water and 1 cup flour. Mix thoroughly. Let stand at room temperature loosely covered for 6 hours, or until the starter foams and doubles in volume. The starter is now ready to use. To keep your starter alive, replace the quantity that has been used with an equal amount of water and flour (for every 1 cup used, replace with ½ cup water and ½ cup flour). Keep covered, stir it every day, and feed it every 5 days by removing some starter and again replacing it with an equal amount of water and flour. If you do not wish to feed it, but want to keep it, cover, airtight, and refrigerate indefinitely, taking it out and repeating the process (removing and replacing 1 cup as before) for 10 days before using it again.

Sourdough Boule

Boule literally means "ball," and indeed these loaves are golden spheres of yummy goodness.

INGREDIENTS | YIELDS 2 LOAVES

1 cup Sourdough Starter (page 69)

1 cup water

1¾ teaspoons active dry yeast (1 package)

1 cup all-purpose flour

1 teaspoon kosher salt

3–4 cups bread flour

2 tablespoons cornmeal

1. To make the sponge, combine starter, ½ cup water, and yeast. Stir to dissolve and let stand 5 minutes. Add all-purpose flour and beat 1 minute. Cover and let stand at room temperature 8–12 hours.

2. Add to the sponge ½ cup water, salt, and enough bread flour to make a soft dough. Turn out onto a floured work surface and knead 8–10 minutes. Add flour only to reduce stickiness. Return to bowl, dust with flour, cover with plastic, and rise at room temperature until doubled in volume, about 1½ hours.

3. Line a baking sheet with parchment, and sprinkle with cornmeal. Turn risen dough onto a floured surface and divide into 2 equal portions. Roll into balls and place on prepared pan, seam-side down. Dust generously with flour, cover again with plastic, and rise until doubled, about 30 minutes. Preheat oven to 475°F.

4. Using a serrated knife, slice decorative slash marks into the surface of the dough, about ½" deep. Place a pan of cold water at the bottom of the oven to create steam. Bake until golden brown and hollow sounding, about 30–40 minutes. Cool completely on a rack.

Sourdough Rye Loaf

The starch content of rye flour makes it exceptional food for sourdough starter. But more important, the sweet, succulent flavor of caraway is the perfect complement to that sour flavor.

INGREDIENTS | YIELDS 2 LOAVES

1 cup Sourdough Starter (page 69)

1 cup water

1¾ teaspoons active dry yeast (1 package)

1 cup light rye flour

1 teaspoon kosher salt

1 cup whole wheat flour

2–3 cups bread flour

2 tablespoons cornmeal

A Baker's Signature

Scoring patterns allow bread to expand decoratively in the oven where the baker wants it to, but they are also a baker's signature. Since most bakeries produce similar breads, one way they differentiate their products from others is by the decorative slash marks in the surface of the dough. Why not create your own decorative, signature slashes?

1. To make the sponge, combine starter, ½ cup water, and yeast. Stir to dissolve and let stand 5 minutes. Add rye flour and beat for 1 minute. Cover and let stand at room temperature 8–12 hours.

2. Add to the sponge ½ cup water, salt, whole wheat flour, and enough bread flour to make a soft dough. Turn out onto a floured work surface and knead 8–10 minutes. Add flour only to reduce stickiness. Return to bowl, dust with flour, cover with plastic, and rise at room temperature until doubled in volume, about 1½ hours.

3. Line a baking sheet with parchment, and sprinkle with cornmeal. Turn risen dough onto a floured surface. Divide into 2 equal portions. Roll into balls and place on prepared pan, seam-side down. Dust generously with flour, cover again with plastic, and rise until doubled, for 30 minutes. Preheat oven to 475°F.

4. Using a serrated knife, slice a pinwheel or star pattern into the top of the dough, about ½" deep. Place a pan of cold water at the bottom of the oven to create steam. Bake until golden brown and hollow sounding, about 30–40 minutes. Cool completely on a rack.

Zoo Bread

This bread is named after the shapes that can be formed. The inspiration came from fanciful bread made for tourists at San Francisco's Fisherman's Wharf, but the shapes are limited only by your imagination.

INGREDIENTS | YIELDS 1–2 LOAVES

1½ cups warm water

1¾ teaspoons active dry yeast (1 package)

½ cup all-purpose flour

1 teaspoon granulated sugar

2 tablespoons unsalted butter

1 teaspoon kosher salt

2–3 cups bread flour

¼ cup cornmeal

1. To make the sponge, combine water and yeast, stir to dissolve, and let stand 5 minutes. Add all-purpose flour and beat 1 minute. Cover and let stand at room temperature 8–12 hours.

2. Add to the sponge the sugar, butter, salt, and enough bread flour to make a soft dough. Turn out onto a floured work surface and knead 8–10 minutes. Add flour only to reduce stickiness. Return to bowl, dust with flour, cover with plastic, and rise at room temperature until doubled in volume, about 1½ hours.

3. Line a baking sheet with parchment, and sprinkle with cornmeal. Turn risen dough onto a floured surface, and form into animal shapes (see instructions below). Place on prepared pans, dust generously with flour, cover again with plastic, and rise until doubled, about 30 minutes. Preheat oven to 475°F. Bake until golden brown and hollow sounding, about 20–30 minutes. Cool completely on a rack before serving.

4. To create Alligator Bread, divide dough into 2 portions, one twice as large as the other. Roll the large portion into a tapered baguette, and place on baking sheet, seam-side down. Divide remaining dough into 4 small teardrop-shaped balls. Tuck the tapered ends of the teardrops under the baguette, 2 on each side, for feet. After proofing, use scissors to cut small V-shaped scales down the back. Snip small Xs for eyes, and snip open a mouth. Bake as instructed.

Zoo Bread *(continued)*

5. To create Crab Bread, divide dough into 2 equal portions. Roll one into a ball, and place on the baking sheet, seam-side down. Divide remaining piece in half. Form one half into a long rope, and the other into 2 large and 2 small balls. Wrap the rope around the back in a U-shape for arms. Place a large ball at each end of the rope for claws. Place the 2 small balls on top of the crab body for eyes. After proofing, use scissors to snip scales across the back, and snip each claw open. Bake as instructed.

6. To create Turtle Bread, divide dough into 2 equal portions. Roll one into a ball, and place on the baking sheet, seam-side down. Divide remaining dough into 5 small balls and 1 medium ball. Roll balls into a teardrop shape. Tuck the tapered ends under the large ball. The medium ball is the head, and the rest are four legs and a tail. After proofing, score the large ball (shell) in a crosshatch pattern, and snip small Xs for eyes. Bake as instructed.

Spinach and Sun-Dried Tomato Bread

This bread is delicious on its own, but it also makes fantastic sandwiches. Try it for your next BLT.

INGREDIENTS | YIELDS 2 LOAVES

1 package frozen chopped spinach, defrosted and squeezed dry

3 tablespoons olive oil, plus more as needed

⅔ cup warm water

1¾ teaspoons active dry yeast (1 package)

1 cup sun-dried tomatoes in oil, drained and finely chopped

2 eggs

1 teaspoon kosher salt

2–3 cups bread flour

1. Using a blender, process spinach and 3 tablespoons oil to a fine purée.

2. In a large bowl, combine water, spinach purée, and yeast. Stir to dissolve and let stand until foamy, about 10 minutes.

3. Add sun-dried tomatoes, eggs, and salt; stir to combine. Add enough bread flour to create a firm dough. Add flour only to reduce stickiness. Turn out onto a floured surface and knead 8–10 minutes. Return to bowl, dust the top with flour, and cover with a damp cloth or plastic wrap. Rise at room temperature until doubled in volume, about 2 hours.

4. Coat two 9" × 5" loaf pans with pan spray and line the bottoms and short sides with a strip of parchment. Turn risen dough onto a floured surface, divide into 2 equal portions, and shape into oblong loaves. Place into prepared pans, seam-side down. Cover loosely with plastic wrap and set aside to proof for 30 minutes, or until dough rises above the pan. Preheat oven to 350°F.

5. Gently brush the surface of the risen dough with oil, and bake until golden brown and hollow sounding, about 30–40 minutes. Cool 10 minutes, remove from pans, and cool completely on a rack.

CHAPTER 5

Braided Breads

Braid Rules

Most of the breads in this chapter specify forming a 3-strand braid, but any of them can be made into more complicated shapes. (Instructions for fancier braids are sprinkled throughout the chapter.)

Bread braiding instructions are written in code. Each strand is numbered from left to right, and instructions indicate strand numbers passing over one another. For example, a 3-strand braid is numbered 1, 2, and 3 from left to right. The instructions start with "1 over 2." This means that the outer left strand is lifted up and over the middle strand, and nestled between the middle strand and the far right strand. Now, the strands are renumbered so that they still read 1, 2, and 3 from left to right, even though strand #2 used to be strand #1. The next instruction is "3 over 2," which means the outer right strand is lifted up and over the middle strand, and nestled between the outer left and middle strands. This pattern is repeated to the end of the strand, tightening the strands toward the end. Pinch the dough together to finish off the end.

Those new to bread braiding often end up with their first few loaves a bit lopsided. This is because the strands are naturally tightened as the loaf is braided, making it thinner at the end. Experienced bakers start a 3-strand braid in the middle of the strands, repeating the pattern, pinching off the end, and flipping the loaf upside-down. Then, with the unbraided strands closest to them, braiding continues as before. By starting the braid in the middle of the loaf, the shape is kept symmetrical, with a center that is full and round.

5-Seed Braid

This mixture of seeds is not only beautiful and delicious; it's healthy, too.

INGREDIENTS | YIELDS 1 LOAF

1 tablespoon white sesame seeds

1 tablespoon black sesame seeds

1 tablespoon fennel seeds

1 tablespoon poppy seeds

1 tablespoon flax seeds

1 cup warm milk

2 tablespoons honey

1¾ teaspoons active dry yeast
(1 package)

¼ cup (½ stick) unsalted butter

1 cup whole wheat flour

1 teaspoon plus 1 pinch kosher salt

2–3 cups bread flour

1 egg

1 tablespoon cream

Seedy Nutrition

Seeds contain a variety of nutrients important for a healthy diet. This mixture contains important omega-3 fatty acids, cholesterol-reducing dietary fiber, vitamins including E and B1, and important minerals such as calcium, copper, zinc, iron, and manganese.

1. Combine sesame, fennel, poppy and flax seeds. Set aside 2 tablespoons of seeds for garnishing the top of the loaf. In a large dry sauté pan over high heat, toast remaining seeds until fragrant, about 30–60 seconds. Remove immediately from the hot pan and cool. Pulse in a coffee grinder to a fine powder. Set aside.

2. In a large bowl stir together milk, honey, and yeast. Set aside at room temperature until foamy, about 10 minutes.

3. Stir in butter, whole wheat flour, 1 teaspoon salt, and ground seeds. Add enough bread flour to create a firm dough. Add flour only to reduce stickiness. Turn out onto a floured surface and knead 8–10 minutes. Return to bowl, dust the top with flour, and cover with a damp cloth or plastic wrap. Rise at room temperature until doubled in volume, about 1½ hours.

4. Line a baking sheet with parchment. Turn risen dough onto a floured surface and divide into 3 equal portions. Shape each into a tight rope, no longer than 12", and form a 3-strand braid. Place onto prepared pan, cover loosely with plastic wrap, and set aside to proof for 30 minutes. Preheat oven to 375°F.

5. Whisk together egg, cream, and a pinch of salt, and brush gently onto the top of the risen loaf. Sprinkle with remaining whole seeds, and bake until golden brown and hollow sounding, about 30–40 minutes. Cool completely on a rack before serving.

Apple Spice Braid

This braiding technique is a standard 3-strand. The secret is in the stuffing. It is not a difficult trick, but it is delicate. Be patient.

INGREDIENTS | YIELDS 1 LOAF

2 tablespoons unsalted butter

¼ cup brown sugar

3 large Fuji Apples, cored, peeled, and diced

¾ cup warm milk

3 tablespoons granulated sugar

1¾ teaspoons active dry yeast (1 package)

2 eggs

Grated zest of 1 lemon

1 teaspoon plus 1 pinch kosher salt

2–3 cups bread flour

1 egg

1 tablespoon cream

2 tablespoons cinnamon sugar

Jellyroll

This recipe can be formed into a spiral loaf instead of a stuffed braid. After Step 3, roll the dough into a 16" x 9" rectangle and spread the apple filling on top in a thin layer. Roll up, starting from the short end. Place in a prepared parchment-lined loaf pan, seam-side down, and then continue with Steps 6 and 7. Slice when cool for a fantastic twist on the stuffed braid.

1. Melt butter in a large sauté pan over high heat. Add brown sugar and apples and cook, stirring until apples begin to caramelize. Reduce heat and cook until tender. Remove from heat and set aside to cool.

2. In a large bowl combine milk, sugar, and yeast. Set aside at room temperature until foamy, about 10 minutes.

3. Stir in eggs, lemon zest, 1 teaspoon salt, and enough bread flour to create a firm dough. Add flour only to reduce stickiness. Turn out onto a floured surface and knead 8–10 minutes. Return to bowl, dust the top with flour, and cover with a damp cloth or plastic wrap. Rise at room temperature until doubled in volume, 2 hours.

4. Line a baking sheet with parchment. Turn risen dough onto a floured surface and roll into a rectangle the size of your baking sheet. Spread cooled apple mixture evenly onto dough, then fold dough in half, like a book. Cover and rise again for 30 minutes.

5. Roll risen dough into an elongated rectangle, approximately 16" × 9". Slice the rectangle into 3 strands, each 16" × 3", Form a 3-strand braid. Place onto prepared pan.

6. Cover shaped loaf loosely with plastic wrap, and proof for 30 minutes. Preheat oven to 375°F.

7. Whisk together egg, cream, and a pinch of salt. Gently brush onto the top of the risen loaf. Sprinkle with cinnamon sugar, and bake until golden brown and hollow sounding, about 30–40 minutes. Cool completely on a rack before serving.

Apricot-Almond Braid

Experience a bite of summer with the classic combination of apricots and almonds.

INGREDIENTS | YIELDS 1 LOAF

1 cup dried apricots, chopped

½ cup amaretto

½ cup boiling water

½ cup milk

1 tablespoon honey

3½ teaspoons active dry yeast (2 packages)

1 cup all-purpose flour

¼ cup (½ stick) unsalted butter, softened

3 whole eggs

2 egg yolks

1 teaspoon plus 1 pinch kosher salt

1 cup skin-on almonds, toasted and finely chopped

4–6 cups bread flour

1 tablespoon water

1 cup apricot jelly

1. Combine chopped apricots and amaretto in a small bowl, and add boiling water until apricots are submerged. Set aside to plump 1 hour or overnight.

2. In a large bowl combine milk, honey, and yeast. Stir to dissolve and let stand until foamy, about 10 minutes.

3. Stir in all-purpose flour, butter, 2 whole eggs, both yolks, and 1 teaspoon salt. Add plumped apricots, almonds, and enough bread flour to create a firm dough. Add flour only to reduce stickiness. Turn out onto a floured surface and knead 8–10 minutes. Return to bowl, dust the top with flour, and cover with a damp cloth or plastic wrap. Rise at room temperature until doubled in volume, about 2 hours.

4. Line a baking sheet with parchment. Turn risen dough onto a floured surface, divide into 3 equal portions, and form a 3-strand braid. Place onto prepared pan, cover loosely with plastic wrap, and proof for 30 minutes. Preheat oven to 375°F.

5. Whisk together remaining egg with 1 tablespoon water and a pinch of salt. Brush gently onto the top of the risen loaf, and bake until golden brown and hollow sounding, about 30–40 minutes. Warm the apricot jelly and brush on top of loaf to glaze. Cool completely on a rack before serving.

Bohemian Houska Braid

Most Eastern European countries sport a rich, eggy Easter bread, laden with fruit or spices. This one, from the Czech Republic, is known for its fragrant flavorings of lemon and nutmeg.

INGREDIENTS | YIELDS 1 LOAF

1 cup raisins

1 cup apple juice

2 cups warm milk

1 cup granulated sugar

3½ teaspoons active dry yeast (2 packages)

3 eggs

1 cup (2 sticks) unsalted butter

½ cup heavy cream

1 tablespoon plus 1 pinch kosher salt

1 teaspoon freshly grated nutmeg

1 cup chopped toasted almonds

Grated zest of 3 lemons

6–8 cups bread flour

1 tablespoon unsalted butter, melted

1 egg yolk

1 tablespoon water

1. Combine raisins and apple juice and set aside to plump 1 hour or overnight.

2. In a large bowl combine milk, 1 tablespoon granulated sugar, and yeast. Stir to dissolve and let stand until foamy, about 10 minutes.

3. Stir in remaining sugar, eggs, butter, cream, 1 tablespoon salt, nutmeg, almonds, lemon zest, and raisins (drained). Add enough bread flour to create a firm dough. Add flour only to reduce stickiness. Turn out onto a floured surface and knead 8–10 minutes. Return to bowl, dust the top with flour, and cover with a damp cloth or plastic wrap. Rise at room temperature until doubled in volume, about 2½ hours.

4. Line a baking sheet with parchment. Turn risen dough onto a floured surface and divide into 3 portions, one large, one medium, and one small. Divide each into 3 equal sections and roll into tight ropes, about 18" long.

5. Starting with the largest ropes, make a 3-strand braid. Place onto prepared pan, press a slight indentation down the center of the braid, and brush with melted butter. Repeat with the medium braid, and place it in on top of the large braid. Brush with melted butter. Finish by braiding the small section, and place it on top of the medium braid. Cover loosely with plastic wrap, and proof for 30 minutes. Preheat oven to 375°F.

6. Whisk the egg yolk with a tablespoon of water and a pinch of salt, and brush onto the top of the risen loaf. Bake 30 minutes. Reduce heat to 250°F and continue baking until golden brown and hollow sounding, about 30–40 minutes. Cool completely on a rack.

Braided Babka

Traditional Polish Babkas, served often at Easter, have some variation of fruit garnish, dried or candied.

INGREDIENTS | YIELDS 1 LOAF

½ cup dried currants

½ cup candied citrus zest

½ cup candied ginger

2 cups orange juice

1 cup warm milk

¼ cup granulated sugar

1¾ teaspoons active dry yeast (1 package)

3 eggs

½ cup (1 stick) unsalted butter

1 teaspoon kosher salt

2–3 cups bread flour

2 tablespoons cream

1 cup powdered sugar

Jewish Babka

The Jewish version of Braided Babka found in the United States is usually without fruit, and is twisted rather than braided. Try this great alternative the next time you make this recipe!

1. Combine currants, citrus zest, ginger, and orange juice, and set aside to plump 1 hour or overnight.

2. In a large bowl combine milk, 1 tablespoon granulated sugar, and yeast. Stir to dissolve and let stand until foamy, about 10 minutes.

3. Stir in remaining sugar, eggs, butter, and salt. Drain the plumped fruits, reserving the liquid, and add the fruits to the mixture. Add enough bread flour to create a firm dough. Add flour only to reduce stickiness. Turn out onto a floured surface and knead 8–10 minutes. Return to bowl, dust the top with flour, and cover with a damp cloth or plastic wrap. Rise at room temperature until doubled in volume, about 2½ hours.

4. Line a baking sheet with parchment. Turn risen dough onto a floured surface, divide into 3 portions, and form a 3-strand braid. Place onto prepared pan, cover loosely with plastic wrap, and proof for 30 minutes. Preheat oven to 375°F.

5. Brush the top of the risen loaf with cream and bake until golden brown and hollow sounding, about 30–40 minutes. Cool on a rack.

6. In a small bowl, whisk together powdered sugar and 1 tablespoon of reserved juice from the plumping. Drizzle over loaf before serving.

Braided Dark Rye

This bread is a classic, perfect for sandwiches, soups, and stews. The recipe gives instructions for a 5-strand braid, but a 3-strand will do.

INGREDIENTS | YIELDS 1 LOAF

⅔ cup lukewarm coffee

1¾ teaspoons active dry yeast (1 package)

3 tablespoons brown sugar

1 tablespoon butter

1 cup medium rye flour

1 teaspoon kosher salt

1 tablespoon caraway seeds, toasted and ground

2–3 cups bread flour

1 tablespoon molasses

1 tablespoon water

Five-Strand Braid

The 5 strand braid looks cool and complicated, but it is actually super-simple. Instead of jumping one strand with each pass, the outer strands jump two. That's it!

1. In a large bowl, combine coffee, yeast, and 1 tablespoon brown sugar. Stir to dissolve and let stand until foamy, about 10 minutes.

2. Add remaining sugar, butter, and rye flour. Stir to combine. Add salt, caraway, and enough bread flour to create a firm dough. Add flour only to reduce stickiness. Turn out onto a floured surface and knead 8–10 minutes. Return to bowl, dust the top with flour, and cover with a damp cloth or plastic wrap. Rise at room temperature until doubled in volume, about 2 hours.

3. Line a baking sheet with parchment. Turn risen dough onto a floured surface and divide into 5 even portions. Shape each into a tight rope, no longer than 12". Lay all 5 ropes pointing toward you, and begin braiding, 1 over 3, 5 over 3, and repeat. (Lift the left strand over the neighboring 2 strands and set it between strands 3 and 4. Next, lift the right strand over its neighboring 2 strands, and set it between strands 2 and 3.) Repeat, until you have reached the end of the braid. Pinch the dough together when you get to the end. Place onto prepared pan, cover loosely with plastic wrap, and proof for 30 minutes. Preheat oven to 375°F.

4. Combine molasses and water, and brush gently onto the top of the risen loaf. Bake until golden brown and hollow sounding, about 30–40 minutes. Cool completely on a rack.

Braided Poppy Seed Bread

*Here is another example of a stuffed braid. The form is simple,
but the filling means a delicate hand is in order.*

INGREDIENTS | YIELDS 1 LOAF

½ cup (1 stick) unsalted butter

¼ cup poppy seeds

2 tablespoons honey

¼ cup candied orange peel

½ cup sliced almonds, toasted

2 eggs

1 tablespoon sour cream

1 cup warm milk

2 tablespoons granulated sugar

1¾ teaspoons active dry yeast
(1 package)

Grated zest of 3 oranges

1 teaspoon plus 1 pinch kosher salt

4–5 cups bread flour

1 tablespoon cream

1. Melt ¼ cup butter in a large sauté pan over high heat. Add 3 tablespoons poppy seeds, honey, and orange peel. Simmer 2–3 minutes. Remove from heat and add almonds. Cool, then stir in 1 egg and sour cream. Set aside.

2. In a large bowl combine milk, sugar, and yeast. Stir to dissolve and let stand until foamy, about 10 minutes.

3. Stir in orange zest, remaining butter, 1 teaspoon salt, and enough bread flour to create a firm dough. Add flour only to reduce stickiness. Turn out onto a floured surface and knead 8–10 minutes. Return to bowl, dust the top with flour, and cover with a damp cloth or plastic wrap. Rise at room temperature until doubled in volume, about 2 hours.

4. Line a baking sheet with parchment. Turn risen dough onto a floured surface and roll into a rectangle the size of your baking sheet. Spread poppy seed mixture evenly onto dough, then fold dough in half, like a book. Cover and rise again for 30 minutes.

5. Roll risen dough into an elongated rectangle, approximately 16" × 9". Slice the rectangle into 3 strands, each 16" × 3", and form a 3-strand braid. Place onto prepared pan, cover loosely with plastic wrap, and proof for 30 minutes. Preheat oven to 375°F.

6. Whisk together remaining egg and cream with a pinch of salt, and brush gently onto the top of the risen loaf. Sprinkle with reserved poppy seeds and bake until golden brown and hollow sounding, about 30–40 minutes. Cool completely on a rack.

Brown Rice Braid

The combination of wheat germ and brown rice imparts a delicious nuttiness to this bread.

INGREDIENTS | YIELDS 1 LOAF

1¼ cups plus 1 tablespoon water

½ cup brown rice

1 cup milk

1 tablespoon granulated sugar

1¾ teaspoons active dry yeast
(1 package)

¼ cup (½ stick) unsalted butter

½ cup wheat germ

1 cup whole wheat flour

1 teaspoon plus 1 pinch kosher salt

2–3 cups bread flour

1 egg

1. Bring 1¼ cups water to a boil over high heat. Add brown rice and stir. When the water returns to the boil, reduce heat to low, cover tightly, and cook for 30 minutes, or until rice is tender and water is absorbed. Spread rice out onto a baking sheet to cool.

2. In a large bowl stir together milk, sugar, and yeast. Set aside at room temperature until foamy, about 10 minutes.

3. Stir in butter, wheat germ, whole wheat flour, 1 teaspoon salt, and cooled rice. Add enough bread flour to create a firm dough. Add flour only to reduce stickiness. Turn onto a floured surface and knead 8–10 minutes. Return to bowl, dust the top with flour, and cover with a damp cloth or plastic wrap. Rise at room temperature until doubled in volume, about 1½ hours.

4. Line a baking sheet with parchment. Turn risen dough onto a floured surface and divide into 3 equal portions. Shape each into a tight rope, no longer than 12", and form a 3-strand braid. Place onto prepared pan, cover loosely with plastic wrap, and proof for 30 minutes. Preheat oven to 375°F.

5. Whisk egg with a pinch of salt and a tablespoon of water, and brush gently onto the top of the risen loaf. Bake until golden brown and hollow sounding, about 30–40 minutes. Cool completely on a rack before serving.

Challah

In the Jewish tradition, challah is served on the Sabbath. Since the first meals of the Sabbath typically contain meat, the challah is made without dairy, although recipes containing butter can be found.

INGREDIENTS | YIELDS 1 LOAF

½ cup plus 1 tablespoon warm water

1 tablespoon honey

3½ teaspoons active dry yeast (2 packages)

1 cup all-purpose flour

¼ cup vegetable or olive oil

3 whole eggs

1 egg white

1 teaspoon plus 1 pinch kosher salt

2–3 cups bread flour

Challah

The blessing of challah on the Sabbath commemorates the manna that fell from heaven when the Israelites wandered the desert after the Exodus from Egypt. In Biblical times a small portion of dough was set aside as an offering, or tithe, to the priesthood in a ritual called hafrashat challah.

1. In a large bowl combine ½ cup water, honey, and yeast. Stir to dissolve and let stand until foamy, about 10 minutes.

2. Stir in all-purpose flour, oil, 2 whole eggs, egg white, and 1 teaspoon salt. Add enough bread flour to create a firm dough. Add flour only to reduce stickiness. Turn onto a floured surface and knead 8–10 minutes. Return to bowl, dust the top with flour, and cover with a damp cloth or plastic wrap. Rise at room temperature until doubled in volume, about 2 hours.

3. Line a baking sheet with parchment. Turn risen dough onto a floured surface, divide into 3 equal portions, and form a 3-strand braid. Place onto prepared pan, cover loosely with plastic wrap, and proof for 30 minutes. Preheat oven to 375°F.

4. Whisk together remaining egg with 1 tablespoon water and a pinch of salt. Brush gently onto the top of the risen loaf, and bake until golden brown and hollow sounding, about 30–40 minutes. Cool completely on a rack before serving.

Cinnamon Raisin Braid

*The unmistakable aroma of cinnamon and raisins will start
mouths watering the minute this loaf hits the oven.*

INGREDIENTS | YIELDS 1 LOAF

½ cup dark raisins

½ cup golden raisins

½ cup dried currants

2 cups brandy

1¼ cups plus 1 tablespoon warm water

½ cup brown sugar

1¾ teaspoons active dry yeast
(1 package)

1 cup all-purpose flour

2 tablespoons ground cinnamon

2 teaspoons plus 1 pinch kosher salt

3–4 cups bread flour

1 egg

2 tablespoons turbinado sugar

1. Combine dark raisins, golden raisins, currants, and brandy. Set aside to plump 1 hour or overnight.

2. In a large bowl combine 1¼ cups water, brown sugar, and yeast. Stir to dissolve and let stand until foamy, about 10 minutes.

3. Stir in plumped raisins (drained), all-purpose flour, cinnamon, 2 teaspoons salt, and enough bread flour to create a firm dough. Add flour only to reduce stickiness. Turn onto a floured surface and knead 8–10 minutes. Return to bowl, dust the top with flour, and cover with a damp cloth or plastic wrap. Rise at room temperature until doubled in volume, about 2 hours.

4. Line a baking sheet with parchment. Turn risen dough onto a floured surface, divide into 3 equal portions, and form a 3-strand braid. Place onto prepared pan, cover loosely with plastic wrap, and proof for 30 minutes. Preheat oven to 375°F.

5. Whisk together egg with 1 tablespoon water and a pinch of salt, and brush gently onto the top of the risen loaf. Sprinkle with turbinado sugar, and bake until golden brown and hollow sounding, about 30–40 minutes. Cool completely on a rack.

Cream Cheese Braid

The natural tanginess of cream cheese gives this bread a subtle but distinctive flavor, reminiscent of cheesecake.

INGREDIENTS | YIELDS 1 LOAF

1 cup warm water

¼ cup honey

3½ teaspoons active dry yeast (2 packages)

2 8-ounce packages cream cheese, diced

½ cup (1 stick) unsalted butter, softened

2 eggs

1 cup all-purpose flour

¾ teaspoon plus 1 pinch kosher salt

3–4 cups bread flour

1 egg white

2 cups powdered sugar

1 teaspoon lemon juice

1 teaspoon vanilla extract

The 4-Strand Braid

The 4-strand braid is a bit trickier than the 3- or 5-strand. The pattern is as follows: 1 over 3, 2 over 3, 4 over 2. It is a little like a standard braid, with an added twist in the middle. The finished product has a raised center that looks like a spiral staircase. It may be necessary to roll the loaf over to find the prettiest side before baking.

1. In a large bowl, combine water, honey, and yeast. Stir to dissolve and let stand until foamy, about 10 minutes.

2. Add 1 (8-ounce) package cream cheese, butter, eggs, all-purpose flour, and ¾ teaspoon salt; stir to combine. Add enough bread flour to create a firm dough. Add flour only to reduce stickiness. Turn out onto a floured surface and knead 8–10 minutes. Return to bowl, dust the top with flour, and cover with a damp cloth or plastic wrap. Rise at room temperature until doubled in volume, about 2 hours.

3. Line a baking sheet with parchment. Turn risen dough onto a floured surface, divide into 4 equal portions, and form a 4-strand braid. Place onto prepared pan, cover loosely with plastic wrap, and proof for 30 minutes. Preheat oven to 375°F.

4. Whisk egg white with a pinch of salt and brush the top of the risen loaf. Bake until golden brown and hollow sounding, about 30–40 minutes. Cool the loaf completely on a rack.

5. In a small bowl combine remaining package cream cheese with powdered sugar, lemon juice, and vanilla. Beat until smooth. Drizzle over bread before serving.

Garlicky Dill Braid

Both dill seed and dried dill weed are used in this recipe, because while they come from the same plant, each has its own distinctive flavor.

INGREDIENTS | YIELDS 1 LOAF

2 heads garlic

1 cup plus 1 tablespoon warm water

1 tablespoon granulated sugar

1¾ teaspoons active dry yeast
(1 package)

½ cup sour cream

2 teaspoons dried dill weed

1 tablespoon olive oil

1 teaspoon plus 1 pinch kosher salt

2–3 cups bread flour

1 egg

1 teaspoon dill seed

1. Preheat oven to 450°F. Wrap garlic in foil and bake until tender, about 30 minutes. Remove from foil and set aside to cool.

2. In a large bowl, combine 1 cup water, sugar, and yeast. Stir to dissolve and let stand until foamy, about 10 minutes.

3. Add sour cream, dill weed, oil, and 1 teaspoon salt. Stir to combine. Cut cooled garlic bulbs in half horizontally and squeeze the soft roasted garlic into the dough. Add enough bread flour to create a firm dough. Add flour only to reduce stickiness. Turn onto a floured surface and knead 8–10 minutes. Return to bowl, dust the top with flour, and cover with a damp cloth or plastic wrap. Rise at room temperature until doubled in volume, about 2 hours.

4. Line a baking sheet with parchment. Turn risen dough onto a floured surface, divide into 3 equal portions, and form a 3-strand braid. Place onto prepared pan, cover loosely with plastic wrap, and proof for 30 minutes. Preheat oven to 375°F.

5. Whisk egg with a tablespoon of water and a pinch of salt and brush gently onto the top of the risen loaf. Sprinkle with dill seed and bake until golden brown and hollow sounding, about 30–40 minutes. Cool completely on a rack.

Molasses Whole Wheat Braid

This bread is sweet and tender, but it can be taken even further with the addition of plumped dried fruits for a hint of sweetness. For a change of pace, try adding currants, raisins, or dates before the bread flour is added.

INGREDIENTS | YIELDS 1 LOAF

1¾ cups plus 1 tablespoon warm water

½ cup brown sugar

1¾ teaspoons active dry yeast
(1 package)

¼ cup molasses

2 tablespoons butter

1 cup whole wheat flour

1 tablespoon plus 1 pinch kosher salt

3–4 cups bread flour

1 egg

The 6-Strand Braid

This braid starts by bringing strand 6 over strand 1, which is not repeated. The repeated sequence is as follows; 2 over 6, 1 over 3, 5 over 1, and 6 over 4. The finished braid looks like a braid-within-a-braid. It's a unique loaf that is sure to make an impression.

1. In a large bowl, combine 1¾ cups water, 1 tablespoon brown sugar, and yeast. Stir to dissolve and let stand until foamy, about 10 minutes.

2. Add remaining brown sugar, molasses, butter, whole wheat flour, and 1 tablespoon salt; stir to combine. Add enough bread flour to create a firm dough. Add flour only to reduce stickiness. Turn onto a floured surface and knead 8–10 minutes. Return to bowl, dust the top with flour, and cover with a damp cloth or plastic wrap. Rise at room temperature until doubled in volume, about 2 hours.

3. Line a baking sheet with parchment. Turn risen dough onto a floured surface, divide into 6 equal portions, and form a 6-strand braid. Place onto prepared pan, cover loosely with plastic wrap, and proof for 30 minutes. Preheat oven to 375°F.

4. Whisk egg with a tablespoon of water and a pinch of salt. Brush gently onto the top of the risen loaf. Bake until golden brown and hollow sounding, about 30–40 minutes. Cool completely on a rack.

Pretzel Bread

*Poaching dough moistens the starch on the crust, giving the crust
a unique chewiness and an all-over golden brown color.*

INGREDIENTS | YIELDS 1 LOAF

1 cup warm water

1 tablespoon brown sugar

1¾ teaspoons active dry yeast
(1 package)

¼ cup milk

2 tablespoons unsalted butter

2 teaspoons plus 1 pinch kosher salt

2–3 cups bread flour

4 quarts plus 1 tablespoon water

½ cup baking soda

¼ cup cornmeal

1 egg

3 tablespoons pretzel or kosher salt

1. In a large bowl, combine water, brown sugar, and yeast. Stir to dissolve and let stand until foamy, about 10 minutes.

2. Add milk, butter, 2 teaspoons salt, and enough bread flour to create a firm dough. Add flour only to reduce stickiness. Turn out onto a floured surface and knead 8–10 minutes. Return to bowl, dust the top with flour, and cover with a damp cloth or plastic wrap. Rise at room temperature until doubled in volume, about 1 hour. Punch risen dough, knead briefly, then cover and rise again until doubled, about 1 hour.

3. In a large saucepan, bring 4 quarts of water to a boil. At the boil, reduce heat to a simmer, and add baking soda. Coat a baking sheet with pan spray, and sprinkle with cornmeal. Preheat oven to 400°F.

4. Turn risen dough onto a floured surface, divide into 3 equal portions, and form a 3-strand braid. Drop braid gently into simmering baking soda bath for about 30 seconds, turning to coat all sides. Carefully remove loaf with 2 slotted spoons or a spider, shake off excess liquid, and place on prepared pan.

5. Whisk egg with a tablespoon of water and a pinch of salt. Brush the top of the risen loaf. Sprinkle with pretzel salt and bake until golden brown and hollow sounding, about 30–40 minutes. Cool completely on a rack.

Swedish Rye Braid

While rye bread is typically flavored with caraway seed, the Swedish rye distinguishes itself with the flavor of anise, fennel, and fragrant orange zest.

INGREDIENTS | YIELDS 1 LOAF

2 cups plus 1 tablespoon warm water

⅓ cup honey

3½ teaspoons active dry yeast (2 packages)

4 cups rye flour

1 cup milk

½ cup molasses

¼ cup (½ stick) unsalted butter

1 tablespoon plus 1 pinch kosher salt

2 teaspoons fennel seed, ground

2 teaspoons anise seed, ground

Grated zest of 4 oranges

3–4 cups bread flour

1 egg

1. To create the sponge, combine 2 cups water, 1 tablespoon honey, and yeast in a large bowl. Stir to dissolve and let stand 10 minutes. Add 1 cup rye flour; beat 1 minute. Cover and let stand at room temperature 8–12 hours.

2. Add to the sponge the milk, remaining honey, molasses, butter, 1 tablespoon salt, fennel, anise, orange zest, and remaining rye flour. Add enough bread flour to make a soft dough. Turn out onto a floured work surface and knead 8–10 minutes. Add flour only to reduce stickiness. Return to bowl, dust with flour, cover with plastic, and rise at room temperature until doubled in volume, about 1½ hours.

3. Line a baking sheet with parchment. Turn risen dough onto a floured surface, divide into 3 equal portions, and form a 3-strand braid. Place onto prepared pan, cover loosely with plastic wrap, and proof for 30 minutes. Preheat oven to 375°F.

4. Whisk egg with a tablespoon of water and a pinch of salt, and brush gently onto the top of the risen loaf. Bake until golden brown and hollow sounding, about 30–40 minutes. Cool completely on a rack.

Tri-Color Braid

Joining three contrasting dough colors makes a great-looking loaf. The combination of flavors in this recipe makes a great-tasting loaf too.

INGREDIENTS | YIELDS 3 LOAVES

1 recipe Braided Dark Rye (page 82)

1 recipe Molasses Whole Wheat Braid (page 89)

1 recipe Basic White Bread (page 21)

1 egg

1 tablespoon water

1 pinch salt

1. Make all three doughs according to their individual recipes. Cover each with plastic, and rise at room temperature until doubled in volume, about 1½ hours.

2. Line a baking sheet with parchment. Turn each risen dough out onto a floured surface and divide each into 3 equal portions. Shape each into a tight rope, no longer than 12". Lay three ropes pointing toward you, one of each color, and form a 3-strand braid. Place onto prepared pan, cover loosely with plastic wrap, and proof for 30 minutes. Repeat with remaining dough. Preheat oven to 375°F.

3. Whisk egg with a tablespoon of water and a pinch of salt, and brush gently onto the top of the risen loaf. Bake until golden brown and hollow sounding, about 30–40 minutes. Cool completely on a rack before serving.

CHAPTER 6

Flatbreads

Armenian Flatbread (Lavash)

This Armenian flatbread is great for wraps or as an accompaniment to a spicy kebab.

INGREDIENTS | YIELDS 6–8 FLATBREADS

⅓ cup water

1 tablespoon honey

1¾ teaspoons active dry yeast (1 package)

2 tablespoons canola oil

½ teaspoon kosher salt

1½–2 cups bread flour

1 tablespoon sesame seeds

Floppy or Crispy?

Lavash is sometimes sold as a crisp cracker, but like many flatbreads from around the world, fresh lavash is meant to be used as a utensil, in lieu of a fork to pinch and roll up foods. If you find yourself in possession of crisp lavash, soften it by surrounding it in a moist towel for a minute or two.

1. In a large bowl, combine water, honey, and yeast. Stir to dissolve and let stand until foamy, about 10 minutes. Add 1 tablespoon oil, salt, and enough bread flour to create a firm dough. Add flour only to reduce stickiness. Turn onto a floured surface and knead 8–10 minutes. Return to bowl, dust the top with flour, and cover with a damp cloth or plastic wrap. Rise at room temperature until doubled in volume, about 1½ hours.

2. Preheat oven to 350°F, and line a baking sheet with parchment. Turn risen dough onto a floured work surface. Using floured fingers, press flat into a disk. Using a rolling pin, roll the entire dough into a paper-thin sheet, the size of the baking sheet. If the dough becomes elastic and springs out of shape, allow it to rest for 5 minutes, then roll again.

3. Brush entire surface of dough lightly with remaining oil, pierce all over with a fork, and sprinkle with sesame seeds. Transfer to prepared baking sheet and bake until lightly golden brown, about 5–10 minutes. Do not to bake too long, or the lavash will become a cracker. Cool completely on a rack.

Whole Wheat Tortillas

These flour tortillas are healthier, heartier, and more flavorful than their white flour counterparts. Once you try them, you'll be a believer.

INGREDIENTS | YIELDS 6–8 TORTILLAS

1 cup whole wheat flour

1 cup all-purpose flour

½ teaspoon kosher salt

2 tablespoons vegetable oil

½–¾ cup cold water

Whole Wheat Flour

Whole wheat flour contains the bran of the grain, which is super-healthy fiber, and the germ, which contains healthful oils, protein, and vitamins. These elements create a dough of a different consistency, so don't be alarmed when kneading feels a little funny.

1. In a large bowl, combine flours and salt. Stir in oil, and enough water to hold dough together. Knead until smooth, about 2–3 minutes, then rest 5 minutes.

2. Turn dough out onto a floured work surface. Pinch off golf-ball-sized pieces of dough and roll into balls. With floured fingers, flatten into thin disks. Using a rolling pin, roll out disks no more than ¼" thick. If the dough becomes elastic and springs out of shape, allow it to rest for 5 minutes, then roll again as necessary.

3. Preheat griddle over medium heat. Cook until lightly golden but still pliable, about 1–2 minutes per side. Serve warm.

Corn Tortillas

Masa harina is a flour made from dried fermented corn, similar to hominy. Its unique flavor is a staple of Central and South American cuisine.

INGREDIENTS | YIELDS 6–8 TORTILLAS

2 cups masa harina

½ teaspoon kosher salt

1¼–1½ cups cold water

Pressed Perfect

A tortilla press is a specialized piece of equipment made for corn tortilla production. Two flat pieces of aluminum or wood sandwich the masa, and a lever presses them together. If you don't have one, you can press your masa thin with a flat cake pan or the bottom of a large bowl, using your own body weight.

1. In a medium bowl, mix together masa, salt, and enough water to make a soft dough. Pinch off golf-ball-sized pieces and roll into balls.

2. Preheat a griddle over medium heat. Sandwich dough between two sheets of paper, place into a tortilla press, and flatten.

3. Place tortillas onto the hot, dry griddle, and cook until lightly golden but still pliable, about 1–2 minutes per side. Serve warm.

Blue Corn Tortillas

Blue cornmeal is made from fermented hominy, like masa harina. It is ground from the dried kernels of blue corn, like the standard yellow and white cornmeal.

INGREDIENTS | **YIELDS 6–8 TORTILLAS**

1½ cups blue cornmeal
1½ cups boiling water
½ teaspoon kosher salt
½–1 cup all-purpose flour

1. In a large bowl, combine cornmeal and boiling water. Stir and set aside to soften and cool for 30 minutes.

2. To the cooled cornmeal, add salt and enough flour to create a soft dough. Turn onto a floured surface and knead for 5 minutes until smooth. Add flour only to reduce stickiness. Cover and rest 20 minutes.

3. Turn dough out onto a floured work surface. Pinch off golf-ball-sized pieces of dough and roll into balls. With floured fingers, flatten into thin disks. Using a rolling pin, roll out disks no more than ¼" thick. If the dough becomes elastic and springs out of shape, allow it to rest for 5 minutes, then roll again as necessary.

4. Preheat a griddle over medium heat. Cook until lightly golden but still pliable, about 1–2 minutes per side. Serve warm.

Flour Tortillas

Flour tortillas are everyone's favorite, especially when they're homemade.

INGREDIENTS	YIELDS 5 LARGE TORTILLAS

2 cups all-purpose flour

1 teaspoon kosher salt

1 teaspoon baking powder

1 tablespoon lard

1¾ cups cold water

1. In a large bowl, combine flour, salt, and baking powder. Cut in lard to a crumb consistency, then add enough water to hold dough together. Knead until smooth, about 2–3 minutes, then rest 5 minutes.

2. Turn dough onto a floured work surface. Divide dough into 5 equal portions, and roll into balls. With floured fingers, flatten each ball into a thin disk. Using a rolling pin, roll the disk into a thin sheet, ¼" thick. If the dough becomes elastic and springs out of shape, allow it to rest for 5 minutes, then roll again.

3. Preheat a cast-iron griddle over medium heat. Place tortillas onto the hot, dry griddle, and cook until lightly golden but still pliable, about 1–2 minutes per side. Serve warm.

Flax and Fennel Crackers

These rustic crackers can be dressed up by cutting the dough into decorative shapes with a cookie cutter before baking.

INGREDIENTS | **YIELDS 12–15 CRACKERS**

⅔ cup warm water
⅓ cup olive oil
½ teaspoon salt
1 teaspoon baking powder
1 tablespoon flax seeds
1 tablespoon fennel seeds
2–3 cups whole wheat flour
1 egg white

1. In a large bowl combine water, oil, and salt. Add baking powder, flax and fennel seeds, and enough flour to create a firm dough. Turn out onto a floured surface and knead, adding flour only to reduce stickiness, for 5 minutes. Return to bowl, dust with flour, cover with plastic wrap, and rest at room temperature for 15 minutes. Preheat oven to 400°F.

2. Coat a baking sheet with pan spray. Turn dough out onto a floured surface and divide it into 3 equal portions. Using a rolling pin, roll each portion to ¼" thick, and pierce each piece all over with a fork. Brush with egg white, arrange on baking sheet, and bake until edges are brown, about 10–15 minutes. When cool, break crackers into serving size pieces.

Ethiopian Injera

Injera is not only used as a utensil. Savory, spicy Ethiopian stews are served on top of the bread too. It catches the juices and gravies, producing a fantastic end-of-the-meal treat.

INGREDIENTS | **YIELDS 5–8 BREADS**

½ cup ground teff
2 cups water
¼ teaspoon kosher salt
1–2 tablespoons canola oil

1. In a large bowl, combine teff and water, stir, and set at room temperature overnight.

2. Preheat griddle on high heat. Stir salt into batter. Lightly oil griddle and ladle out about ¼ cup of batter. Cook until holes bubble up into the batter, and the edges begin to contract slightly. Do not flip. Repeat with remaining batter, stacking finish injera between sheets of plastic wrap. Serve with rich and spicy curries.

Fry Bread

This bread, also known as Navajo bread, or squaw bread, is often found plain, without scallions and coriander, and served as a sweet bread with honey or jam.

INGREDIENTS | YIELDS 5–8 BREADS

2 cups all-purpose flour

1 teaspoon baking powder

1 teaspoon kosher salt

2 scallions, minced

1 tablespoon ground coriander

¾–1 cup cold milk

2 cups canola oil

Deep-Frying

Deep-frying can be accomplished on the stovetop easily. Use a heavy, high-sided pan, such as cast iron, which heats up evenly and holds the heat at an even temperature. The weight of cast iron makes it the safer choice, as it is less likely to tip over. Be sure pot handles are turned inward to prevent accidental tipping.

1. In a large bowl, combine flour, baking powder, salt, scallions, and coriander. Stir in enough milk to hold dough together. Cover and rest 5 minutes.

2. Turn dough out onto a floured work surface. Pinch off golf-ball-sized pieces of dough and roll into balls. With floured fingers, flatten into disks. Using a rolling pin, roll out disks no more than ¼" thick.

3. In a heavy skillet, heat oil over high heat. Oil is ready when a small bit of dough dropped in sizzles immediately. Carefully drop disks of dough into oil, and cook until golden brown, about 30 seconds per side. Do not crowd. Adjust oil temperature as needed. Drain on paper towels, and serve warm.

Nigella Naan

This Indian bread, flavored with traditional peppery nigella (also called black onion seeds) is traditionally cooked on the side of a piping hot tandori oven. A good griddle will suffice.

INGREDIENTS | YIELDS 8 BREADS

1 cup warm water

1 tablespoon sugar

1¾ teaspoons active dry yeast (1 package)

¼ cup plain yogurt

1 tablespoon nigella

1 teaspoon kosher salt

3–4 cups bread flour

2–4 tablespoons ghee

Ghee

Ghee is clarified butter from which all the moisture has been evaporated, leaving the fat, which browns and takes on a nutty flavor. It can be made at home fairly easily. Start by slowly melting a pound of butter, carefully skimming off the foam, and pouring off the pure fat, leaving the sediment in the pan. This fat is the clarified butter. Cook the clarified butter slowly until it turns a deep golden brown. Ghee can be stored in the refrigerator for several weeks.

1. In a large bowl, combine water, sugar, and yeast. Stir to dissolve and let stand until foamy, about 5 minutes. Add yogurt, nigella, and salt, and enough bread flour to create firm dough. Turn dough onto a lightly floured surface and knead 8–10 minutes, or until dough is smooth and elastic. Add flour only to reduce stickiness. Cover dough with a warm, damp towel, and rise until double in volume.

2. Preheat griddle on high heat. Divide dough into 8 portions and roll into balls. Pat balls flat into disks and elongate each into an oval about ½" thick. Oil griddle lightly with ghee, and cook 2–4 minutes, until golden brown and puffy. Brush uncooked side with ghee, flip, and brown again. Serve warm.

Norwegian Lefse

Lefse is eaten as a sweet treat, with sugar and jam, or as an accompaniment to a savory meal, with nothing but butter.

INGREDIENTS | **YIELDS 8–10 BREADS**

2 pounds russet potatoes

Water, as needed

2 teaspoons kosher salt

3–4 cups all-purpose flour

1. Peel and halve potatoes. Place in a large pot, cover with cold water and bring to a boil over high heat. Reduce to a simmer and cook until tender, about 30 minutes. Drain and cool.

2. Pass cooled potatoes through a ricer or mesh strainer, and combine in a large bowl with salt and enough flour to create a firm dough. Turn out onto a floured work surface and knead 3–5 minutes, until smooth. Add flour only to reduce stickiness. Cover and rest 20 minutes.

3. Turn dough out onto a floured work surface. Pinch off golf-ball-sized pieces and roll into balls. With floured fingers, flatten into thin disks, then use a rolling pin to roll out disks ¼" thick. If the dough becomes elastic and springs out of shape, allow it to rest for 5 minutes, then roll again as necessary.

4. Preheat a griddle over medium heat. Cook on hot, dry griddle until lightly golden but still pliable, about 1–2 minutes per side. Serve warm.

Pita Bread

The key to the pocket is the thickness, and the rest period between rolling and baking. This rest allows a skin to form, which traps the steam and forces it to build up inside the dough.

INGREDIENTS | **YIELDS 5 BREADS**

1½ cups warm water

1 tablespoon honey

3½ teaspoons active dry yeast
(2 packages)

1 tablespoon olive oil

1 tablespoon kosher salt

3–4 cups bread flour

Perfect Pita

This bread must remain pale if it is to be flexible. If it gets too browned it will be too hard, like a cracker, and impossible to use as pocket bread. Watch the clock carefully.

1. In a medium bowl, stir together warm water, honey, and yeast, and set aside until foamy, about 10 minutes.

2. Stir in oil, salt, and enough bread flour to create a firm dough. Turn the dough out onto a floured surface and knead, adding flour only as necessary, until the dough becomes smooth and elastic, about 8–10 minutes. Return to bowl, cover with plastic wrap, and set in a warm place to rise until doubled in volume, about 1½ hours.

3. Preheat oven to 500°F, and preheat a dry baking sheet. Turn dough onto a floured surface, divide into 5 equal portions, and roll each into a tight ball. Using a rolling pin, roll out each ball into a flat disk, ¼" thick. Rest 20 minutes, uncovered. Place one disk onto the preheated baking sheet. Bake exactly 3 minutes. Remove carefully with tongs, and repeat with remaining disks. Finished bread will be puffed and very pale. Cool completely before slicing and opening.

Greek Olive Pita

*Black kalamata olives add a salty note to these herby breads. Use them
for falafel, or as the perfect vessel for your best tzatziki.*

INGREDIENTS | YIELDS 5 BREADS

1½ cups warm water

1 tablespoon honey

3½ teaspoons active dry yeast
(2 packages)

1 tablespoon olive oil

1 teaspoon kosher salt

1 cup kalamata olives, pitted and
chopped

2 teaspoons dried oregano

1 teaspoon dried mint

3–4 cups bread flour

1. In a medium bowl, stir together warm water, honey, and yeast. Set aside until foamy, about 10 minutes.

2. Stir in oil, salt, olives, oregano, mint, and enough bread flour to create a firm dough. Turn the dough out onto a floured surface and knead, adding flour only to reduce stickiness, until the dough becomes smooth and elastic, about 8–10 minutes. Return to bowl, cover with plastic wrap, and set in a warm place to rise until doubled in volume, about 1½ hours.

3. Preheat oven to 500°F, and preheat a dry baking sheet. Turn dough out onto a floured surface, divide into 5 equal portions, and roll each into a tight ball. Using a rolling pin, roll out each ball into a flat disk ¼" thick. Rest 20 minutes, uncovered. Place one disk onto the preheated baking sheet. Bake exactly 3 minutes. Remove carefully with tongs, and repeat with remaining disks. Finished bread will be puffed and very pale. Cool completely before slicing and opening.

Whole Wheat Pita

Whole wheat adds a delicious nutty flavor and boosts the health benefits of this pita.
However, the gluten of bread flour is still needed for proper rolling and puffing.

INGREDIENTS | **YIELDS 5 BREADS**

1½ cups warm water

1 tablespoon honey

3½ teaspoons active dry yeast
(2 packages)

1 tablespoon olive oil

1 teaspoon kosher salt

1 cup whole wheat flour

2–3 cups bread flour

1. In a medium bowl, stir together warm water, honey, and yeast. Set aside until foamy, about 10 minutes.

2. Stir in oil, salt, whole wheat flour, and enough bread flour to create a firm dough. Turn the dough out onto a floured surface and knead, adding flour only to reduce stickiness, until the dough becomes smooth and elastic, about 8–10 minutes. Return to bowl, cover with plastic wrap, and set in a warm place to rise until doubled in volume, about 1½ hours.

3. Preheat oven to 500°F, and preheat a dry baking sheet. Turn dough out onto a floured surface, divide into 5 equal portions, and roll each into a tight ball. Using a rolling pin, roll out each ball into a flat disk ¼" thick. Rest 20 minutes, uncovered. Place one disk onto the preheated baking sheet. Bake exactly 3 minutes. Remove carefully with tongs, and repeat with remaining disks. Finished bread will be puffed and very pale. Cool completely before slicing and opening.

Whole Grain Wraps

These wraps are delicious and nutritious!

INGREDIENTS | YIELDS 5 WRAPS

1 cup all-purpose flour
½ cup whole wheat flour
¼ cup rolled oats (not quick cooking)
2 tablespoons brown rice flour
2 tablespoons cornmeal
1 teaspoon kosher salt
1 teaspoon baking powder
1 tablespoon lard
½–¾ cup cold water

1. In a large bowl, combine all-purpose flour, whole wheat flour, oats, rice flour, cornmeal, salt, and baking powder. Cut in lard to a crumb consistency. Add enough water to hold dough together. Knead until smooth, about 2–3 minutes, then rest 5 minutes.

2. Turn dough out onto a floured work surface, divide and roll into 5 balls. With floured fingers, flatten into a thin disk. Using a rolling pin, roll into a thin sheet, no more than ¼" thick. If the dough becomes elastic and springs out of shape, rest for 5 minutes, then roll again.

3. Preheat a dry griddle over medium heat. Cook until lightly golden about 1–2 minutes per side.

Wild Mushroom Wraps

Buy mushroom powder at gourmet markets, or make your own by pulverizing dried mushrooms in a coffee grinder.

INGREDIENTS | YIELDS 5 WRAPS

2 cups all-purpose flour
1 teaspoon kosher salt
1 teaspoon baking powder
¼ teaspoon dried onion
¼ cup powdered dried mushrooms
1 tablespoon lard
½–¾ cup cold water

1. In a large bowl, combine flour, salt, baking powder, dried onion, and powdered mushrooms. Cut in lard to a crumb consistency, then add enough water to hold dough together. Knead until smooth, about 2–3 minutes. Rest 5 minutes.

2. Turn dough onto a floured work surface, divide and roll into 5 balls. With floured fingers, flatten into thin disks. Using a rolling pin, roll out into disks no more than ¼" thick. If the dough becomes elastic and springs out of shape, rest for 5 minutes, then roll again.

3. Preheat a dry griddle over medium heat. Cook until lightly golden, about 1–2 minutes per side.

Roasted Garlic Flatbread

*Roasted whole, the sugar in a garlic bulb concentrates. It loses its
bitter, sharp tang and becomes rich, sweet, and creamy.*

INGREDIENTS | **MAKES 4 LARGE
FLATBREADS**

1 head garlic

1 cup water

1 tablespoon honey

1¾ teaspoons active dry yeast
(1 package)

½ cup whole wheat flour

¾ cup olive oil

1 tablespoon kosher salt

3–4 cups bread flour

2 tablespoons cornmeal

1. Preheat oven to 500°F. Wrap garlic bulb in foil and roast until tender, about 45 minutes. Cool completely.

2. In a large bowl, combine water, honey, and yeast. Set aside until foamy, about 10 minutes. Stir in whole wheat flour, cover, and set in a warm spot until it begins to bubble, about 30–60 minutes. This is the sponge.

3. Cut cooled garlic bulb in half and squeeze out softened roasted garlic. Add it to the sponge, along with ½ cup of olive oil, salt, and enough bread flour to create a firm dough. Turn dough out onto a floured surface and knead, adding flour only as necessary, until it becomes smooth and elastic, about 8–10 minutes. Return to bowl, cover with plastic wrap, and set in a warm place to rise until doubled in volume, about 1 hour.

4. Preheat oven to 450°F. Coat two baking sheets with pan spray and sprinkle with cornmeal. Turn dough onto a floured work surface and divide into 4 equal portions. With floured fingers, flatten into thin disks, about ½" thick. Place on prepared baking sheets, brush lightly with remaining olive oil, and bake until golden brown, about 10–15 minutes.

Spinach and Basil Flatbread

*Flecked with dark green and full of pungent herby goodness, this
bread is the perfect accompaniment to pasta, soup, or salad.*

INGREDIENTS | **YIELDS 4 LARGE
FLATBREADS**

3 tablespoons plus ¾ cup olive oil

2 cloves garlic, minced

1 cup fresh spinach leaves, washed and chopped

2 cups fresh basil leaves, washed and chopped

1 cup water

1 tablespoon honey

1¾ teaspoons active dry yeast
(1 package)

1 tablespoon kosher salt

3–4 cups bread flour

2 tablespoons cornmeal

1. Heat 2 tablespoons oil in a large sauté pan over high heat. Add garlic and cook until just tender, about 30 seconds. Add spinach and basil, and cook, stirring constantly, until wilted and dry, about 5 minutes. Remove from heat and cool completely.

2. In a large bowl, combine water, honey, and yeast. Stir together and set aside until bubbly, about 10 minutes. Add cooled spinach mixture, ¾ cup oil, salt, and enough bread flour to create a firm dough. Turn dough onto a floured surface and knead until smooth and elastic, about 8–10 minutes. Add flour only to reduce stickiness. Return to bowl, cover with plastic wrap, and set in a warm place to rise until doubled in volume, about 1½ hours.

3. Preheat oven to 450°F. Coat two baking sheets with pan spray and sprinkle lightly with cornmeal. Turn dough out onto a floured work surface and divide into 4 equal portions. With floured fingers, flatten into thin disks, about ½" thick. Place on prepared baking sheets, brush lightly with remaining olive oil and bake until golden brown, about 10–15 minutes.

Tomato Wraps

*These red wraps make fantastic sandwiches, and can be rolled up
with bright salads or spread with creamy cheeses.*

INGREDIENTS | YIELDS 5 WRAPS

2 cups all-purpose flour

1 teaspoon kosher salt

1 teaspoon baking powder

1 tablespoon lard

1 teaspoon Italian seasoning

¼ teaspoon powdered garlic

2 tablespoons tomato paste

¼–½ cup cold water

1. In a large bowl, combine flour, salt, and baking powder. Cut in lard to a crumb consistency. In a small bowl mix together Italian seasoning, garlic, tomato paste, and ¼ cup water. Stir wet mixture into dry, adding extra water as needed to hold dough together. Knead until smooth, about 2–3 minutes. Rest 5 minutes.

2. Turn dough out onto a floured work surface, divide dough into 5 equal portions, and roll into balls. With floured fingers, flatten each into a thin disk. Using a rolling pin, roll out disks no more than ¼" thick. If the dough becomes elastic and springs out of shape, rest for 5 minutes, then roll again.

3. Preheat a dry cast-iron griddle over medium heat. Cook until lightly golden but still pliable, about 1–2 minutes per side.

CHAPTER 7

Rolls

Anadama Rolls

This classic bread, made with cornmeal and molasses, is a New England favorite.

INGREDIENTS | YIELDS APPROXIMATELY
1 DOZEN ROLLS

1½ cups water

⅓ cup molasses

1¾ teaspoons active dry yeast
(1 package)

2 tablespoons unsalted butter, softened

⅔ cup cornmeal

4–5 cups bread flour

1. In a large bowl, combine water, molasses, and yeast. Stir to dissolve and let stand until foamy, about 10 minutes.

2. Add butter, cornmeal, and enough bread flour to create a firm dough. Add flour only to reduce stickiness. Turn out onto a floured surface and knead 8–10 minutes. Return to bowl, dust the top with flour, and cover with a damp cloth or plastic wrap. Rise at room temperature until doubled in volume, about 2 hours.

3. Line a baking sheet with parchment. Turn risen dough onto a floured surface and shape into a rope, about 3" thick. Slice 2" pieces off the rope, then roll each into a tight ball. Place balls 2" apart on the prepared pan, seam-side down. Dust with flour, cover loosely with plastic wrap, and proof for 30 minutes. Preheat oven to 375°F.

4. Bake until golden brown, about 20–25 minutes. Cool completely.

Bagels

Embellishing this recipe for plain bagels is as easy as sprinkling on your favorite topping just before baking.

INGREDIENTS | YIELDS 6–8 BAGELS

1 cup plus 1 quart water

1 tablespoon granulated sugar

1¾ teaspoons active dry yeast (1 package)

1 tablespoon vegetable oil

½ teaspoon plus 1 pinch kosher salt

3–5 cups bread flour

2 tablespoons cornmeal

1 quart whole milk

1 egg

Poaching

Poaching gives bagels their distinctive chewy texture. The softening of the outer starches keeps the crust from becoming crispy, and promotes all-over coloring. The poaching liquid chosen also adds a specific flavor. Some bakers use milk or fruit juice, and some are even said to import New York City tap water for authenticity.

1. In a large bowl, combine 1 cup water, sugar, and yeast. Stir to dissolve and let stand until foamy, about 10 minutes.

2. Add oil, ½ teaspoon salt, and enough bread flour to create a firm dough. Add flour only to reduce stickiness. Turn out onto a floured surface and knead 8–10 minutes. Return to bowl, dust the top with flour, and cover with a damp cloth or plastic wrap. Rise at room temperature until doubled in volume, about 1 hour.

3. Spray a baking sheet with pan spray and sprinkle with cornmeal. Turn risen dough onto a floured surface and shape into a rope, about 3" thick. Slice 2" pieces off the rope, then roll each into a tight ball. Leave balls on the floured surface, dust with flour, cover loosely with plastic wrap, and proof for 10 minutes.

4. Preheat oven to 425°F. Combine milk and 1 quart water in a large, deep skillet. Bring to a boil, then reduce to a simmer. Working with 1 roll at a time, poke your finger down through its center, and on a well-floured surface, begin spinning the roll to open up a large center hole. Make the hole large, as it will close in during baking.

5. Drop each formed bagel into simmering milk and water mixture, and poach 30 seconds on each side. Remove, tap off excess liquid, and place on prepared baking sheet, seam-side down. Mix egg with a pinch of salt and brush lightly onto bagels. Place a pan of water on the oven floor to create steam, and bake until brown, about 20–25 minutes. Cool completely on a rack.

Bialy

If you've never had a bialy before, you're in for a treat. This flattened filled bagel is hard to find but easy to make.

INGREDIENTS | YIELDS 6–8 ROLLS

2 tablespoons unsalted butter

1 large yellow onion, minced

2 teaspoons poppy seeds

1 teaspoon plus 1 pinch kosher salt

¼ teaspoon black pepper

1 cup plus 1 quart water

1 tablespoon granulated sugar

1¾ teaspoons active dry yeast (1 package)

1 tablespoon vegetable oil

3–5 cups bread flour

1 quart milk

2 tablespoons cornmeal

1 egg

Baking Poached Breads

Most baking is done on parchment for ease of removal and preservation of bakeware. But poached breads are wet, which causes the dough to stick to the paper. To eliminate sticky paper headaches, baked poached breads on greased pans coated with cornmeal for easy removal.

1. Melt butter in a large sauté pan over medium heat. Add onion and cook, stirring, until translucent, about 5 minutes. Add poppy seeds, ½ teaspoon salt, and pepper. Cook an additional minute. Remove from heat.

2. In a large bowl, combine 1 cup water, sugar, and yeast. Stir to dissolve and let stand for 10 minutes. Add oil, ½ teaspoon salt, and enough bread flour to create a firm dough. Add flour only to reduce stickiness. Turn onto a floured surface and knead 8–10 minutes. Return to bowl, dust the top with flour, and cover with a damp cloth or plastic wrap. Rise at room temperature until doubled in volume, about 1 hour.

3. Preheat oven to 425°F. Combine milk and 1 quart water in a large, deep skillet. Bring to a boil, then reduce to a simmer. Line a baking sheet with parchment and sprinkle with cornmeal. Turn risen dough onto a floured surface. Shape into a rope, about 3" thick. Slice 2" pieces off the rope, then roll each into a tight ball. Leave balls on the floured surface, dust with flour, cover loosely with plastic wrap, and proof for 10 minutes. Use floured fingers to press rolls into disks, about ½" thick. Press fingers in the center firmly to make a hollow. Press hard, but do not punch through the dough or make a hole.

4. Drop each formed bialy into simmering milk and water mixture, and poach 30 seconds on each side. Remove, tap off excess liquid, and place on prepared baking sheet. Mix egg with a pinch of salt and brush lightly onto bialy. Divide onion filling evenly between each roll, filling the center indentation of each. Place a pan of water on the oven floor and bake until brown, 20–25 minutes. Cool completely on a rack.

Butterfly Rolls

These rolls make a great accompaniment to a meat-and-potatoes meal. You can also replace the Parmesan cheese with cinnamon sugar for a morning treat.

INGREDIENTS | **YIELDS ABOUT 1 DOZEN ROLLS**

1 cup milk

½ cup sugar

1¾ teaspoons active dry yeast (1 package)

3 eggs

1 teaspoon plus 1 pinch kosher salt

¾ cup (1½ sticks) unsalted butter, softened

4–5 cups all-purpose flour

1 cup grated Parmesan cheese

Seam-Side Down Rolls

Forming rolls is an easy task, but to keep their shape in the oven, be sure to set them on the pan properly. A tightly rolled bun should be smooth all over, with the exception of one patch of wrinkled skin. If the wrinkled patch is on the bottom of the bun, gravity will help to ensure that the roll keeps its shape.

1. In a large bowl, combine milk, sugar, and yeast. Stir to dissolve and let stand until foamy, about 10 minutes.

2. Add 2 eggs, 1 teaspoon salt, ½ cup butter, and enough all-purpose flour to create a firm dough. Add flour only to reduce stickiness. Turn out onto a floured surface and knead 8–10 minutes. Return to bowl, dust the top with flour, and cover with a damp cloth or plastic wrap. Rise at room temperature until doubled in volume, about 2 hours.

3. Line two baking sheets with parchment. Turn risen dough onto a floured surface, divide into 2 equal pieces, and roll each into a rectangle the size of the baking sheets. Melt remaining butter and brush evenly over both rectangles. Sprinkle generously with Parmesan cheese. Starting from the long side, roll up rectangle jellyroll-style. Cut rolled dough into 2" pieces, then, using a floured wooden spoon handle, press firmly across each roll in the center. This pushes the spiral edges out and up, resembling butterfly wings.

4. Preheat oven to 425°F. Place balls onto prepared pans, 2" apart. Cover loosely with plastic wrap, and proof for 10 minutes. Mix 1 egg with a pinch of salt and brush lightly across rolls. Bake until golden brown, about 15–20 minutes. Cool completely on a rack.

Buttermilk Buns

Soft, white, and slightly sweet, these buns make fantastic dinner rolls or mini buns for burgers.

INGREDIENTS | **YIELDS 8–12 ROLLS**

¾ cup water

1¼ cups buttermilk

¼ cup sugar

1¾ teaspoons active dry yeast (1 package)

½ cup (1 stick) unsalted butter, softened

2 teaspoons plus 1 pinch kosher salt

2 teaspoons baking powder

4–6 cups bread flour

1 egg

1. In a large bowl, combine water, buttermilk, 1 teaspoon sugar, and yeast. Stir to dissolve and let stand until foamy, about 10 minutes.

2. Add remaining sugar, butter, 2 teaspoons salt, baking powder, and enough bread flour to create a firm dough. Add flour only to reduce stickiness. Turn out onto a floured surface and knead 8–10 minutes. Return to bowl, dust the top with flour, and cover with a damp cloth or plastic wrap. Rise at room temperature until doubled in volume, about 1 hour.

3. Line a baking sheet with parchment. Turn risen dough onto a floured surface. Shape into a rope, about 3" thick. Slice 2" pieces, then roll each into a tight ball. Place balls 2" apart on the prepared pan, seam-side down. Dust with flour, cover loosely with plastic wrap, and proof for 30 minutes. Preheat oven to 375°F.

4. Mix egg with a pinch of salt and brush lightly across proofed rolls. Bake until golden brown, about 25–30 minutes. Cool completely.

Cloverleaf Rolls

Nestled together in muffin tins, three tiny rolls become one large pull-apart clover, both tasty and fun to eat.

INGREDIENTS | YIELDS 12–15 ROLLS

¾ cup water

1 cup milk

¼ cup sugar

3½ teaspoons active dry yeast (2 packages)

1 egg

½ cup (1 stick) unsalted butter, softened

1 teaspoon kosher salt

4–6 cups bread flour

1. In a large bowl, combine water, milk, 1 teaspoon sugar, and yeast. Stir to dissolve and let stand until foamy, about 10 minutes.

2. Add remaining sugar, egg, ¼ cup butter, salt, and enough bread flour to create a firm dough. Add flour only to reduce stickiness. Turn out onto a floured surface and knead 8–10 minutes. Return to bowl, dust the top with flour, and cover with a damp cloth or plastic wrap. Rise at room temperature until doubled in volume, about 2 hours.

3. Coat muffin tin with pan spray. Turn risen dough onto a floured surface and shape into a rope, about 1" thick. Slice 2" pieces, then roll each into a tight ball. Place 3 balls next to each other in each muffin cup, forming a clover. Dust with flour, cover loosely with plastic wrap, and proof for 30 minutes. Preheat oven to 375°F.

4. Bake until golden brown, about 15–20 minutes. Melt remaining butter and brush over hot rolls as they come out of the oven. Serve warm.

French Ballons

Ballon is French for "balloon," which is what these puffy round rolls resemble when they are done.

INGREDIENTS | YIELDS 12–15 ROLLS

3 cups water

1¾ teaspoons active dry yeast (1 package)

5–6 cups bread flour

¼ cup (½ stick) unsalted butter, softened

2 tablespoons granulated sugar

2 teaspoons kosher salt

2 tablespoons cornmeal

Crusty Rolls

The steam in this recipe is essential to the form. These rolls will not expand as much, have as light a crust, or be round enough without an oven full of steam. The moist air softens the outer crust, creating the perfect balloon buns.

1. To make the sponge, combine 1 cup water and half the yeast, stir to dissolve, and let stand 5 minutes. Add 1 cup flour and beat 1 minute. Cover and let stand at room temperature 8–12 hours.

2. Add to the sponge 2 cups water, remaining yeast, butter, sugar, salt, and enough bread flour to make a soft dough. Turn out onto a floured work surface and knead 8–10 minutes. Add flour only to reduce stickiness. Return to bowl, dust with flour, cover with plastic wrap, and rise at room temperature until doubled in volume, about 1 hour. Punch dough down, fold it in half, and rise again until doubled, about 45 minutes.

3. Line two baking sheets with parchment and sprinkle with cornmeal. Turn risen dough onto a floured surface. Shape into a rope, about 2" thick. Slice 2" pieces off the rope, then roll each into a tight ball. Place balls onto prepared pans, 2" apart. Dust with flour, cover loosely with plastic wrap, and proof for 30 minutes. Preheat oven to 375°F.

4. Place a pan of cold water at the bottom of the oven to create steam. Bake until golden brown and hollow sounding, about 15–20 minutes. Cool completely on a rack.

Hamburger and Hot Dog Buns

The all-American backyard barbeque is taken to new heights with these homemade buns. You'll be the envy of the block party.

INGREDIENTS | **YIELDS 4–6 BUNS**

¾ cup water

2 teaspoons granulated sugar

1¾ teaspoons active dry yeast (1 package)

2 eggs

¼ cup (½ stick) unsalted butter, softened

1 teaspoon plus 1 pinch kosher salt

3–5 cups bread flour

2 tablespoons sesame seeds

1. In a large bowl, combine water, sugar, and yeast. Stir to dissolve and let stand until foamy, about 10 minutes.

2. Add 1 egg, butter, 1 teaspoon salt, and enough bread flour to create a firm dough. Add flour only to reduce stickiness. Turn out onto a floured surface and knead 8–10 minutes. Return to bowl, dust the top with flour, and cover with a damp cloth or plastic wrap. Rise at room temperature until doubled in volume, about 2 hours.

3. Line two baking pans with parchment. Turn risen dough onto a floured surface. Shape into a rope, about 2" thick. For hamburger buns, slice 3" pieces off the rope, then roll each into a tight ball. For hot dog buns, cut rope into 4" pieces and gently round the ends. Place on prepared pan, dust with flour, cover loosely with plastic wrap, and proof for 30 minutes. Preheat oven to 375°F.

4. Mix remaining egg with a pinch of salt and brush lightly across proofed rolls. Top with sesame seeds and bake until golden brown, about 15–20 minutes. Cool completely.

Italian Panini

Panini is an Italian sandwich roll, but in the United States it has come to mean specifically a grilled sandwich. These rolls make a great sandwich, grilled or not.

INGREDIENTS | YIELDS 8–10 ROLLS

1 cup water

1¾ teaspoons active dry yeast (1 package)

6–8 cups bread flour

2 teaspoons sugar

½ cup olive oil

2 teaspoons kosher salt

2 tablespoons cornmeal

1. To make the sponge, combine water and yeast, stir to dissolve and let stand 5 minutes. Add 1 cup bread flour and beat 1 minute. Cover and let stand at room temperature 8–12 hours.

2. Add to the sponge the sugar, oil, salt, and enough bread flour to make a soft dough. Turn out onto a floured work surface and knead 8–10 minutes. Add flour only to reduce stickiness. Return to bowl, dust with flour, cover with plastic, and rise at room temperature until doubled in volume, about 2 hours.

3. Line a baking sheet with parchment and sprinkle with cornmeal. Turn risen dough onto a floured surface. Shape into a rope, about 2" thick. Slice 3" pieces, then roll each into a tight ball. Place on prepared pan, dust with flour, cover loosely with plastic wrap, and proof for 30 minutes. Preheat oven to 375°F.

4. Place a pan of cold water at the bottom of the oven to create steam, and bake until golden brown, about 10–20 minutes. Cool completely on a rack.

Orange-Scented Pumpkin Buns

These heavenly rolls are great spread with honey at brunch, or dipped in turkey gravy at dinner.

INGREDIENTS | YIELDS 8–12 ROLLS

¾ cup water

¼ cup sugar

1¾ teaspoons active dry yeast
(1 package)

½ cup (1 stick) unsalted butter, softened

1 cup pumpkin purée

2 teaspoons plus 1 pinch kosher salt

½ teaspoon freshly grated nutmeg

Grated zest of 2 oranges

4–6 cups bread flour

1 egg

1. In a large bowl, combine water, 1 teaspoon sugar, and yeast. Stir to dissolve and let stand about 10 minutes.

2. Add remaining sugar, butter, pumpkin, 2 teaspoons salt, nutmeg, orange zest, and enough bread flour to create a firm dough. Add flour only to reduce stickiness. Turn out onto a floured surface and knead 8–10 minutes. Return to bowl, dust the top with flour, and cover with a damp cloth or plastic wrap. Rise at room temperature until doubled in volume, about 1 hour.

3. Line a baking sheet with parchment. Turn risen dough onto a floured surface. Shape into a rope, about 3" thick. Slice 2" pieces off the rope, then roll each into a tight ball. Place balls on prepared pan, seam-side down. Dust lightly with flour, cover loosely with plastic wrap, and proof for 30 minutes. Preheat oven to 375°F.

4. Mix egg with a pinch of salt and brush lightly across proofed rolls. Bake until golden brown, about 20–25 minutes. Cool completely.

Parker House Rolls

This recipe originated at Boston's Parker House Hotel in the 1850s. They're sometimes called pocket-book rolls because of their shape.

INGREDIENTS | **YIELDS 12–15 ROLLS**

2 cups milk

½ cup granulated sugar

3½ teaspoons active dry yeast
(2 packages)

1 egg

1 cup (2 sticks) unsalted butter, softened

2 teaspoons kosher salt

6–8 cups bread flour

1. In a large bowl, combine milk, 1 tablespoon sugar, and yeast. Stir to dissolve and let stand until foamy, about 10 minutes.

2. Add egg, half the butter, remaining sugar, salt, and enough bread flour to create a firm dough. Add flour only to reduce stickiness. Turn onto a floured surface and knead 8–10 minutes. Return to bowl, dust the top with flour, and cover with a damp cloth or plastic wrap. Rise at room temperature until doubled in volume, about 2 hours.

3. Line two baking sheets with parchment. Melt remaining butter. Let it cool, but remain liquid. Turn risen dough onto a floured surface. Using a rolling pin, roll flat to ½" thick. Using a 3" round biscuit cutter, cut dough into circles. Dip both sides of circles into melted butter, fold in half, and place on prepared pan, ⅓" apart (rolls should grow together in oven). Cover loosely with plastic wrap, and proof for 30 minutes. Preheat oven to 375°F.

4. Bake proofed rolls until golden brown, about 15–20 minutes. Cool completely.

Poppy Seed Kaiser Rolls

Supposedly invented in Vienna and named for Kaiser Franz Joseph, these rolls make the perfect foundation for your favorite sandwich.

INGREDIENTS | **YIELDS 6–8 ROLLS**

1¼ cups plus 1 tablespoon water

1 tablespoon sugar

1¾ teaspoons active dry yeast (1 package)

2 eggs

1 tablespoon vegetable oil

1 teaspoon plus 1 pinch kosher salt

4–6 cups bread flour

2–3 tablespoons poppy seeds

1. In a large bowl, combine 1¼ cups water, sugar, and yeast. Stir to dissolve and let stand until foamy, about 10 minutes.

2. Add 1 egg, oil, 1 teaspoon salt, and enough bread flour to create a firm dough. Add flour only to reduce stickiness. Turn out onto a floured surface and knead 8–10 minutes. Return to bowl, dust the top with flour, and cover with a damp cloth or plastic wrap. Rise at room temperature until doubled in volume, about 2 hours.

3. Line two baking pans with parchment. Turn risen dough onto a floured surface. Shape into a rope, about 3" thick. Slice into 3" pieces, then roll each into a tight ball. Place on prepared pan, dust with flour, cover loosely with plastic wrap, and rest for 10 minutes.

4. Preheat oven to 375°F. Using a rolling pin, roll buns into flat ½"-thick disks. Mix remaining egg with a pinch of salt and a tablespoon of water, and brush onto surface of disks, reserving egg wash that remains. Fold edges of disks into the center, making 5 folds in all (creating a pentagon-shaped roll). Place on prepared pans and proof 15 minutes.

5. Gently brush proofed rolls with remaining egg wash, sprinkle with poppy seeds, and bake until golden brown, about 15–20 minutes. Cool completely.

Potato Egg Bagels

Store-bought egg bagels usually contain yellow food coloring, so don't be discouraged by this paler homemade version. The flavor is superior to anything at the market.

INGREDIENTS | YIELDS 6–8 BAGELS

1 large russet (baking) potato (about 1 pound)

Water, as needed, plus 1 quart

1 tablespoon granulated sugar

1¾ teaspoons active dry yeast (1 package)

5 eggs

2 tablespoons vegetable oil

½ teaspoon plus 1 pinch kosher salt

4–6 cups bread flour

2 tablespoons cornmeal

1 quart whole milk

1. Peel and quarter potato, place in a small saucepan, cover with cold water, and bring to a boil. Cook until tender, drain, and reserve liquid. Mash with a fork and set aside. In a large bowl, combine 1 cup potato water, sugar, and yeast. Stir to dissolve and let stand until foamy, about 10 minutes.

2. Add mashed potato, 4 eggs, oil, ½ teaspoon salt, and enough bread flour to create a firm dough. Add flour only to reduce stickiness. Turn out onto a floured surface and knead 8–10 minutes. Return to bowl, dust the top with flour, and cover with plastic wrap. Rise at room temperature until doubled in volume, about 1 hour.

3. Spray a baking sheet with pan spray and sprinkle with cornmeal. Turn risen dough onto a floured surface. Shape into a rope, about 3" thick. Slice into 2" pieces, then roll each into a tight ball. Leave balls on the floured surface, dust with flour, cover loosely with plastic wrap, and proof for 10 minutes.

4. Preheat oven to 425°F. Combine milk and 1 quart water in a large, deep skillet. Bring to a boil, then reduce to a simmer. Working with one roll at a time, poke your finger down through its center, and on a well-floured surface, begin spinning the roll to open up a large center hole. Make the hole large, as it will close in during baking.

5. Drop each bagel into liquid, and poach 30 seconds on each side. Remove, tap off excess liquid, then place on baking sheet, seam-side down. Mix remaining egg with a pinch of salt and brush lightly onto bagels. Place a pan of water on the oven floor, and bake until brown, 20–25 minutes. Cool completely on a rack.

Pretzels

The traditional shape of the pretzel is said to show children's arms formed in prayer, creating three holes that represent the holy trinity.

INGREDIENTS | YIELDS 8–10 PRETZELS

2 cups plus 2 quarts water

1¾ teaspoons active dry yeast (1 package)

4–5 cups bread flour

1 tablespoon sugar

¼ cup vegetable oil

2 teaspoons plus 4 teaspoons kosher salt

¼ cup cornmeal

3 tablespoons baking soda

1 egg

1 pinch salt

¼ cup pretzel salt

Pretzel Salt

Salt is obtained through evaporation of sea water, and by mining veins of salt deposits left from ancient seas. Pretzel salt, a lighter crystal that flakes easily into flat, square pieces, comes from uncommon salt domes that formed when the earth's pressure forced salt up to the surface through cracks in the bedrock. If you can't find pretzel salt, kosher is the next best alternative.

1. To make the sponge, combine 1 cup water and yeast, stir to dissolve, and let stand 5 minutes. Add 1 cup bread flour and beat 1 minute. Cover and let stand at room temperature 8–12 hours.

2. Add to the sponge additional 1 cup water, sugar, oil, 2 teaspoons salt, and enough flour to make a soft dough. Turn out onto a floured surface and knead 8–10 minutes. Add flour only to reduce stickiness. Return to bowl, dust with flour, cover with plastic, and rise at room temperature until doubled in volume, about 1 hour.

3. Spray a baking sheet with pan spray and sprinkle with cornmeal. Turn risen dough onto a floured surface. Shape into a rope, about 3" thick. Slice into 2" pieces, then roll each into a tight ball. Leave balls on the floured surface, dust with flour, cover loosely with plastic wrap, and proof for 10 minutes.

4. Preheat oven to 425°F. Combine 2 quarts water with baking soda and remaining kosher salt in a large, deep skillet. Bring to a boil, then reduce to a simmer. Working with one roll at a time, roll into a thin rope about 1½" long. Form into a pretzel knot by bringing the ends of the rope into the center, crossing them, and attaching to opposite ends by pressing firmly.

5. Drop each pretzel into simmering liquid and poach 30 seconds on each side. Remove, tap off excess water, and place on baking sheet, seam-side down. Mix egg with a pinch of salt and brush lightly onto bagels. Sprinkle with pretzel salt. Bake until brown, about 15–20 minutes. Cool completely on a rack.

Scottish Baps

These traditional Scottish rolls are meant to be smeared with butter, topped with meat, and eaten like a sandwich. Do not mistake them for the Irish version containing sweet currants.

INGREDIENTS | YIELDS 8–12 ROLLS

1 cup milk

⅔ cup water

1 teaspoon sugar

1¾ teaspoons active dry yeast (1 package)

2 teaspoons kosher salt

3–6 cups bread flour

1. In a large bowl, combine 2/3 cup milk, water, sugar, and yeast. Stir to dissolve and let stand until foamy, about 10 minutes.

2. Add salt and enough bread flour to create a firm dough. Add flour only to reduce stickiness. Turn out onto a floured surface and knead 8–10 minutes. Return to bowl, dust the top with flour, and cover with a damp cloth or plastic wrap. Rise at room temperature until doubled in volume, about 2 hours.

3. Line two baking pans with parchment. Turn risen dough onto a floured surface. Shape into a rope, about 3" thick. Slice into 3" pieces, then roll each into a tight ball. Place on prepared pan, dust with flour, cover loosely with plastic wrap, and rest for 15 minutes.

4. Preheat oven to 375°F. Using floured fingers, press proofed buns into flat ½"-thick disks. Cover and rest another 15 minutes. Again using floured fingers, press firmly into the center, making an indentation. (This keeps the baps flat, preventing the center from rising up into a ball during baking.) Place on prepared pans, brush with remaining milk, and bake until golden brown, about 15–20 minutes. Cool completely.

Sourdough Hoagie Rolls

No matter what you call it (hoagie, sub, grinder, Italian, or hero), these rolls make one heck of a sandwich.

INGREDIENTS | **YIELDS 4–6 ROLLS**

1 cup Sourdough Starter (page 69)
1 cup milk
1 tablespoon honey
1¾ teaspoons active dry yeast
(1 package)
1 tablespoon olive oil
2 eggs
2 teaspoons plus 1 pinch kosher salt
4–6 cups bread flour

1. In a large bowl, combine sourdough starter, milk, honey, and yeast. Stir to dissolve and let stand until foamy, about 10 minutes.

2. Add oil, 1 egg, 2 teaspoons salt, and enough bread flour to create a firm dough. Add flour only to reduce stickiness. Turn onto a floured surface and knead 8–10 minutes. Return to bowl, dust the top with flour, and cover with a damp cloth or plastic wrap. Rise at room temperature until doubled in volume, about 1½ hours.

3. Line two baking pans with parchment. Turn risen dough onto a floured surface. Shape into a rope, about 3" thick. Slice into 3" pieces, then roll each into a ball. Form into a tapered football shapes by rolling the ends, pressing the outside of hands (the palm beneath your pinky fingers) toward the table. Place on prepared pan, dust with flour, cover loosely with plastic wrap, and proof for 30 minutes. Preheat oven to 375°F.

4. Mix remaining egg with a pinch of salt and brush lightly across proofed rolls. Bake until golden brown, about 15–20 minutes. Cool completely.

Walnut Rye Bagels

The natural nuttiness of rye flour is enhanced by the addition of toasted walnuts.

INGREDIENTS | YIELDS 6–8 BAGELS

1 cup plus 1 quart water

½ cup Sourdough Starter (page 69)

1 tablespoon honey

1¾ teaspoons active dry yeast
(1 package)

1 tablespoon vegetable oil

½ teaspoon plus 1 pinch kosher salt

1 cup medium rye flour

1 tablespoon caraway seeds, toasted
and ground

1 cup walnuts, toasted and chopped

3–5 cups bread flour

2 tablespoons cornmeal

1 quart whole milk

1 egg

1. In a large bowl, combine 1 cup water, starter, honey, and yeast. Stir to dissolve and let stand until foamy, about 10 minutes.

2. Add oil, ½ teaspoon salt, rye flour, caraway seeds, walnuts, and enough bread flour to create a firm dough. Add flour only to reduce stickiness. Turn onto a floured surface and knead 8–10 minutes. Return to bowl, dust the top with flour, and cover with a damp cloth or plastic wrap. Rise at room temperature until doubled in volume, about 1 hour.

3. Spray a baking sheet with pan spray and sprinkle with cornmeal. Turn risen dough onto a floured surface. Shape into a rope, about 3" thick. Slice into 2" pieces, then roll each into a tight ball. Leave balls on the floured surface, dust with flour, cover loosely with plastic wrap, and proof for 10 minutes.

4. Preheat oven to 425°F. Combine milk and 1 quart water in a large, deep skillet. Bring to a boil, then reduce to a simmer. Working with one roll at a time, poke your finger down through its center, and on a well-floured surface, spin the roll to open up a large center hole. Make the hole large, as it will close in during baking.

5. Drop each formed bagel into simmering milk and water, and poach 30 seconds on each side. Remove, tap off excess liquid, and place on baking sheet, seam-side down. Mix egg with a pinch of salt and brush lightly onto bagels. Place a pan of water on the oven floor to create steam, and bake until brown, about 20–25 minutes. Cool completely on a rack.

CHAPTER 8

Breadsticks

Sea Salt Breadsticks

Sea salt has a distinctively oceanic flavor, which makes these sticks perfect for a summer seaside picnic.

INGREDIENTS | YIELDS 24–35 STICKS

½ cup warm water

1 tablespoon granulated sugar

1¾ teaspoons active dry yeast (1 package)

4–5 cups bread flour

1 cup warm milk

¼ cup olive oil

¼ cup coarse sea salt

Better Browning

Because of their thin shape, breadsticks bake very quickly. Watch them carefully so they don't burn. It may also be necessary to turn the pans in the oven for even browning.

1. To make the sponge, combine water, sugar, and yeast in a large bowl. Stir to dissolve, and let stand 5 minutes. Add 1 cup bread flour and beat 1 minute. Cover and let stand at room temperature 8–12 hours.

2. Add to the sponge the milk, 2 tablespoons oil, 1 teaspoon salt, and enough remaining bread flour to make a soft dough. Turn onto a floured work surface and knead 8–10 minutes. Add flour only to reduce stickiness. Return to bowl, dust with flour, cover with plastic, and rise at room temperature until doubled in volume, about 1 hour.

3. Preheat oven to 400°F. Line three baking sheets with parchment. Turn dough onto a floured surface and pinch into golf-ball-sized pieces. Roll each piece into a 3"–4" rope, and set aside to rest 2–3 minutes. Once rested, pull the ropes into longer, free-form sticks, and place on prepared pans, ½" apart.

4. Brush remaining olive oil across sticks. Evenly sprinkle the remaining sea salt. Bake until golden brown and crisp, about 8–10 minutes. Cool and serve.

Cracked Pepper Breadsticks

A touch of subtle heat from black pepper makes these mouthwatering sticks the perfect appetizer.

INGREDIENTS | **YIELDS 24–36 STICKS**

2 cups warm water

1 tablespoon granulated sugar

2½ teaspoons active dry yeast
(2 packages)

4–5 cups bread flour

1 tablespoon kosher salt

2–3 tablespoons olive oil

2–3 tablespoons fresh cracked pepper

Pepper Perfect

The intense flavor of these sticks is best achieved with pepper ground fresh from a peppermill. Don't worry about measuring the pepper precisely. Just grind it liberally over the formed sticks before they hit the oven.

1. To make the sponge, combine water, sugar, and yeast in a large bowl. Stir to dissolve and let stand 5 minutes, until foamy. Add 1 cup bread flour and beat 1 minute. Cover and let stand at room temperature 8–12 hours.

2. Add to the sponge the salt and enough remaining bread flour to make a soft dough. Turn onto a floured work surface and knead 8–10 minutes. Add flour only to reduce stickiness. Return to bowl, dust with flour, cover with plastic, and rise at room temperature until doubled in volume, about 1 hour.

3. Preheat oven to 400°F. Line three baking sheets with parchment. Turn dough onto a floured surface and pinch off golf-ball-sized pieces. Roll each piece into a thin rope, about ½" in diameter. Place on prepared pans, ½" apart.

4. Brush olive oil across each stick. Evenly sprinkle cracked pepper. Bake until golden brown and crisp, about 8–10 minutes. Cool and serve.

Espresso Rye Sticks

These tangy sticks are perfect for hearty soups and stews. Or eat them with a little dip of mustard.

INGREDIENTS | YIELDS 24–36 STICKS

1½ cups strong coffee, cooled

½ cup buttermilk

1 tablespoon granulated sugar

1¾ teaspoons active dry yeast
(1 package)

1½ cups light rye flour

1 teaspoon kosher salt

1 tablespoon caraway seeds, toasted and ground

1 tablespoon cocoa powder

3–4 cups bread flour

2 tablespoons olive oil

2 tablespoons caraway seeds, whole and untoasted

1. Combine coffee, buttermilk, sugar, and yeast. Stir to dissolve and let stand 5 minutes, until foamy. Add rye flour, salt, ground caraway, cocoa, and enough bread flour to make a soft dough. Turn onto a floured work surface and knead 8–10 minutes. Add flour only to reduce stickiness. Return to bowl, dust with flour, cover with plastic, and rise at room temperature until doubled in volume, about 2 hours.

2. Preheat oven to 400°F. Line three baking sheets with parchment. Turn dough onto a floured surface and pinch off golf-ball-sized pieces. Roll each piece into a thin rope, about ½" in diameter. Place on prepared pans, ½" apart.

3. Brush olive oil across each stick. Evenly sprinkle on whole caraway seeds. Bake until golden brown and crisp, about 8–10 minutes. Cool and serve.

Fennel and Sage Breadsticks

The combination of fennel seed and dried sage gives these sticks an unmistakably Italian flavor. Make them a part of your next antipasto plate.

INGREDIENTS | YIELDS 24–36 STICKS

½ cup warm water

1 tablespoon granulated sugar

1¾ teaspoons active dry yeast (1 package)

4–5 cups bread flour

1 cup warm milk

2 teaspoons rubbed sage

2 teaspoons ground fennel

¼ cup olive oil

1 teaspoon kosher salt

¼ cup whole fennel seeds

Shapely Sticks

Any stick can be made in any shape: free-form, rolled tight and thin, or curled on the end like a fancy shepherd's crook. Feel free to shape the sticks to suit your mood.

1. To make the sponge, combine water, sugar, and yeast in a large bowl. Stir to dissolve and let stand 5 minutes. Add 1 cup bread flour and beat 1 minute. Cover and let stand at room temperature 8–12 hours.

2. Add to the sponge the milk, rubbed sage, ground fennel, 2 tablespoons oil, 1 teaspoon salt, and enough remaining bread flour to make a soft dough. Turn onto a floured work surface and knead 8–10 minutes. Add flour only to reduce stickiness. Return to bowl, dust with flour, cover with plastic, and rise at room temperature until doubled in volume, about 1½ hours.

3. Preheat oven to 400°F. Line three baking sheets with parchment. Turn risen dough onto a floured surface and pinch off golf-ball-sized pieces. Roll each piece into a very thin rope, no longer than the baking pan. Place on prepared pans, ½" apart.

4. Brush remaining olive oil across the sticks. Evenly sprinkle on fennel seeds. Bake until golden brown and crisp, about 8–10 minutes. Cool and serve.

Garlic, Lemon, and Poppy Seed Breadsticks

Lemon and poppy seeds are commonly paired in sweet baked goods. But don't overlook their savory possibilities. The pungent oil from the lemon zest compliments a variety of foods, including meats, fish, vegetables, and cheeses.

INGREDIENTS | **YIELDS 24–36 STICKS**

3 tablespoons olive oil

2 cloves garlic, minced

1 cup water

2 tablespoons sugar

1¾ teaspoons active dry yeast
(1 package)

1 cup milk

¾ teaspoon kosher salt

Grated zest of 3 lemons

3 tablespoons poppy seeds

4–6 cups bread flour

Grating Zest

Citrus zest is the most flavorful part of the fruit. Be careful to remove only the colored outer layer. The white pith underneath is bitter. Use the finest-holed grater you can find. The microplane, a fancy carpenter's rasp for the kitchen, is the best.

1. In a small sauté pan, heat 2 tablespoons of olive oil over medium heat. Add minced garlic, reduce heat to low, and cook until tender and barely browned, about 2–3 minutes. Remove from heat and set aside to cool.

2. Combine water, sugar, and yeast. Stir to dissolve and let stand until foamy, about 5 minutes.

3. Add milk, sautéed garlic and its oil, salt, lemon zest, 2 tablespoons poppy seeds, and enough flour to make a soft dough. Turn out onto a floured work surface and knead 8–10 minutes. Add flour only to reduce stickiness. Return to bowl, dust with flour, cover with plastic, and rise at room temperature until doubled in volume, about 1½ hours.

4. Preheat oven to 400°F. Line three baking sheets with parchment. Turn risen dough onto a floured surface and pinch off golf-ball-sized pieces. Roll each piece into a thin rope, about ¼" thick. Place on prepared pans, ½" apart.

5. Brush remaining olive oil across sticks, then evenly sprinkle on the remaining poppy seeds. Bake until golden brown and crisp, about 8–10 minutes. Cool and serve.

Little Loaf Soft Breadsticks

Although a similar product is called "breadsticks" at popular Italian chain restaurants, they are not considered as such by most bakers, because they are not long or crisp. But what's in a name?

INGREDIENTS | YIELDS 8–10 STICKS

1½ cups milk

1 teaspoon granulated sugar

1¾ teaspoons active dry yeast (1 package)

¼ cup (½ stick) unsalted butter, room temperature

1½ teaspoons kosher salt

3–4 cups bread flour

1. Combine milk, sugar, and yeast. Stir to dissolve and let stand 5 minutes. Add 2 tablespoons butter, salt, and enough bread flour to make a soft dough. Turn onto a floured work surface and knead 8–10 minutes. Add flour only to reduce stickiness. Return to bowl, dust with flour, cover with plastic, and rise at room temperature until doubled in volume, about 1 hour.

2. Preheat oven to 400°F. Line three baking sheets with parchment. Turn risen dough onto a floured surface and pinch off golf-ball-sized pieces. Roll each piece into a 3"–4" rope. Place on prepared pans, 2" apart.

3. Melt remaining butter and brush evenly on sticks. Using a serrated knife, slash one cut down the length of each stick, about ⅛" deep. Bake until golden brown, about 10–15 minutes. Serve warm.

Martini Breadsticks

Juniper berries give gin its distinctive flavor. Added here, with the addition of martini olives, these breadsticks are good enough for 007.

INGREDIENTS | **YIELDS 24–36 STICKS**

1½ cups water

1 tablespoon granulated sugar

1¾ teaspoons active dry yeast (1 package)

2 tablespoons juniper berries, crushed

¼ cup green pimento-stuffed olives, chopped

¼ cup olive oil

½ teaspoon kosher salt

4–6 cups bread flour

1. Combine water, sugar, and yeast. Stir to dissolve and let stand 5 minutes. Add juniper berries, olives, 2 tablespoons olive oil, salt, and enough bread flour to make a soft dough. Turn onto a floured work surface and knead 8–10 minutes. Add flour only to reduce stickiness. Return to bowl, dust with flour, cover with plastic, and rise at room temperature until doubled in volume, about 1 hour.

2. Preheat oven to 400°F. Line three baking sheets with parchment. Turn risen dough onto a floured surface and pinch off golf-ball-sized pieces. Roll each piece into a thin breadstick, about ¼" thick. Place on prepared pans, ½" apart.

3. Brush remaining olive oil across sticks. Bake until golden brown and crisp, about 8–10 minutes. Cool and serve.

North Beach Sourdough Sticks

This recipe is an homage to an Italian bakery in the Italian district of San Francisco, called North Beach, where you can find the finest breadsticks, a yard long, with knobby ends that make them look like bones.

INGREDIENTS | YIELDS 12–20 STICKS

1 cup Sourdough Starter (page 69)

1 cup water

1¾ teaspoons active dry yeast (1 package)

1 cup all-purpose flour

1 teaspoon kosher salt

3–4 cups bread flour

2 tablespoons olive oil

1. To make the sponge, combine sourdough starter, ½ cup water, and yeast. Stir to dissolve and let stand 5 minutes. Add all-purpose flour and beat 1 minute. Cover and let stand at room temperature 8–12 hours.

2. Add to the sponge ½ cup water, salt, and enough bread flour to make a soft dough. Turn onto a floured work surface and knead 8–10 minutes. Add flour only to reduce stickiness. Return to bowl, dust with flour, cover with plastic, and rise at room temperature until doubled in volume, about 1½ hours.

3. Preheat oven to 400°F. Line three baking sheets with parchment. Turn risen dough onto a floured surface and pinch off golf-ball-sized pieces. Roll each piece into a rope, 3"–4" long. Set aside to rest for 5 minutes. Pull the ends of the ropes to create thin, freeform sticks. Place on prepared pans, ½" apart.

4. Brush olive oil across the sticks, and bake until golden brown and crisp, about 8–10 minutes. Cool and serve.

Oatmeal Pull-Apart Breadsticks

Pull-apart sticks are more like mini loaves than sticks, baked close together to keep their sides tender and soft.

INGREDIENTS | YIELDS 20–36 BREADSTICKS

1 cup cold buttermilk

1 cup rolled oats (not quick cook)

2 tablespoons honey

1¾ teaspoons active dry yeast (1 package)

1 egg

2 tablespoons canola oil

2 teaspoons ground cinnamon

1½ teaspoons kosher salt

3–4 cups bread flour

2 tablespoons unsalted butter, melted

2 tablespoons granulated sugar

1. Combine buttermilk, oats, honey, and yeast. Stir to dissolve and let stand until foamy, about 5 minutes. Add egg, oil, 1 teaspoon cinnamon, salt, and enough bread flour to make a soft dough. Turn onto a floured work surface and knead 8–10 minutes. Add flour only to reduce stickiness. Return to bowl, dust with flour, cover with plastic, and rise at room temperature until doubled in volume, about 1 hour.

2. Preheat oven 400°F. Line three baking sheets with parchment. Turn risen dough onto a floured surface and pinch off golf-ball-sized pieces. Roll each piece into a 4"–5" rope. Place on prepared pans, ⅛" apart.

3. Brush melted butter across each stick. Combine sugar with remaining cinnamon and evenly sprinkle on the sticks. Bake until golden brown, about 10–15 minutes. Cool and serve.

Pepperoni Sticks

The addition of pepperoni, sun-dried tomatoes, and pepperoncini turns these sticks into a satisfying snack for all the pizza lovers in your life.

INGREDIENTS | **YIELDS 24–30 STICKS**

1½ cups warm water

1 tablespoon honey

1¾ teaspoons active dry yeast
(1 package)

½ cup pepperoni, diced finely

¼ cup sun-dried tomatoes, finely diced

¼ cup pepperoncini, finely diced

¼ cup olive oil

½ teaspoon kosher salt

4–6 cups bread flour

¼ cup Parmesan cheese

1. Combine water, honey, and yeast. Stir to dissolve and let stand 5 minutes. Add pepperoni, sun-dried tomatoes, pepperoncini, 2 tablespoons oil, salt, and enough bread flour to make a soft dough. Turn onto a floured work surface and knead 8–10 minutes. Add flour only to reduce stickiness. Return to bowl, dust with flour, cover with plastic, and rise at room temperature until doubled in volume, about 1½ hours.

2. Preheat oven to 400°F. Line three baking sheets with parchment. Turn risen dough onto a floured surface and pinch off golf-ball-sized pieces. Roll each piece into a thin rope, about ½" thick. Place on prepared pans, ½" apart.

3. Brush remaining olive oil across sticks, then evenly sprinkle on Parmesan cheese. Bake until golden brown and crisp, about 8–10 minutes. Cool and serve.

Prosciutto Breadsticks

Prosciutto is fairly salty, and paired with the Parmesan cheese on the surface of these breadsticks, greatly reduces the amount of salt needed for the dough.

INGREDIENTS | **YIELDS 24–30 STICKS**

2 cups warm water

1 tablespoon granulated sugar

2½ teaspoons active dry yeast (2 packages)

¾ cup prosciutto, minced finely

½ teaspoon kosher salt

4–5 cups bread flour

2 tablespoons olive oil

¼ cup grated Parmesan cheese

Prosciutto

Prosciutto means "ham" in Italian, but it generally refers to a salt-cured, air-dried, pressed ham from Parma. It's readily available in most large supermarkets, but any salty cured meat, like ham or salami, can successfully be substituted.

1. Combine water, sugar, and yeast. Stir to dissolve and let stand until foamy, about 5 minutes. Add prosciutto, salt, and enough bread flour to make a soft dough. Turn onto a floured work surface and knead 8–10 minutes. Add flour only to reduce stickiness. Return to bowl, dust with flour, cover with plastic, and rise at room temperature until doubled in volume, about 2 hours.

2. Preheat oven to 400°F. Line three baking sheets with parchment. Turn risen dough onto a floured surface and pinch off golf-ball-sized pieces. Roll each piece into a thin rope, about ¼" thick. Place on prepared pans, ½" apart.

3. Brush olive oil across each stick. Evenly sprinkle on Parmesan cheese. Bake until golden brown and crisp, about 8–10 minutes. Cool and serve.

Sesame Soy Breadsticks

These sticks have a decidedly Asian flair. Although breadsticks are rare in Asia, these would make a fantastic accompaniment to your favorite bowl of soba or ramen.

INGREDIENTS | YIELDS 24–30 STICKS

1¼ cups warm milk

4 tablespoons honey

1¾ teaspoons active dry yeast (1 package)

1 teaspoon sesame oil

½ teaspoon ground ginger

3 scallions, minced finely

1 egg

2 teaspoon kosher salt

3–4 cups bread flour

1 tablespoon soy sauce

¼ cup sesame seeds

Open Sesame

Originally from North Africa, the sesame seed is available in either white or black. They can be used interchangeably, but both share a rich, nutty flavor that's greatly improved by toasting. *Benné* is the Nigerian name for the seeds, and they are considered lucky in West Africa. Slaves brought sesame seeds to the United States, where they remain a popular baking ingredient.

1. Combine milk, 2 tablespoons honey, and yeast. Stir to dissolve and let stand until foamy, about 5 minutes. Add sesame oil, ginger, scallions, egg, salt, and enough bread flour to make a soft dough. Turn onto a floured work surface and knead 8–10 minutes. Add flour only to reduce stickiness. Return to bowl, dust with flour, cover with plastic, and rise at room temperature until doubled in volume, about 2 hours.

2. Preheat oven to 400°F. Line three baking sheets with parchment. Turn risen dough onto a floured surface and pinch off golf-ball-sized pieces. Roll each piece into a thin rope about ¼" thick. Place on prepared pans, ½" apart.

3. Combine remaining honey with soy sauce. Brush across each stick, then evenly sprinkle on sesame seeds. Bake until golden brown and crisp, about 8–10 minutes. Cool and serve.

Sesame Tahini Breadsticks

Sesame, garlic, and parsley give this recipe a distinctively Middle Eastern flair.

INGREDIENTS | **YIELDS 24–30 STICKS**

4 tablespoons olive oil

4 cloves garlic, minced

1¼ cups warm milk

2 teaspoons honey

1¾ teaspoons active dry yeast
(1 package)

¼ cup tahini

¼ cup fresh parsley, minced

½ teaspoon kosher salt

3–4 cups bread flour

½ teaspoon sesame seeds

Tahini

Tahini is a sesame paste used extensively throughout the Middle East. It is thinner than peanut butter, and is used as both a condiment and recipe ingredient. It is widely available in most supermarkets and health-food stores in the U.S. If tahini eludes you, make your own by toasting and then pulverizing the warm seeds in a food processor, blender, or mortar.

1. Heat 2 tablespoons olive oil in a small saucepan over medium heat. Add garlic, reduce heat to low, and cook until tender and barely golden. Remove from heat and set aside to cool.

2. Combine milk, honey, and yeast. Stir to dissolve and let stand 5 minutes, until foamy. Add tahini, parsley, salt, and enough bread flour to make a soft dough. Turn out onto a floured work surface and knead 8–10 minutes. Add flour only to reduce stickiness. Return to bowl, dust with flour, cover with plastic, and rise at room temperature until doubled in volume, about 1 hour.

3. Preheat oven to 400°F. Line three baking sheets with parchment. Turn risen dough onto a floured surface and pinch off golf-ball-sized pieces. Roll each piece into a thin rope, about ¼" thick. Place on prepared pans, ½" apart.

4. Brush remaining olive oil across sticks. Evenly sprinkle on the sesame seeds. Bake until golden brown and crisp, about 8–10 minutes. Cool and serve.

Sour Cream and Onion Breadsticks

Like the popular potato chips, this recipe is based on the flavor of ranch dressing.
Try serving these sticks on the side of your best salad, in lieu of croutons.

INGREDIENTS | **YIELDS 24–30 STICKS**

¼ cup warm water

2 tablespoons granulated sugar

1¾ teaspoons active dry yeast
(1 package)

1 cup buttermilk

1 cup sour cream

4 scallions, minced

¼ cup chives, minced

¼ small Bermuda onion, minced

1½ teaspoons kosher salt

1 egg

4–6 cups bread flour

¼ cup olive oil

2 tablespoons dried onion flakes

1. Combine water, sugar, and yeast. Stir to dissolve and let stand until foamy, about 5 minutes. Add buttermilk, sour cream, scallions, chives, Bermuda onion, salt, egg, and enough bread flour to make a soft dough. Turn onto a floured work surface and knead 8–10 minutes. Add flour only to reduce stickiness. Return to bowl, dust with flour, cover with plastic, and rise at room temperature until doubled in volume, about 1 hour.

2. Preheat oven to 400°F. Line three baking sheets with parchment. Turn risen dough onto a floured surface and pinch off golf-ball-sized pieces. Roll each piece into a thin stick, about ½" thick. Place on prepared pans, ½" apart, bending the tips into decorative squiggles and curly-Qs.

3. Brush olive oil across each stick. Evenly sprinkle on onion flakes. Bake until golden brown and crisp, about 8–10 minutes. Cool and serve.

Tapenade Sticks

Tapenade is a traditional dish of Provence used as a spread, pasta topping, or condiment.

INGREDIENTS | YIELDS 24–30 STICKS

1½ cups warm water

1 tablespoon sugar

1¾ teaspoons active dry yeast
(1 package)

¼ cup kalamata olives, pitted and minced

2 tablespoons capers, drained and chopped

Grated zest of 1 lemon

2 anchovy fillets, minced

3–4 grinds fresh cracked black pepper

3–4 cups bread flour

2 tablespoons olive oil

1. Combine water, sugar, and yeast. Stir to dissolve and let stand until foamy, about 5 minutes. Add olives, capers, lemon zest, anchovy, pepper, and enough bread flour to make a soft dough. Turn onto a floured work surface and knead 8–10 minutes. Add flour only to reduce stickiness. Return to bowl, dust with flour, cover with plastic, and rise at room temperature until doubled in volume, about 1 hour.

2. Preheat oven to 400°F. Line three baking sheets with parchment. Turn dough out onto a floured surface and pinch off golf-ball-sized pieces. Roll each piece into a thin stick, about ½" thick. Place on prepared pans, ½" apart.

3. Brush olive oil across each stick, and bake until golden brown and crisp, about 8–10 minutes. Cool and serve.

CHAPTER 9

Decadently Rich Breads

Brie en Brioche

Brie wrapped in brioche ranks among the top ten best appetizers of all time.

INGREDIENTS | YIELDS 1 BRIE EN BRIOCHE

⅔ cup milk

2¾ cups sugar

1¾ teaspoons active dry yeast (1 package)

4 eggs

6 ounces (1½ sticks) unsalted butter, softened

1 teaspoon plus 1 pinch kosher salt

4–6 cups bread flour

1 2-pound wheel Brie cheese

1 tablespoon water

1. In a large bowl, combine milk, 1 cup sugar, and yeast. Stir to dissolve and let stand until foamy, about 10 minutes.

2. Add 3 eggs, butter, remaining sugar, and 1 teaspoon salt; stir to combine. Add enough bread flour to create a firm dough. Turn onto a floured surface and knead 8–10 minutes. Add flour only to reduce stickiness. Return to bowl, dust the top lightly with flour, and cover with plastic wrap. Rise at room temperature until doubled in volume, about 2–3 hours. Punch dough down, fold in half, and rise again, until doubled, about 45 minutes.

3. Line a baking sheet with parchment. Turn risen dough onto floured surface and with a rolling pin, roll out into a circle 3"–4" wider than the wheel of Brie. Place Brie into center of circle, and fold edges over to completely conceal cheese. Place on prepared baking sheet, seam-side down. Whisk together remaining egg with a pinch of salt and a tablespoon of water. Brush egg wash across surface of dough, then bake until puffed and golden, 30–45 minutes. Cool on a rack to lukewarm before serving.

Brioche à Tête

Tête means "head," and these traditional buns have them. They look like tiny, buttery, luscious snowmen. Serve them with plenty of marmalade, jam, and honey.

INGREDIENTS | **YIELDS 12 ROLLS**

⅔ cup milk

2¾ cups sugar

1¾ teaspoons active dry yeast (1 package)

4 eggs

6 ounces (1½ sticks) unsalted butter, softened

1 teaspoon plus 1 pinch kosher salt

4–6 cups bread flour

No Sweat

Any bread baked in a high-sided pan will sweat as it cools. In tiny brioche molds, this phenomenon can be particularly detrimental, leading to soggy bottoms. As soon as the pans can be handled, invert them and remove the buns to cool on a rack to encourage evaporation of moisture. Taking the bread out hot also prevents sticking.

1. In a large bowl, combine milk, 1 cup sugar, and yeast. Stir to dissolve and let stand until foamy, about 10 minutes.

2. Add 3 eggs, butter, remaining sugar, and 1 teaspoon salt; stir to combine. Add enough bread flour to create a firm dough. Turn onto a floured surface and knead 8–10 minutes. Add flour only to reduce stickiness. Return to bowl, dust the top lightly with flour, and cover with plastic wrap. Rise at room temperature until doubled in volume, about 2–3 hours. Punch dough down, fold it in half, and rise again, until doubled, about 45 minutes.

3. Coat twelve brioche tins with pan spray. Turn risen dough onto floured surface and divide into 12 equal pieces. Roll each piece into a tight ball. Turn the ball on its side, and using a sawing motion, almost pinch off the top third . . . but not quite. Turn roll upright again. Give the top knot a little twist. Place into prepared tins so the rolls resemble snowmen. Cover loosely with plastic wrap, and set aside to proof for 15–20 minutes. Preheat oven to 375°F.

4. Combine remaining egg with a pinch of salt and a tablespoon of water, and brush lightly onto surface of brioche. Do not let egg wash pool between tin and dough. Bake until golden brown, about 15–20 minutes. Cool 10 minutes, then remove from tins while still warm to prevent sweating. Finish cooling on a rack.

Chocolate Brioche

Though brioche is typically a breakfast bread, these buns are more suited to dessert. (Although, as a breakfast, they will certainly motivate your sleepyheads out of bed.)

INGREDIENTS | YIELDS 10–12 BUNS

⅔ cup milk

2¾ cups sugar

1¾ teaspoons active dry yeast
(1 package)

¼ cup cocoa powder

4 eggs

6 ounces (1½ sticks) unsalted butter, softened

1 teaspoon plus 1 pinch kosher salt

4–6 cups bread flour

12 ounces bittersweet chocolate chips

1 tablespoon water

1. In a large bowl, combine milk, 1 cup sugar, and yeast. Stir to dissolve and let stand until foamy, about 10 minutes.

2. Add cocoa powder, 3 eggs, butter, remaining sugar, and 1 teaspoon salt; stir to combine. Add enough bread flour to create a firm dough. Turn onto a floured surface and knead 8–10 minutes. Add flour only to reduce stickiness. Return to bowl, dust the top lightly with flour, and cover with plastic wrap. Rise at room temperature until doubled in volume, about 2–3 hours. Punch dough down, fold it in half, and rise again, until doubled, about 45 minutes.

3. Line a baking sheet with parchment. Turn risen dough onto floured surface and pinch off baseball-sized pieces of dough. Roll each piece into a tight ball and rest 10 minutes. Using floured fingers, press each ball into a flat disk, about ½" thick. Place 1 tablespoon chocolate chips in the center, bring edges together to conceal chocolate, and pinch to close. Place onto prepared baking sheet seam-side down. Cover loosely with plastic wrap, and proof for 15–20 minutes. Preheat oven to 375°F.

4. Combine remaining egg with a pinch of salt and a tablespoon of water, and brush lightly onto surface of brioche. Bake until golden brown, about 15–20 minutes. Cool on a rack.

Egg Bread

Richer than challah, but not quite as rich as brioche, this golden loaf gets its color from the egg yolks. Don't despair if it is not identical to store-bought versions, which usually add yellow food coloring.

INGREDIENTS | YIELDS 1 LOAF

½ cup milk

1 tablespoon honey

3½ teaspoons active dry yeast
(2 packages)

1 cup all-purpose flour

¼ cup (½ stick) unsalted butter, softened

3 whole eggs

2 egg yolks

1 teaspoon plus 1 pinch kosher salt

2–3 cups bread flour

1 tablespoon water

1. In a large bowl combine milk, honey, and yeast. Stir to dissolve and let stand until foamy, about 10 minutes.

2. Stir in all-purpose flour, butter, 2 eggs, both yolks, and 1 teaspoon salt. Add enough bread flour to create a firm dough. Add flour only to reduce stickiness. Turn onto a floured surface and knead 8–10 minutes. Return to bowl, dust the top with flour, and cover with plastic wrap. Rise at room temperature until doubled in volume, about 2 hours.

3. Coat a 9" × 5" loaf pan with pan spray, and line its length with a strip of parchment. Turn risen dough onto a lightly floured work surface, and shape into an oblong loaf. Place in prepared pan, seam-side down. Dust lightly with flour, cover loosely with plastic wrap, and proof until doubled in volume, about 1 hour.

4. Preheat oven to 350°F. Whisk together remaining egg with 1 tablespoon water and a pinch of salt. Brush gently onto the top of the risen loaf, and bake until golden brown and hollow sounding, about 30–40 minutes. Cool completely on a rack before serving.

Croissants

There is nothing more decadent than a croissant, unless it's a homemade croissant.

INGREDIENTS | YIELDS 15–20 CROISSANTS

Butter Block:

1½ cups (3 sticks) unsalted butter, softened

1 tablespoon lemon juice

½ cup all-purpose flour

Deutremp:

2 cups milk

1¾ teaspoons active dry yeast (1 package)

2 tablespoons granulated sugar

2 teaspoons plus 1 pinch kosher salt

4–6 cups bread flour

1 egg

1 tablespoon water

Laminated Dough

Croissant is a laminated dough, which means it contains two components, butter and dough (known as the "deutremp"), which are pressed and folded to created multiple layers. Other doughs in that category include puff pastry and Danish dough.

1. Beat butter with lemon juice and all-purpose flour until it is creamy and lump-free. Form it into a square 1" thick. Refrigerate no longer than 1 hour.

2. Combine milk, yeast, and sugar in a large bowl and set aside 10 minutes until foamy. Add 2 teaspoons salt and enough bread flour to make a firm dough. Turn onto a floured surface and knead 8–10 minutes. Add flour only to reduce stickiness. Wrap well and chill for 30 minutes.

3. Working on a floured surface, roll out dough into a square 2" larger than the butter block. Place butter on top so than it forms a diamond inside the dough square. Wrap dough over, completely encasing butter. Dust with flour, turn over, and with a rolling pin, using short, light motions, roll into a rectangle, ½" thick. Fold the dough into thirds, like a business letter, (called a single turn) and refrigerate 30 minutes.

4. Remove chilled dough from the fridge, place on a floured surface, and roll again, using short, light motions, into a rectangle, ½" thick. Make another single turn and refrigerate. Repeat this process for a total of 4 single turns, chilling between each. After the last turn, roll to ¼" thick. The puff pastry is now ready to be formed and baked. It can also be stored in the refrigerator for up to 24 hours, or frozen for long term storage.

Croissants (*continued*)

5. Line two baking sheets with parchment. Preheat oven to 400°F. To form classic croissants, roll dough into a large rectangle, 12" high and ¼" thick. Rest dough for 5 minutes, then cut into two parallel rectangles each 6" high. Cut every 6" along the length, creating 6" squares. Cut each square in half on the bias, creating 2 triangles. Roll up triangle from the wide side, and shape into crescents. Place on prepared pan. Combine egg with a pinch of salt and a tablespoon of water, and brush lightly onto surface of croissants. Bake until golden brown, about 15–20 minutes. Cool completely.

Eggplant Artichoke Bread

This savory bread is so good, you may just end up eating the whole loaf yourself.

INGREDIENTS | YIELDS 2 LOAVES

1 large eggplant, diced

1 tablespoon plus 1 teaspoon kosher salt

½ cup olive oil

4 cloves garlic, minced

1 8-ounce can artichoke hearts, drained

⅔ cup warm water

1 teaspoon granulated sugar

1¾ teaspoons active dry yeast (1 package)

2 eggs

1 cup whole wheat flour

3–5 cups bread flour

¼ cup cornmeal

1. Toss together eggplant and 1 tablespoon salt, place in a colander, and drain for 30 minutes. Heat 2 tablespoons olive oil in a large sauté pan over high heat. Rinse eggplant, add to oil and cook until tender, about 5 minutes. Add garlic, and cook 1 minute. Add artichokes and cook 1 minute until warmed through. Set aside to cool.

2. In a large bowl, combine water, sugar, and yeast. Stir to dissolve and let stand until foamy, about 10 minutes.

3. Add cooled eggplant mixture, eggs, 2 tablespoons olive oil, 1 teaspoon salt, and whole wheat flour; stir to combine. Add enough bread flour to create a firm dough. Add flour only to reduce stickiness. Turn onto a floured surface and knead 8–10 minutes. Return to bowl, dust the top with flour, and cover with plastic wrap. Rise at room temperature until doubled in volume, about 1 hour.

4. Line a baking sheet with parchment, and sprinkle with cornmeal. Turn risen dough onto a floured surface, divide into 2 equal portions, and shape into round loaves. Place onto prepared pan and proof for 30 minutes. Preheat oven to 375°F.

5. Brush the top of the risen loaves with remaining olive oil, and using a serrated knife, cut an X into the surface of the dough, about ½" deep. Place a pan of cold water at the bottom of the oven to create steam. Bake until golden brown and hollow sounding, about 30–40 minutes. Cool completely on a rack before serving.

Extra-Virgin Olive Oil Bread

Good olive oil adds a rich and fruity flavor to this yeast bread, and brushed on the outside it creates an extra crispy crust.

INGREDIENTS | YIELDS 1 LOAF

½ cup water

1¾ teaspoons active dry yeast (1 package)

4–6 cups bread flour

2 teaspoons honey

¾ cup extra-virgin olive oil, plus more as needed

1 teaspoon kosher salt

2 tablespoons cornmeal

1. To make the sponge, combine water and yeast, stir to dissolve, and let stand 5 minutes. Add ½ cup bread flour and beat 1 minute. Cover and let stand at room temperature for 8–12 hours.

2. Add to the sponge the honey, ¾ cup oil, salt, and enough bread flour to make a soft dough. Turn onto a floured work surface and knead 8–10 minutes. Add flour only to reduce stickiness. Return to bowl, brush with more oil, cover with plastic, and rise at room temperature until doubled in volume, about 1 hour. Punch dough down, fold in half, and rise again, until doubled, about 45 minutes.

3. Line a baking sheet with parchment, and sprinkle with cornmeal. Turn risen dough onto a floured surface, and shape into a round loaf. Place onto prepared pan, brush with more oil, cover loosely with plastic wrap, and proof for 15 minutes. Preheat oven to 375°F.

4. Using a serrated knife, cut decorative slash marks into the surface of the dough, about ½" deep. Place a pan of cold water at the bottom of the oven to create steam. Bake until golden brown and hollow sounding, about 30–40 minutes. Cool completely on a rack.

Gorgonzola Black Pepper Bread

Gorgonzola is the richest of the blue cheeses, buttery and soft, but deliciously tangy. Paired with fresh cracked pepper, it makes a mouthwatering loaf.

INGREDIENTS | YIELDS 2 LOAVES

1 cup warm water

1 tablespoon honey

3½ teaspoons active dry yeast (2 packages)

1 cup milk

½ cup Gorgonzola cheese, softened

2 tablespoons olive oil, plus more as needed

1 tablespoon kosher salt

2 tablespoons fresh cracked black pepper

4–6 cups bread flour

¼ cup cornmeal

Gorgonzola

Gorgonzola is an Italian blue cheese named for a town near Milan that was once a center of dairy trade. The cheese is creamy and pungent and becomes stronger with age. Other blue cheeses may be substituted if necessary.

1. Combine water, honey, and yeast. Stir to dissolve and let stand until foamy, about 10 minutes.

2. Add milk, Gorgonzola, 2 tablespoons oil, salt, pepper, and enough bread flour to make a soft dough. Turn onto a floured work surface and knead 8–10 minutes. Add flour only to reduce stickiness. Return to bowl, dust with flour, cover with plastic, and rise at room temperature until doubled in volume, about 2 hours.

3. Coat a baking sheet with pan spray and sprinkle with cornmeal. Turn dough onto a floured surface and divide into 2 equal portions. Roll each piece into a tight football shape and taper the ends slightly. Place loaves on prepared pan, dust with flour, cover with plastic wrap, and rise 30 minutes. Preheat oven to 400°F.

4. Brush loaves lightly with olive oil, and using a serrated knife, cut decorative slash marks into the surface of the dough, about ½" deep. Place a pan of cold water at the bottom of the oven to create steam. Bake until golden brown and hollow sounding, about 30–40 minutes. Cool completely on a rack before serving.

Marzipan Bread

The addition of marzipan, a heavenly confection made from ground almonds and sugar, takes the term "decadence" to a whole new level.

INGREDIENTS | **YIELDS 2 LOAVES**

⅔ cup milk

2¾ cups sugar

1¾ teaspoons active dry yeast (1 package)

¼ cup (1 stick) unsalted butter, softened

2 ounces marzipan

4 eggs

¼ teaspoon almond extract

1 cup skin-on almonds, toasted and finely chopped

1 teaspoon plus 1 pinch kosher salt

4–6 cups bread flour

1 tablespoon water

1. In a large bowl, combine milk, 1 tablespoon sugar, and yeast. Stir to dissolve and let stand until foamy, about 10 minutes.

2. Beat together butter, marzipan, and remaining sugar until smooth and creamy. Add to the yeast mixture along with 3 eggs, almond extract, almonds, and 1 teaspoon salt. Stir to combine, then add enough bread flour to create a firm dough. Turn onto a floured surface and knead 8–10 minutes. Add flour only to reduce stickiness. Return to bowl, dust the top lightly with flour, and cover with plastic wrap. Rise at room temperature until doubled in volume, about 2–3 hours. Punch dough down, fold in half, and rise again, until doubled, about 45 minutes.

3. Coat two 9" × 5" loaf pans with pan spray, and line the length of each with a strip of parchment. Turn risen dough onto a lightly floured work surface, divide into 2 equal portions, and shape into oblong loaves. Place in prepared pans, seam-side down. Dust lightly with flour, cover loosely with plastic wrap, and proof until doubled in volume, about 1 hour.

4. Preheat oven to 350°F. Whisk together remaining egg with 1 tablespoon water and a pinch of salt. Brush gently onto the top of the risen loaves, and bake until golden brown and hollow sounding, about 30–40 minutes. Cool completely on a rack before serving.

Pain au Chocolate

Also called chocolate croissants, these classic pastries are a fixture in every self-respecting French bakery.

INGREDIENTS | **YIELDS 10–12 CROISSANTS**

1 batch Croissants dough (page 148)

1 egg

1 pinch salt

1 tablespoon water

12 ounces bittersweet chocolate chips

½ cup granulated sugar

Pain au Chocolate

Professional bakers use chocolate batons instead of chips when making this popular bread. Batons are skinny chocolate bars of exquisite quality, made to fit perfectly into the rectangle of croissant dough. Fine culinary retailers carry them, as do several Internet sources. (See Appendix B.)

1. Prepare croissant dough as directed in that recipe. When all four turns of the croissant dough are completed, roll out the dough into a rectangle ¼" thick, and cut into 6" × 4" rectangles.

2. Line two baking sheets with parchment. Whisk the egg with a pinch of salt and a tablespoon of water, and brush it onto the long edges of each rectangle. Reserve remaining egg wash. Place a tablespoon of chocolate chips at one short end of each rectangle and roll up, jellyroll-style. Pinch edges to seal, and place on prepared pan. Cover loosely with plastic wrap and proof for 10–15 minutes. Preheat oven to 375°F.

3. Brush the top of each croissant with remaining egg wash, and sprinkle generously with sugar. Bake until deep golden brown, about 15–20 minutes. Cool completely on a rack.

Roasted Garlic Potato Bread

Potato is a well-loved addition to bread, used for centuries as a way to stretch nutritious leftovers.

INGREDIENTS | YIELDS 2 LOAVES

2 heads garlic

1 large russet (baking) potato, peeled and quartered

Water, as needed

1½ cups milk

1 teaspoon granulated sugar

1¾ teaspoons active dry yeast (1 package)

¼ cup (½ stick) unsalted butter, softened

2 teaspoons kosher salt

5–6 cups bread flour

2 tablespoons cornmeal

1. Preheat oven to 400°F. Wrap garlic bulbs together in one sheet of foil. Bake until soft to the touch, about 45 minutes. Remove from foil and cool completely.

2. In a small saucepan, cover potato with cold water and bring to a boil. At the boil, reduce to a simmer and cook until tender, about 30 minutes. Strain and pass potato through a ricer or mesh strainer. Cool completely.

3. Combine milk, sugar, and yeast. Stir to dissolve and let stand until foamy, about 10 minutes. Cut garlic bulbs in half and squeeze softened garlic bulbs into yeast mixture. Add butter, salt, potatoes, and enough bread flour to make a soft dough. Turn onto a floured work surface and knead 8–10 minutes. Add flour only to reduce stickiness. Return to bowl, dust with flour, cover with plastic, and rise at room temperature until doubled in volume, about 2 hours.

4. Preheat oven to 400°F. Line baking sheet with parchment and sprinkle with cornmeal. Turn risen dough onto a floured surface and divide into 2 equal portions. Form each into a round loaf, and place on prepared pan. Dust with flour, and using a serrated knife, slash a decorative mark into the crust, about ¼" deep. Bake until golden brown and crisp, about 35–45 minutes. Cool completely on a rack.

Sausage Roll

Sausage wrapped in dough is commonly referred to as toad-in-the-hole,
or pig in a blanket. Whatever you call it, it's sure to be a hit.

INGREDIENTS | YIELDS 10–12 ROLLS

⅔ cup milk

1 tablespoon sugar

1¾ teaspoons active dry yeast
(1 package)

4 eggs

¼ cup (½ stick) unsalted butter, softened

1 teaspoon plus 1 pinch kosher salt

4–6 cups bread flour

1 tablespoon water

8 English banger sausages, fully cooked

Sausage Selection

This recipe calls for bangers, but if you have a different sausage preference, by all means, use it. Kielbasa, bratwurst, knock-wurst, chorizo, Italian, or your favorite hot dog will all work. Just be sure the meat is fully cooked and cooled before rolling it up in the dough.

1. In a large bowl, combine milk, sugar, and yeast. Stir to dissolve and let stand until foamy, about 10 minutes.

2. Add 3 eggs, butter, 1 teaspoon salt, and enough bread flour to create a firm dough. Turn onto a floured surface and knead 8–10 minutes. Add flour only to reduce stickiness. Return to bowl, dust the top lightly with flour, and cover with plastic wrap. Rise at room temperature until doubled in volume, about 2–3 hours. Punch dough down, fold in half, and rise again, until doubled, about 45 minutes.

3. Line a baking sheet with parchment. Turn risen dough onto floured surface and with a rolling pin, roll out into a rectangle ¼" thick. Rest 5 minutes, then cut into 6" × 4" rectangles. Whisk together 1 egg with a pinch of salt and a tablespoon of water, and brush onto the long edges of each rectangle. Reserve remaining egg wash. Cut sausages into 2" lengths. Place 1 piece of sausage at the short end of each rectangle and roll up, jellyroll-style. Pinch edges to seal, and place on prepared pan. Cover loosely with plastic wrap and proof for 10–15 minutes.

4. Preheat oven to 375°F. Brush the top of each roll with remaining egg wash. Bake until deep golden brown, about 15–20 minutes. Cool 10 minutes on a rack before serving warm.

Sticky Buns

These upside-down rolls are a crowd pleaser. You can up the ante by adding to the cinnamon swirl more nuts, dried fruits, or even chocolate chips.

INGREDIENTS | **YIELDS 10–12 BUNS**

Buns:

1 cup milk

1 teaspoon granulated sugar

1¾ teaspoons active dry yeast (1 package)

½ cup (1 stick) unsalted butter

3 eggs

1 teaspoon kosher salt

4–6 cups bread flour

Topping:

1 cup brown sugar

2 tablespoons honey

1¼ cups (2½ sticks) unsalted butter

2 cups chopped pecans

Cinnamon Swirl:

1 cup granulated sugar

3 tablespoons cinnamon

Danger:

The sticky part of sticky buns comes from melted sugar, which is extremely hot when it emerges from the oven. Even though the recipe calls for waiting 10 minutes before inverting, the topping will still be quite hot. Unfortunately, if the sticky topping is allowed to cool completely before inverting, the entire loaf will stick in the pan. So, turn it out while hot, but use caution. Use oven mitts and work over a sink, away from other people, especially small children.

1. In a large bowl combine milk, 1 teaspoon sugar, and yeast. Stir to dissolve and let stand until foamy, about 10 minutes.

2. Stir in 1 stick butter, eggs, salt, and enough bread flour to create a firm dough. Add flour only to reduce stickiness. Turn onto a floured surface and knead 8–10 minutes. Return to bowl, dust the top with flour, and cover with a damp cloth or plastic wrap. Rise at room temperature until doubled in volume, about 2 hours.

3. Spray a 9" × 13" baking pan with pan spray, and line with parchment. Sprinkle the bottom evenly with the brown sugar, honey, dot with 2 sticks butter, and pecans. Set aside.

4. Turn risen dough onto a floured surface and with a rolling pin, roll into a 9" × 40" rectangle. Melt remaining butter and brush over the entire surface. Combine 1 cup granulated sugar and cinnamon and sprinkle evenly over butter. Starting on a long edge, roll up the dough into a log. Slice log into 3" wheels, and place on prepared pan, ½" apart. Dust lightly with flour, cover with plastic wrap, and rise for 30 minutes. Preheat oven to 350°F.

5. Bake buns 15–20 minutes, until golden brown and bubbly. Remove from oven; cool 10 minutes. While still warm, carefully invert onto serving platter or tray. Cool before serving.

Sweet Vanilla Bay Bread

It may sound unusual, but bay and vanilla make a classic Mediterranean combo. Once you try it, you'll be hooked.

INGREDIENTS | YIELDS 1 LOAF

1 cup milk

¼ cup granulated sugar

1¾ teaspoons active dry yeast (1 package)

½ cup (1 stick) unsalted butter

3 eggs

5 bay leaves, ground finely, plus 3–4 whole leaves

1 vanilla bean, scraped

1 tablespoon vanilla extract

1 teaspoon plus 1 pinch kosher salt

4–6 cups bread flour

1 tablespoon water

1. Combine milk, sugar, and yeast. Stir to dissolve and let stand until foamy, about 10 minutes.

2. Add butter, 2 eggs, ground bay, vanilla bean and extract, 1 teaspoon salt, and enough bread flour to make a soft dough. Turn onto a floured work surface and knead 8–10 minutes. Add flour only to reduce stickiness. Return to bowl, dust with flour, cover with plastic, and rise at room temperature until doubled in volume, about 2 hours.

3. Coat a 9" × 5" loaf pan with pan spray, and line its length with a strip of parchment. Turn risen dough onto a lightly floured work surface, and shape into an oblong loaf. Place in prepared pan, seam-side down. Dust lightly with flour, cover loosely with plastic wrap, and proof until doubled in volume, about 1 hour.

4. Preheat oven to 350°F. Whisk together remaining egg, 1 tablespoon water, and a pinch of salt. Brush gently onto the top of the risen loaf. With a sharp knife, make a few decorative cuts, and insert a whole bay leaf into each. Bake until golden brown and hollow sounding, about 30–40 minutes. Cool completely on a rack before serving.

Wild Mushroom Bread

The combination of yeast and earthy mushrooms is mouthwatering. Serve this bread alongside your favorite pasta, or use it for the world's best bruschetta.

INGREDIENTS | YIELDS 2 LOAVES

½ cup mixed dried wild mushrooms

2 cups hot water

2 tablespoons olive oil, plus more as needed

1 shallot, minced

8 ounces shiitake mushrooms, sliced

8 ounces cremini mushrooms, sliced

1 tablespoon sugar

3½ teaspoons active dry yeast (2 packages)

1 teaspoon kosher salt

4–6 cups bread flour

¼ cup cornmeal

1. In a small bowl, combine dried mushrooms and hot water, and set aside to steep and soften at least 1 hour, or overnight.

2. Heat 2 tablespoons oil in a large sauté pan over medium heat. Add shallots and cook, stirring, until tender and translucent, about 3 minutes. Add shiitake and cremini mushrooms and continue cooking until softened and dry, 8–10 minutes. Remove from heat and cool completely.

3. Strain dried mushrooms from water. Reserve water and chop reconstituted mushrooms. Add the sugar and yeast to the water. Stir to dissolve and let stand until foamy, about 10 minutes. Add sautéed mushrooms, reconstituted mushrooms, salt, and enough bread flour to make a soft dough. Turn onto a floured work surface and knead 8–10 minutes. Add flour only to reduce stickiness. Return to bowl, dust with flour, cover with plastic, and rise at room temperature until doubled in volume, about 2 hours.

4. Preheat oven to 400°F. Line baking sheet with parchment and sprinkle with cornmeal. Turn risen dough onto a floured surface and divide into 2 equal portions. Form each into a round loaf, and place on prepared pan. Brush olive oil across each loaf. Bake until golden brown, about 35–45 minutes. Cool completely on a rack.

Antipasto Bread

Meaning "before the meal," antipasto is the first course of a traditional Italian meal, and typically includes cured meats and fish, marinated vegetables, olives, and cheese.

INGREDIENTS | YIELDS 1 LOAF

1 cup water

1 tablespoon honey

1¾ teaspoons active dry yeast (1 package)

1 tablespoon Italian seasoning

½ cup Italian salami, diced finely

¼ cup pepperoncini, diced finely

¼ cup roasted red peppers, finely diced

¼ cup black olives

2 tablespoons olive oil, plus more as needed

½ teaspoon kosher salt

4–6 cups bread flour

2 tablespoons cornmeal

1 tablespoon shredded Parmesan cheese

1 teaspoon red chili pepper flakes

Italian Seasoning

A blend of dried Italian herbs is easy to find in any market, or you can make your own fresh blend. Combine ¼ cup each chopped fresh oregano and basil, 2 tablespoons each fresh chopped sage and rosemary, 3 minced cloves garlic, and 1 tablespoon crushed fennel seeds.

1. Combine water, honey, and yeast. Stir to dissolve and let stand until foamy, about 10 minutes.

2. Add Italian seasoning, salami, pepperoncini, roasted red peppers, olives, 2 tablespoons oil, salt, and enough bread flour to make a soft dough. Turn onto a floured work surface and knead 8–10 minutes. Add flour only to reduce stickiness. Return to bowl, dust with flour, cover with plastic, and rise at room temperature until doubled in volume, about 2 hours.

3. Preheat oven to 400°F. Line a baking sheet with parchment and sprinkle with cornmeal. Turn risen dough onto a floured surface and form into an oblong loaf. Place on prepared pan, brush with olive oil, and sprinkle with Parmesan cheese and red chili pepper flakes. Place a pan of cold water on the oven floor to create steam. Bake until golden brown about 35–45 minutes. Cool completely on a rack.

CHAPTER 10

Breakfast Breads

Cinnamon Swirl Bread

This bread creates a welcoming smell in the morning when warmed gently in the toaster.

INGREDIENTS | YIELDS 2 LOAVES

1½ cups plus 1 tablespoon water

½ cup honey

1¾ teaspoons active dry yeast
(1 package)

3 eggs

¼ cup canola oil

1 teaspoon kosher salt

4–5 cups bread flour

⅓ cup cinnamon

⅔ cup sugar

1. In a large bowl, combine 1½ cups water, 2 tablespoons honey, and yeast. Stir to dissolve and let stand until foamy, about 10 minutes.

2. Add 2 eggs, oil, salt, and enough bread flour to create a firm dough. Turn onto a floured surface and knead 8–10 minutes. Add flour only to reduce stickiness. Return to bowl, dust the top lightly with flour, and cover with plastic wrap. Rise at room temperature until doubled in volume, about 2–3 hours. Punch dough down, fold in half, and rise again, until doubled, about 45 minutes.

3. Coat two 9" × 5" loaf pans with pan spray and line with a strip of parchment. Turn risen dough onto a floured surface, and with a rolling pin, roll into an 18" × 24" rectangle. Warm remaining honey and brush over the entire surface of dough. Combine cinnamon and sugar, and sprinkle on top of honey. Starting on a long edge, roll the dough up into a log. Cut the log into two 9" loaves. Place each loaf in a pan, seam-side down, dust with flour, cover with plastic wrap, and rise for 30 minutes. Combine remaining egg with a tablespoon of water and brush over the surface of the breads. Bake until golden brown and firm, about 50–60 minutes. Cool completely on a rack before slicing.

Apple Fritters

Don't let the addition of fresh fruit fool you. These are doughnuts, through and through.

INGREDIENTS | YIELDS 12 FRITTERS

4–6 cups canola oil

1 cup sifted all-purpose flour

¼ cup sugar

1 teaspoon kosher salt

1½ teaspoons baking powder

1 egg

⅓ cup milk

2 large apples, peeled and grated

½ cup powdered sugar

1. In a heavy, high-sided frying pan, heat oil to 350°F. Sift together flour, sugar, salt and baking powder into a large bowl. In a separate bowl whisk together egg and milk, then add to dry ingredients, and stir until just combined. Fold in apples.

2. Drop tablespoons of batter into hot oil. Working in batches, fry 2–3 minutes, until evenly browned. Drain on paper towels and roll warm fritters in powdered sugar.

Old-Fashioned Doughnuts

The tangy cake and crisp crust of the old-fashioned doughnut, plain or glazed, makes it an American favorite.

INGREDIENTS | YIELDS 10–15 DOUGHNUTS

2 tablespoons unsalted butter

2 cups sugar

2 eggs

2 teaspoons vanilla extract

3½ cups all-purpose flour

4 teaspoons baking powder

1 teaspoon baking soda

½ teaspoon kosher salt

1 cup sour cream

4-6 cups canola oil

1. Beat together butter and 1 cup sugar until smooth. Add eggs and vanilla. Sift together flour, baking powder, baking soda, and salt, and add to butter mixture alternately with sour cream. Chill dough for at least 3 hours, or overnight.

2. In a heavy, high-sided frying pan, heat canola oil to 350°F. Turn out dough onto a floured surface, knead briefly, and using a rolling pin, roll to ½" thick. Cut into doughnut shapes and fry in hot oil, 1–2 minutes on each side, until evenly browned. Drain on paper towels. While hot, dredge in remaining sugar.

Autumn Harvest Ring

*This loaf makes a beautiful presentation for a buffet or an
edible centerpiece for a celebration brunch table.*

INGREDIENTS | YIELDS 1 LARGE LOAF
(15–20 SLICES)

1½ cups plus 1 tablespoon water

½ cup honey

1¾ teaspoons active dry yeast
(1 package)

3 eggs

¼ cup canola oil

1 teaspoon kosher salt

4–5 cups bread flour

1 tablespoon ground cinnamon

1 teaspoon ground nutmeg

1 teaspoon ground ginger

¼ teaspoon ground cloves

½ cup dried cranberries

½ cup dried apricots, chopped

½ cup golden raisins

½ cup chopped toasted walnuts

1. In a large bowl, combine 1½ cups water, 2 tablespoons honey, and yeast. Stir to dissolve and let stand until foamy, about 10 minutes.

2. Add 2 eggs, oil, salt, and enough bread flour to create a firm dough. Turn onto a floured surface and knead 8–10 minutes. Add flour only to reduce stickiness. Return to bowl, dust the top lightly with flour, and cover with plastic wrap. Rise at room temperature until doubled in volume, about 2–3 hours. Punch dough down, fold in half, and rise again, until doubled, about 45 minutes.

3. Coat a baking sheet with pan spray. Turn risen dough onto a floured surface and with a rolling pin, roll into an 18" × 24" rectangle. Warm remaining honey and brush over entire surface. Mix together cinnamon, nutmeg, ginger, and cloves, and sprinkle over honey. Evenly distribute cranberries, apricots, raisins, and walnuts over the spices. Starting on a long edge, roll the dough up into a log. Join both ends of the log to make a circle, and place on baking sheet, seam-side down. Cover with plastic wrap, and rise again 30 minutes.

4. Preheat oven to 325°F. Combine remaining egg with a tablespoon of water and brush over the surface of the bread. Slice two-thirds of the way into the log every 2" all round the ring. Turn each slice into a slight angle, so the resulting ring looks like a flower. Bake until golden brown and firm, about 50–60 minutes. Cool completely before slicing.

Beignets

In France, a beignet is fruit that is dipped in batter and fried, what we would call a fritter. But in the United States, a beignet is a square doughnut, made popular in New Orleans, at the Café du Monde.

INGREDIENTS | YIELDS 10–12 BEIGNETS

¾ cup warm milk

2 tablespoons honey

1¾ teaspoons active dry yeast (1 package)

2 tablespoons melted butter

2–3 cups bread flour

1 teaspoon kosher salt

3–4 cups canola oil

¼ cup powdered sugar

Safety First

Keep deep-frying painless by remembering a few simple safety tips. First, keep pot handles turned toward the wall, to prevent accidental tipping. Second, drop items into the oil using an "away-from-you" motion, to prevent hot oil splashing on you. Finally, drain items on paper towels, but keep the paper towels well away from the flame.

1. Stir together milk, honey, and yeast. Rest 10 minutes until foamy. Add butter, 1 cup bread flour, and salt. Stir together to form a smooth paste. Add enough remaining flour to form a firm dough. Turn onto a floured surface and knead 8–10 minutes. Add flour only to reduce stickiness. Return to bowl, dust with flour, cover with a warm, moist towel, and rise until doubled in volume, about 1 hour.

2. In a heavy, high-sided frying pan, heat canola oil to 350°F. Turn dough onto a floured surface and with a rolling pin, roll to ¼" thick; then cut into 2" squares. Working in batches, fry 1–2 minutes on each side, until evenly browned. Drain on paper towels. Dust with powdered sugar before serving.

Brown Sugar Coffee Cake

This simple cake is as comforting as it gets. Served with a steaming cup of coffee or tea, it's a perfect start to the day.

INGREDIENTS | YIELDS 1 CAKE, YIELDING 10–12 SLICES

2¼ cups cake flour

1 cup brown sugar

1½ teaspoons baking soda

½ teaspoon baking powder

¼ teaspoon kosher salt

1 cup (2 sticks) unsalted butter (keep 1 stick cold)

1 egg

1 cup milk

¼ cup molasses

1 cup all-purpose flour

Streusel

Also known as crumb or crisp topping, streusel is a staple ingredient in every bake shop. A simple combination of flour, butter, and sugar, it can be easily jazzed up with the addition of spices, nuts, and cereals. Try cinnamon walnut oat streusel, or ginger almond puffed rice. Be creative!

1. Preheat oven to 375°F. Coat a 9" round cake pan (2" deep) with pan spray. Cut a circle of parchment to fit in the bottom, and then coat the top of the parchment with pan spray. In a large bowl sift together cake flour, ½ cup brown sugar, baking soda, baking powder, and salt. Melt ½ cup of butter, and in a separate bowl, mix it with the egg, milk, and molasses. Add butter mixture to flour mixture, stir to blend thoroughly, and pour into prepared pan.

2. In a large bowl, combine all-purpose flour with remaining brown sugar. Mix well, then cut in 1 stick cold butter using fingertips or a pastry blender, until chunks are pea-sized. The streusel is ready when it holds together when squeezed, but easily crumbles apart. Be careful not to over mix. Generously crumble streusel over the batter, then bake until risen and firm to the touch, about 30–40 minutes. Cool before removing from pan.

Chocolate Fig Bread

*Sweet and rich, dried black figs are perfectly enhanced by
deep, dark chocolate. The combination is sublime.*

INGREDIENTS | **YIELDS 2 LOAVES**

1½ cups milk

¼ cup brown sugar

1¾ teaspoons active dry yeast
(1 package)

½ cup cocoa powder

3 eggs

¼ cup butter

1 teaspoon kosher salt

1½ cups dried black mission figs,
chopped

1½ cups chocolate chips

4–5 cups bread flour

1. In a large bowl, combine milk, brown sugar, and yeast. Stir to dissolve and let stand until foamy, about 10 minutes.

2. Add cocoa powder, eggs, butter, salt, figs, chocolate chips, and enough bread flour to create a firm dough. Turn onto a floured surface and knead 8–10 minutes. Add flour only to reduce stickiness. Return to bowl, dust the top lightly with flour, and cover with plastic wrap. Rise at room temperature until doubled in volume, about 2–3 hours. Punch dough down, fold in half, and rise again, until doubled, about 45 minutes.

3. Line a baking sheet with parchment. Turn risen dough onto floured surface. Divide evenly and form into round loaves. Place on prepared pan seam-side down, dust generously with flour, and cover loosely with plastic wrap. Proof for 30 minutes. Preheat oven to 400°F.

4. Using a serrated knife, slash a decorative cut into the surface of the risen dough about ¼" deep. Bake until golden brown and firm, about 30–40 minutes. Cool completely on a rack before slicing.

Cinnamon Peach Coffee Cake

This breakfast bread is a bread only in the loosest sense of the word. But with fresh peaches and the tang of buttermilk, who cares what it's called!

INGREDIENTS | YIELDS 1 CAKE
(10–12 SLICES)

1½ cups (3 sticks) butter, 2 softened, 1 kept cold

1 cup sugar

2 eggs

2 teaspoons vanilla

3½ cups cake flour

3 teaspoons cinnamon

1 teaspoon baking powder

1 teaspoon salt

1 cup buttermilk

1½ cups fresh peaches, peeled and diced

1 cup all-purpose flour

½ cup brown sugar

½ cup sliced almonds

The Creaming Method

This method refers to beating butter and sugar together until creamy. This ensures there are no lumps, which allows the remaining ingredients to be mixed in smoothly and evenly. Most recipes that call for creaming also call for the dry and wet ingredients to be added alternately. This means the sifted dry and measured liquids are each divided into thirds, and added, one-third at a time, first dry, then wet. This guarantees easy, even mixing.

1. Preheat oven to 375°F. Coat a 9" round (2" deep) cake pan with pan spray. Cut a circle of parchment to fit in the bottom, then coat the top of the parchment with pan spray. In a large bowl beat 1 cup (2 sticks) butter with sugar until smooth and lump-free. Add eggs and vanilla, and mix thoroughly. Sift together cake flour, 2 teaspoons cinnamon, baking powder, and salt. Add to batter alternately with buttermilk. Pour into prepared pan, and top with peaches.

2. In a large bowl, combine all-purpose flour, brown sugar, almonds, and remaining teaspoon of cinnamon. Mix well, then cut in 1 stick cold butter, using fingertips or a pastry blender, until chunks are pea-sized. The streusel is ready when it holds together when squeezed, but easily crumbles apart. Be careful not to over mix. Generously crumble streusel over the peaches, then bake until risen and firm, about 30–40 minutes. Cool before removing from pan.

Espresso Bean Bread

*This unusual dark, rich bread is perfect with butter and a cup
of coffee. It also makes fantastic French toast.*

INGREDIENTS | **YIELDS 1 LOAF**

1 cup milk

1 cup espresso beans, finely ground

¼ cup granulated sugar

1¾ teaspoons active dry yeast
(1 package)

½ cup (1 stick) unsalted butter, softened

3 eggs

1 tablespoon instant espresso powder

1 teaspoon plus 1 pinch kosher salt

4–6 cups bread flour

2 tablespoons cornmeal

1 tablespoon water

2 tablespoons turbinado sugar

1. In a small saucepan, heat milk until just below the boil. Remove from heat, add ground coffee beans, stir, and steep 15 minutes. Strain through a fine mesh strainer or a coffee filter. Combine coffee milk with sugar and yeast. Stir to dissolve and let stand until foamy, about 10 minutes.

2. Add butter, 2 eggs, espresso powder, 1 teaspoon salt, and enough bread flour to make a soft dough. Turn onto a floured work surface and knead 8–10 minutes. Add flour only to reduce stickiness. Return to bowl, dust with flour, cover with plastic, and rise at room temperature until doubled in volume, about 2 hours.

3. Line a baking sheet with parchment, and sprinkle with cornmeal. Turn risen dough onto a lightly floured work surface, and shape into an oblong loaf. Place in prepared pan, seam-side down. Dust lightly with flour, cover loosely with plastic wrap, and proof until doubled in volume, about 1 hour.

4. Preheat oven to 350°F. Whisk together remaining egg with 1 tablespoon water and a pinch of salt. Brush gently onto the top of the risen loaf, then sprinkle with turbinado sugar. With a sharp knife, make a few decorative cuts. Bake until golden brown and hollow sounding, about 30–40 minutes. Cool completely on a rack before serving.

Honey Pecan Rolls

The rich, sticky topping of these nutty rolls makes them irresistible.

INGREDIENTS | **YIELDS 12–15 ROLLS**

1 cup brown sugar

½ cup honey

1 cup (2 sticks) butter, softened

¼ cup milk

2 tablespoons all-purpose flour

4 cups chopped pecans

1½ cups water

1¾ teaspoons active dry yeast (1 package)

3 eggs

¼ cup canola oil

1 teaspoon kosher salt

4–5 cups bread flour

1. Generously coat two muffin tins with pan spray. Mix brown sugar, 2 tablespoons honey, butter, milk, flour, and 2 cups pecans into a paste. Divide the paste evenly among the muffin cups.

2. In a large bowl, combine water, remaining honey, and yeast. Stir to dissolve and let stand until foamy, about 10 minutes.

3. Add eggs, oil, salt, and enough bread flour to create a firm dough. Turn onto a floured surface and knead 8–10 minutes. Add flour only to reduce stickiness. Return to bowl, dust the top lightly with flour, and cover with plastic wrap. Rise at room temperature until doubled in volume, about 2–3 hours. Punch dough down, fold in half, and rise again, until doubled, about 45 minutes.

4. Turn risen dough onto a floured surface and shape into a rope, about 3" thick. Slice 2" pieces off the rope, then roll each into a tight ball. Place balls into prepared muffin tins, dust with flour, cover loosely with plastic wrap, and proof for 30 minutes. Preheat oven to 375°F.

5. Bake buns for 15–20 minutes, until golden brown and bubbly. Remove from oven, cool 10 minutes, and while still warm, carefully invert onto a serving platter or tray. Cool before serving.

Lemon Poppy Seed Sugar Rolls

The zest of fresh lemons gives these rolls a bright yellow hue, and a blast of citrus flavor.

INGREDIENTS | YIELDS 12–15 ROLLS

1 cup granulated sugar

Grated zest of 5 lemons

1 cup water

½ cup milk

1¾ teaspoons active dry yeast (1 package)

2 eggs

1 teaspoon vanilla extract

¼ cup poppy seeds

½ cup (1 stick) unsalted butter

1 teaspoon kosher salt

4–5 cups bread flour

1 cup heavy cream

Maximizing Your Citrus

The citrus oil, found in the colorful zest, is the most potent part of any citrus fruit. Sugar attracts the oil naturally, so combining the two will yield the best results. Using a hand grater to remove the zest works best if it is done over a bowl of sugar. When finished, rub the grater with excess sugar to absorb every bit of flavor.

1. Combine sugar and grated lemon zest in a food processor and process 1–2 minutes until zest is pulverized and sugar is deep yellow and moist. Combine 2 tablespoons of this lemon sugar with water, milk, and yeast. Stir to dissolve and let stand until foamy, about 10 minutes.

2. Add eggs, vanilla, poppy seeds, butter, salt, and enough bread flour to create a firm dough. Turn out onto a floured surface and knead 8–10 minutes. Add flour only to reduce stickiness. Return to bowl, dust the top lightly with flour, and cover with plastic wrap. Rise at room temperature until doubled in volume, about 2 hours.

3. Line a baking sheet with parchment. Turn risen dough onto a floured surface and shape into a rope, about 3" thick. Slice 2" pieces off the rope, then roll each into a tight ball. Place balls into prepared pan, seam-side down. Dust with flour, cover loosely with plastic wrap, and proof for 15 minutes. Preheat oven to 375°F.

4. Brush risen rolls gently with cream, and top generously with remaining lemon sugar. Bake until golden brown, about 15–20 minutes. Cool completely.

Maple Nut Snails

Is there a flavor more suited to breakfast than maple? Just the word conjures up images of PJs and messy hair.

INGREDIENTS | YIELDS 12–15 ROLLS

1½ cups milk

2 tablespoons brown sugar

1¾ teaspoons active dry yeast (1 package)

3 eggs

¼ cup (½ stick) unsalted butter, softened

1 teaspoon kosher salt

1 cup whole wheat flour

3–4 cups bread flour

¼ cup maple syrup

1½ cups walnuts, chopped

1 cup maple sugar

1 teaspoon nutmeg

1 tablespoon water

1. In a large bowl, combine milk, brown sugar, and yeast. Stir to dissolve and let stand until foamy, about 10 minutes.

2. Add 2 eggs, butter, salt, whole wheat flour, and enough bread flour to create a firm dough. Turn onto a floured surface and knead 8–10 minutes. Add flour only to reduce stickiness. Return to bowl, dust the top lightly with flour, and cover with plastic wrap. Rise at room temperature until doubled in volume, about 2 hours.

3. Coat a baking sheet with parchment. Turn risen dough onto floured surface, and with a rolling pin, roll into an 18" × 24" rectangle. Brush maple syrup over the entire surface of dough. Combine walnuts, ¼ cup maple sugar, and nutmeg, and sprinkle across the dough on top of maple syrup. Starting on a long edge, roll the dough into a log. Cut the log into 3" wheels, and place on prepared pan, 2" apart. Dust with flour, cover with plastic wrap, and rise for 30 minutes.

4. Combine remaining egg with a tablespoon of water and brush gently over risen rolls. Sprinkle with remaining maple sugar, and bake until golden brown and firm, about 15–20 minutes. Cool completely.

Monkey Bread

Also called pull-apart bread or bubble loaf, this recipe is sure to please all your monkeys.

INGREDIENTS | YIELDS 1 LOAF

1 cup milk

½ cup sugar

1¾ teaspoons active dry yeast
(1 package)

1 cup (2 sticks) unsalted butter, softened

1 tablespoon kosher salt

3–5 cups bread flour

2 tablespoons cinnamon

1. In a large bowl, combine milk, ¼ cup sugar, and yeast. Stir to dissolve and let stand until foamy, about 10 minutes.

2. Add ½ cup butter, salt, and enough bread flour to create a firm dough. Turn onto a floured surface and knead 8–10 minutes. Add flour only to reduce stickiness. Return to bowl, dust the top lightly with flour, and cover with a damp cloth or plastic wrap. Rise at room temperature until doubled in volume, about 1½ hours.

3. Coat a 9" round (2" deep) cake pan with pan spray. Cut a circle of parchment to fit in the bottom, then coat the top of the parchment with pan spray. Melt remaining butter, and mix remaining sugar with cinnamon. Turn risen dough onto floured surface, and with a rolling pin, roll to ½" thickness. Using a 1" diameter biscuit cutter, cut dough into as many circles as possible. Re-roll scraps, and continue cutting until all dough is used.

4. Dip each circle of dough into melted butter, then into cinnamon sugar. Arrange dough in concentric circles, overlapping as needed, in prepared cake pan. Cover loosely and rise again for 30 minutes. Preheat oven to 375°F.

5. Bake until golden brown, about 35–45 minutes. Remove from oven and brush again with melted butter while still hot. Cool 15–20 minutes before inverting bread onto a serving platter. To serve, allow guests to pull pieces apart.

Orange Vanilla Buns

Candied orange peel gives this bread a festive flavor, reminiscent of fruitcake or figgy pudding.

INGREDIENTS | **YIELDS 12–15 BUNS**

1½ cups water

2 tablespoons granulated sugar

1¾ teaspoons active dry yeast (1 package)

3 eggs

1 vanilla bean, scraped

1 teaspoon vanilla extract

½ cup (1 stick) unsalted butter

1 teaspoon kosher salt

Grated zest of 2 oranges

1 cup candied orange peel, diced

4–5 cups bread flour

¼ cup orange juice

1 tablespoon lemon juice

4 cups powdered sugar, sifted

Homemade Candied Citrus

Peel the rind off citrus in large sections, then dice finely. Blanch in boiling water, drain, then cook in simple syrup (equal parts sugar and water) at a bare simmer, until tender and translucent, about 2 hours. Drain and dredge in granulated sugar. (Reserve syrup for a great lemonade!)

1. Combine water, sugar, and yeast. Stir to dissolve and let stand until foamy, about 10 minutes.

2. Add eggs, vanilla bean, vanilla extract, butter, salt, orange zest, orange peel, and enough bread flour to create a firm dough. Turn onto a floured surface and knead 8–10 minutes. Add flour only to reduce stickiness. Return to bowl, dust the top lightly with flour, and cover with plastic wrap. Rise at room temperature until doubled in volume, about 2 hours.

3. Generously coat two muffin tins with pan spray. Turn risen dough onto a floured surface and shape into a rope, about 3" thick. Slice 2" pieces off the rope, then roll each into a tight ball. Place balls into prepared muffin tins, dust with flour, cover loosely with plastic wrap, and proof for 30 minutes. Preheat oven to 375°F.

4. Bake buns for 15–20 minutes, until golden brown. Remove from oven, cool 10 minutes, and while still warm, carefully invert onto serving platter. In a large bowl, whisk orange juice and lemon juice with powdered sugar until smooth, then drizzle over cooled buns before serving.

Sopapilla

These luscious fried breads fill restaurant bread baskets throughout the Southwest. Omit the cinnamon sugar and honey to serve them as a savory accompaniment.

INGREDIENTS | YIELDS 10–12
SOPAPILLA

1 tablespoon unsalted butter

1 cup milk

½ teaspoon kosher salt

½ cup water

1¾ teaspoon active dry yeast (1 package)

½ cup whole wheat flour

2–3 cups bread flour

½ cup granulated sugar

2 tablespoons ground cinnamon

1 cup honey

Grated zest and juice of 1 orange

Grated zest and juice of 1 lemon

1 whole star anise

4-6 cups canola oil

1. Combine butter, milk, and salt in a small saucepan. Bring to a simmer over medium heat, then set aside to cool.

2. Meanwhile, whisk together water and yeast, and rest 10 minutes until foamy. Add cooled butter mixture and whole wheat flour. Stir together to form a smooth paste. Add enough bread flour to form a firm dough. Turn out onto a floured surface and knead 8–10 minutes. Add flour only to reduce stickiness. Return to bowl, dust with flour, cover with a warm, moist towel, and rise until doubled in volume, about 1 hour.

3. Mix together sugar and cinnamon and set aside. Combine honey, orange zest and juice, lemon zest and juice, and star anise. Warm gently over low heat. Keep warm.

4. In a heavy, high-sided frying pan, heat canola oil to 350°F. Turn dough onto floured surface and with a rolling pin, roll to ¼" thick. Cut into 2" squares. Fry in hot oil, 1–2 minutes on each side, until evenly browned. Drain on paper towels, dust with cinnamon sugar, and serve immediately with honey mixture for dipping.

Popovers

Jazz up this batter with a handful of cheese, a tablespoon of cinnamon sugar, or a few fresh blueberries. Or boost the nutritional value by using whole wheat flour instead.

INGREDIENTS	YIELDS ABOUT 12 POPOVERS

4 eggs, room temperature

2 cups milk, room temperature

1 teaspoon kosher salt

2 cups all-purpose flour

Pop Secrets

Temperature is the key to well-poufed popovers. If the ingredients or the oven are too cold, there will not be enough energy to push the batter up into a beautiful crown. Be sure the ingredients have lost the chill from the fridge, preheat the pan, and don't open the oven door during the first 30 minutes of baking. If you do, the temperature will drop dramatically, and the popovers will fall.

1. Preheat oven to 400°F. Place the popover pan into the oven to preheat as well.

2. Combine eggs, milk, salt, and flour in a blender, and blend until well combined.

3. Pour the batter into the heated pan, filling each cup to the rim. Bake at 400°F for 15 minutes, then turn the heat down to 375°F and bake for 20 minutes longer, until golden brown. Serve immediately.

CHAPTER 11

Pancakes

Old-Fashioned Buttermilk Pancakes

The sweet tang of buttermilk makes this morning favorite worth getting up for.

INGREDIENTS | YIELDS 10–12 PANCAKES

1½ cups all-purpose flour

2½ teaspoons baking powder

3 tablespoons granulated sugar

½ teaspoon kosher salt

3 eggs

2 tablespoons canola oil

1½ cups buttermilk

1 teaspoon vanilla extract

Griddle Smarts

Cast iron holds heat well, and even over a low flame it will continue to heat up during prolonged cooking. If the pancakes are browning too fast, turn down the heat, wait about 5 minutes, then resume cooking. If your griddle is well seasoned, food will not stick. If, however, it has been washed with soap or scrubbed hard, the seasoning will have been removed, and it will benefit from a light coat of oil as it heats up for the first batch.

1. In a large bowl, sift together flour, baking powder, sugar, and salt. Set aside.

2. In a second bowl whisk together eggs and oil until light and airy, then add buttermilk and vanilla. Pour wet mixture into dry and mix briefly, until just combined. Set aside to rest 10 minutes.

3. Preheat griddle over medium heat. Sprinkle a few drops of water on the griddle. when they sizzle and evaporate, it is ready. Ladle batter out in half-cup puddles, and cook until bubbles appear on surface, about 1 minute. Flip and cook 1 minute on the opposite side, until firm in the center. Keep pancakes warm in a low oven and repeat with remaining batter. Serve with syrup, butter, or jam.

Sourdough Pancakes

Sourdough lends a welcome savory element to your morning stack.

INGREDIENTS | YIELDS 10–12 PANCAKES

1¼ cups all-purpose flour
¼ cup whole wheat flour
2½ teaspoons baking powder
3 tablespoons granulated sugar
½ teaspoon kosher salt
3 eggs
2 tablespoons canola oil
1 cup milk
½ cup Sourdough Starter (page 69)

1. In a large bowl, sift together all-purpose flour, whole wheat flour, baking powder, sugar, and salt. Set aside.

2. In a second bowl whisk together eggs and oil until light and airy, then add milk and sourdough starter. Pour wet mixture into dry and mix briefly, just until combined. Set aside to rest 10 minutes.

3. Preheat griddle over medium heat. When hot, ladle batter out in half-cup puddles, and cook until bubbles appear on surface, about 1 minute. Flip and cook 1 minute on the opposite side, until firm in the center.

Buckwheat Pancakes

*Nutty buckwheat has been a breakfast grain since ancient times.
Top pancakes with sour cream for a rich brunch treat.*

INGREDIENTS | YIELDS 10–12 PANCAKES

1 cup all-purpose flour
½ cup buckwheat flour
2½ teaspoons baking powder
3 tablespoons brown sugar
½ teaspoon kosher salt
3 eggs
2 tablespoons canola oil
1½ cups buttermilk

1. In a large bowl, sift together all-purpose flour, buckwheat flour, baking powder, brown sugar, and salt. Set aside.

2. In a second bowl whisk together eggs and oil until light and airy, then add buttermilk. Pour wet mixture into dry and mix briefly, just until combined. Set aside to rest 10 minutes.

3. Preheat griddle over medium heat. When hot, ladle batter out in half-cup puddles, and cook until bubbles appear on surface, about 1 minute. Flip and cook 1 minute on the opposite side, until firm in the center.

Blueberry Orange Pancakes

Blueberries are a welcome element to any breakfast. If using frozen berries, be sure to add them frozen. If they defrost first, they will be too wet, make the batter too thin, and turn the pancakes purple.

INGREDIENTS | YIELDS 10–12 PANCAKES

3 tablespoons granulated sugar

Grated zest of 2 oranges

1½ cups all-purpose flour

2½ teaspoons baking powder

½ teaspoon kosher salt

3 eggs

2 tablespoons canola oil

1½ cups milk

1 cup fresh or frozen blueberries

Fruit Compote

Fresh fruit is a great topping, but a compote can be even better. Get creative by mixing 3–4 cups of chopped seasonal fruits with a touch of sweetener, and your choice of herbs or spices, citrus zest, and juice or liquor. Let it macerate at least 30 minutes. Any fruit will work, including dried fruits.

1. Combine sugar and zest in a small food processor or coffee grinder, and pulse until it becomes a moist orange sugar.

2. In a large bowl, sift together flour, baking powder, salt, and orange sugar. Set aside.

3. In a second bowl whisk together eggs and oil until light and airy, then add milk. Pour wet mixture into dry and mix briefly, just until combined. Set aside to rest 10 minutes.

4. Preheat griddle over medium heat. When hot, stir berries into batter. Ladle batter out in half-cup puddles, and cook until bubbles appear on surface, about 1 minute. Flip and cook 1 minute on the opposite side, until firm in the center. Keep pancakes warm in a low oven while repeating with remaining batter. Serve with syrup, butter, or jam.

Buckwheat Blinis

Blinis are a classic pancake used not for breakfast, but for savory snacks. Serve them classically, topped with sour cream and caviar or smoked salmon.

INGREDIENTS | YIELDS 18–20 CAKES

⅔ cup milk

½ cup (1 stick) unsalted butter

2 teaspoons granulated sugar

1¾ teaspoons active dry yeast (1 package)

2 eggs, separated

1 teaspoon kosher salt

¾–1 cup buckwheat flour

1. In a small saucepan, combine milk, butter, and sugar. Bring to a boil. Remove from heat and set aside to cool to lukewarm.

2. Stir yeast into the lukewarm milk. Set aside until foamy, about 10 minutes.

3. Beat the egg yolks until light and foamy, and stir into batter. Add salt and enough buckwheat flour to create a loose batter. Cover with a moist towel and set aside until doubled, about 1 hour.

4. Whip egg whites to stiff peaks, and fold into risen batter. Rest 10 minutes.

5. Preheat griddle over medium heat. When hot, ladle batter out in ¼ cup puddles, and cook until bubbles appear on surface, about 30 seconds. Flip and cook 1 minute on the opposite side, until firm in the center. Keep pancakes warm in a low oven while repeating with remaining batter.

Flannel Cakes

These thin, tender, old-fashioned griddlecakes are a staple at the Hollywood landmark restaurant Musso and Frank, where they have been on the breakfast menu since 1919.

INGREDIENTS | **YIELDS 10–12 CAKES**

½ cup all-purpose flour
½ cup cake flour
2 tablespoons granulated sugar
1 teaspoon kosher salt
6 eggs
2 cups milk
1 tablespoon canola oil

1. In a large bowl, sift together all-purpose flour, cake flour, sugar, and salt. Set aside.

2. In a second bowl whisk eggs until light and foamy. Add milk and oil; mix thoroughly. Pour wet mixture into dry and mix briefly, just until combined.

3. Preheat griddle over medium heat. When hot, ladle batter out in ⅓ cup puddles, and cook until bubbles appear on surface, about 1 minute. Flip and cook 1 minute on the opposite side, until firm in the center. Keep pancakes warm in a low oven, and repeat with remaining batter.

Johnnycakes

These traditional American cakes can be served with syrup, like pancakes, or served alongside a savory meal, like traditional corn bread.

INGREDIENTS | **YIELDS 10–12 CAKES**

1 cup milk
1 tablespoon unsalted butter
1 cup cornmeal (fine ground)
1 teaspoon granulated sugar
1 teaspoon kosher salt
1 egg
½ cup all-purpose flour

1. In a small saucepan bring milk and butter to a boil over medium heat. At the boil, remove from heat and stir in cornmeal. Set aside to soften for 15 minutes.

2. Add sugar, salt, and egg to the softened cornmeal. Mix thoroughly, then stir in all-purpose flour.

3. Preheat griddle over medium heat. When hot, ladle batter out small spoonfuls of batter and cook until golden brown, about 1 minute per side. Keep cakes warm in a low oven, and repeat with remaining batter.

Pumpkin Pecan Pancakes

Serve these autumnal cakes on a brisk fall morning. Top them with warm cranberry sauce.

INGREDIENTS | YIELDS 10–12 CAKES

1½ cups all-purpose flour

2½ teaspoons baking powder

3 tablespoons brown sugar

½ teaspoon kosher salt

½ teaspoon cinnamon

½ teaspoon ground nutmeg

¼ teaspoon ground cloves

3 eggs

2 tablespoons canola oil

1 cup milk

½ cup pumpkin purée

1 cup chopped pecans

1. In a large bowl, sift together flour, baking powder, brown sugar, salt, cinnamon, nutmeg, and clove. Set aside.

2. In a second bowl whisk together eggs and oil until light and airy, then add milk and pumpkin. Pour wet mixture into dry and mix briefly, just until combined. Set aside to rest 10 minutes.

3. Preheat griddle over medium heat. When hot, stir pecans into batter, then ladle batter out in half-cup puddles. Cook until bubbles appear on surface, about 1 minute. Flip and cook 1 minute on the opposite side, until firm in the center.

Coconut Pineapple Pancakes

Cane syrup, made from sugar cane, is a delicious tropical alternative to maple syrup.

INGREDIENTS | YIELDS 10–12 CAKES

1½ cups all-purpose flour

2½ teaspoons baking powder

½ teaspoon ground allspice

½ teaspoon kosher salt

3 eggs

¼ cup cane syrup (or 2 tablespoons molasses)

2 tablespoons canola oil

½ cup milk

1 13 ½-14-ounce can coconut milk

1 8-ounce can crushed pineapple, drained

1. In a large bowl, sift together flour, baking powder, allspice, and salt. Set aside.

2. In a second bowl whisk together eggs, cane syrup, and oil until light and airy, then add milk, coconut milk, and pineapple. Pour wet mixture into dry and mix briefly, just until combined. Set aside to rest 10 minutes.

3. Preheat griddle over medium heat. When hot, ladle batter out in half-cup puddles, and cook until bubbles appear on surface, about 1 minute. Flip and cook for 1 minute on the opposite side, until firm in the center. Serve with sliced fresh mango and papaya.

Whole Wheat Banana Walnut Pancakes

Top these pancakes with the usual maple syrup, or try with warmed Fruit Compote (page 180).

INGREDIENTS | YIELDS 10–12 CAKES

1½ cups whole wheat flour
2½ teaspoons baking powder
½ teaspoon cinnamon
½ teaspoon kosher salt
3 eggs
2 tablespoons honey
2 ripe bananas, mashed
2 tablespoons canola oil
1½ cups milk
½ teaspoon rum extract
1 cup chopped walnuts

1. In a large bowl, sift together whole wheat flour, baking powder, cinnamon, and salt. Set aside.

2. In a second bowl whisk together eggs and honey until light and airy. Add bananas, oil, milk, and rum extract. Pour wet mixture into dry and mix briefly, just until combined. Set aside to rest 10 minutes.

3. Preheat griddle over medium heat. When hot, stir walnuts into batter, then ladle batter out in half-cup puddles. Cook until bubbles appear on surface, about 1 minute. Flip and cook 1 minute on the opposite side, until firm in the center. Keep pancakes warm in a low oven while repeating with remaining batter.

Brown Butter Crepes

These crepes make a terrific wrapping for rich chocolate mousse, fresh fruit, or ice cream. But don't discount them for chicken or seafood!

INGREDIENTS | YIELDS 15–20 CREPES

6–7 tablespoons unsalted butter
Grated zest of 1 orange
½ vanilla bean, scraped
3 eggs
2 tablespoons all-purpose flour
1 tablespoon milk
1 tablespoon water
¼ teaspoon kosher salt

1. Melt 3 tablespoons butter in a sauté pan over medium heat. Let butter sizzle, and cook until solids sink to the bottom to toast and blacken. Remove from heat, add zest and vanilla, and set aside to cool.

2. In a blender, combine cooled brown butter, eggs, flour, milk, water, and salt, and mix to the consistency of thin cream. Refrigerate 1–3 hours.

3. Heat a nonstick pan over high heat. Add 1 tablespoon butter, let it sizzle, then add enough batter to thinly coat the bottom of the pan. Cook, swirling the pan, for 1 minute. Flip and cook the other side 1 minute, until golden brown. Turn onto a plate, and repeat with remaining batter.

Crepes Sucre

*This is the classic plain crepe. Serve it with sugar, as described,
or use it to create your own culinary masterpiece.*

INGREDIENTS | **YIELDS 15–20 CREPES**

3 eggs

2 tablespoons all-purpose flour

1 tablespoon milk

1 tablespoon water

¼ teaspoon kosher salt

3–4 tablespoons unsalted butter

¼–½ cup granulated sugar

2–3 tablespoons powdered sugar

Crepe Creations

Crepes can be filled with anything, sweet or savory, hot or cold. Or slice them into thin strips and use them like noodles in broth. Crepes can also be made ahead of time and stored in the fridge for a day or two, or in the freezer for a week. To serve, warm them briefly in a dry nonstick pan.

1. Combine eggs, flour, milk, water, and salt in a blender, and mix to the consistency of thin cream. Refrigerate 1–3 hours.

2. Heat a small nonstick sauté pan over high heat. Add a teaspoon of butter, let it sizzle, then add enough batter to thinly coat the bottom of the pan. Cook, swirling the pan, 1 minute. Flip and cook the other side 1 minute, until golden brown. Turn onto a plate, and repeat with remaining batter. Additional butter is not necessary with each crepe, unless they start to stick.

3. Heat a dry skillet or griddle over medium-high heat. Place a crepe in the pan, add a small pat of butter (about 1 teaspoon), then sprinkle the surface generously with granulated sugar. When butter and sugar begin to melt together, fold crepe in half, warm for a moment, then fold again into quarters. Serve immediately, dusted with powdered sugar.

Nutella Crepes

If you have ever been to Paris, you will recognize this flavor right away. If not, prepare yourself for the taste treat of a lifetime. (And call your travel agent.)

INGREDIENTS | YIELDS 15–20 CREPES

3 eggs

2 tablespoons all-purpose flour

2 tablespoons hazelnuts, ground finely

1 tablespoon milk

1 tablespoon water

¼ teaspoon kosher salt

3–4 tablespoons unsalted butter

1–2 cups Nutella

Nutella

Nutella, which is made from ground hazelnuts and milk chocolate, was first developed in Italy during World War II as a way to extend rationed chocolate. The combination of milk chocolate and hazelnuts can also be found in *giandujia*, a delicious alternative to milk chocolate. It is available for baking as well as in candy.

1. Combine eggs, flour, nuts, milk, water, and salt in a blender, and mix to the consistency of thin cream. Refrigerate 1–3 hours.

2. Heat a nonstick pan over high heat. Add 1 tablespoon butter, let it sizzle, then add enough batter to thinly coat the bottom of the pan. Cook, swirling the pan, 1 minute. Flip and cook the other side 1 minute, until golden brown. Turn out onto a plate, and repeat with remaining batter. Additional butter is not necessary with each crepe, unless they start to stick.

3. To serve, heat crepe in a dry skillet or griddle over medium-high heat. Spread a thin layer of Nutella evenly across crepe, heat for 30 seconds, then fold into quarters and serve.

Herb and Nut Crepes

Fill these savory gems with melted cheese, roasted chicken, sautéed seafood, or whatever your imagination creates.

INGREDIENTS | **YIELDS 15–20 CREPES**

3 eggs

2 tablespoons all-purpose flour

2 tablespoons sliced almonds, finely chopped

1 teaspoon fresh chervil, chopped

1 teaspoon fresh chives, chopped

1 teaspoon fresh Italian parsley, chopped

¼ teaspoon dried thyme

1 tablespoon milk

1 tablespoon water

¼ teaspoon kosher salt

¼ teaspoon black pepper

3–4 tablespoons unsalted butter

1. Combine eggs, flour, almonds, herbs, milk, water, salt, and pepper in a blender. Mix to the consistency of thin cream. Refrigerate 1–3 hours.

2. Heat a nonstick pan over high heat. Add 1 tablespoon butter, let it sizzle, then add enough batter to thinly coat the bottom of the pan. Cook, swirling the pan, 1 minute. Flip and cook the other side 1 minute, until golden brown. Turn onto a plate, and repeat with remaining batter. Additional butter is not necessary with each crepe, unless they start to stick.

Creamy Spinach Crepes

This is a great brunch dish because it can be assembled the night before and baked just prior to serving.

INGREDIENTS | **YIELDS 15–20 CREPES**

2 tablespoons olive oil

1 shallot, minced

1 10-ounce package frozen chopped spinach, thawed and well drained

¼ teaspoon kosher salt

½ teaspoon freshly grated nutmeg

4 ounces cream cheese

1 recipe Brown Butter Crepes (page 184)

1 cup sour cream

1. Heat oil in a large sauté pan over high heat. Add shallot and cook until tender, about 1 minute. Add well-drained spinach, salt, and nutmeg. Cook, stirring, to warm through. Add cream cheese and continue to stir until cheese is well blended into the mixture. Set aside to cool.

2. Preheat oven to 350°F. Roll 2 tablespoons of spinach filling into each crepe, and place side by side in a baking dish, seam-side down. Top with sour cream and bake until lightly browned and bubbly. Serve immediately.

Strawberry Lemon Crepes

It's hard to believe there is a way to improve strawberries and cream, but this dessert is a strong contender.

INGREDIENTS | SERVES 4–6

3 tablespoons granulated sugar

Grated zest of 2 lemons

3 eggs

2 tablespoons whole wheat flour

1 tablespoon milk

1 tablespoon water

¼ teaspoon kosher salt

2–4 tablespoons unsalted butter

2 cups fresh strawberries

2 tablespoons strawberry jam

1 tablespoon honey

2 cups Crème Chantilly (see below)

Crème Chantilly

In a large bowl, combine 2 cups heavy whipping cream, 3 tablespoons sugar, and 1 teaspoon vanilla. Whip with a whisk or an electric mixer, watching carefully as the cream begins to stiffen. Stop when it reaches medium peaks. (When the cream is lifted out of the bowl on the whisk, a medium peak will hold its shape as the whisk is turned upside-down.) Use immediately, or chill for up to 30 minutes.

1. Combine sugar and lemon zest on a cutting board and mince it finely, until it becomes bright yellow sugar. (You can also do this job in a food processor).

2. In a blender, combine the lemon sugar with eggs, flour, milk, water, and salt; mix to the consistency of thin cream. Refrigerate 1–3 hours.

3. Heat a nonstick pan over high heat. Add 1 tablespoon butter, let it sizzle, then add enough batter to thinly coat the bottom of the pan. Cook, swirling the pan, 1 minute. Flip and cook the other side 1 minute, until golden brown. Turn onto a plate, and repeat with remaining batter. Additional butter is not necessary with each crepe, unless they start to stick.

4. In a small bowl, combine berries, jam, and honey, and toss to combine. Set aside for 30 minutes.

5. To serve, fill each crepe with ¼ cup berry mixture, roll up to conceal the filling, and top with Crème Chantilly.

CHAPTER 12

Waffles and Griddle Breads

Belgian Waffles

Slice some fresh, ripe peaches or nectarines and serve them on the side.
Or try your favorite jam or marmalade as a topping.

INGREDIENTS | YIELDS 8–10 WAFFLES

1½ cups cake flour

2½ teaspoons baking powder

1 tablespoon granulated sugar

½ teaspoon kosher salt

3 eggs, separated

¼ cup (½ stick) unsalted butter, melted

1 cup milk

½ cup sour cream

1. Preheat waffle iron according to manufacturer's instructions. Triple-sift flour, baking powder, sugar, and salt into a large bowl. Set aside.

2. In a separate bowl combine the egg yolks, melted butter, milk, and sour cream. Whisk together thoroughly. In another bowl, whip the egg whites until they are stiff, and set aside.

3. Pour the egg yolk mixture into the flour and stir together briefly. Lumps are okay. Add the stiffened egg whites to this mixture and fold together gently until they are just combined. Cook batter in a waffle iron. Serve immediately with butter and syrup.

Malted Waffles

Malt is a classic, and distinctive, waffle ingredient, but it is usually only found in waffle mixes. You can buy malt powder at most large supermarkets.

INGREDIENTS | SERVES 4

1½ cups cake flour

2½ teaspoons baking powder

3 tablespoons malt powder

½ teaspoon kosher salt

3 eggs, separated

¼ cup (½ stick) unsalted butter, melted

1½ cups milk

1. Preheat waffle iron according to manufacturer's instructions. Triple-sift flour, baking powder, malt powder, and salt into a large bowl. Set aside.

2. In a separate bowl combine the egg yolks, melted butter, and milk. Whisk together thoroughly. In another bowl, whip the egg whites until they are stiff.

3. Pour the egg yolk mixture into the flour and stir together briefly. Lumps are okay. Add the stiffened egg whites to this mixture and fold together gently until they are just combined. Cook batter in a waffle iron. Serve immediately with butter and syrup.

Honey Whole Wheat Waffles

Sweet honey and nutty whole wheat are a naturally healthful pair. Serve these with a sprinkle of toasted nuts and dried fruits to complete the effect.

INGREDIENTS | YIELDS 8–12 WAFFLES

¾ cup cake flour
¾ cup whole wheat flour
2½ teaspoons baking powder
½ teaspoon kosher salt
3 eggs, separated
2 tablespoons honey
¼ cup (½ stick) unsalted butter, melted
1½ cups milk

1. Preheat waffle iron according to manufacturer's instructions. Triple-sift cake flour, whole wheat flour, baking powder, and salt into a large bowl. Set aside.

2. In a separate bowl combine the egg yolks, honey, melted butter, and milk. Whisk together thoroughly. In another bowl, whip the egg whites until they are stiff.

3. Pour the egg yolk mixture into the flour and stir together briefly. Lumps are okay. Add the stiffened egg whites to this mixture and fold together gently until they are just combined. Cook batter in a waffle iron. Serve immediately.

Apple Oat Waffles

Top these apple-licious waffles with apple butter and sour cream for an autumn waffle treat.

INGREDIENTS | YIELDS 8–12 WAFFLES

1¼ cups cake flour
2½ teaspoons baking powder
1 tablespoon brown sugar
1 teaspoon cinnamon
½ teaspoon kosher salt
½ cup rolled oats (not quick cooking)
2 Fuji apples, grated
3 eggs, separated
¼ cup (½ stick) unsalted butter, melted
1½ cups milk

1. Preheat waffle iron according to manufacturer's instructions. Triple-sift flour, baking powder, brown sugar, cinnamon, and salt into a large bowl. Stir in oats and apples and set aside.

2. In a separate bowl, combine the egg yolks, melted butter, and milk, and whisk together thoroughly. In another bowl, whip the egg whites until they are stiff.

3. Pour the egg yolk mixture into the flour and stir together briefly. Lumps are okay. Add the stiffened egg whites to this mixture and fold together gently until they are just combined. Cook batter in a waffle iron. Serve immediately.

Chocolate Waffles

Who says waffles are just for breakfast? Serve these for dessert
with a scoop of ice cream and a ladle of hot fudge.

INGREDIENTS | **YIELDS 8–12 WAFFLES**

1¼ cups cake flour

¼ cup cocoa powder

2½ teaspoons baking powder

1 tablespoon granulated sugar

½ teaspoon kosher salt

3 eggs, separated

¼ cup (½ stick) unsalted butter, melted

1½ cups milk

1 teaspoon vanilla extract

¾ cup grated bittersweet chocolate

Grated Chocolate

Large pieces of chocolate that come into direct contact with a hot waffle iron will scorch and burn. Small pieces are more easily coated and protected by the batter. Buy baking chocolate in small blocks, and grate with a standard cheese grater for this recipe. Do not substitute chocolate chips.

1. Preheat waffle iron according to manufacturer's instructions. Triple-sift flour, cocoa, baking powder, sugar, and salt into a large bowl. Set aside.

2. In a separate bowl combine the egg yolks, melted butter, milk, and vanilla. Whisk together thoroughly.

3. In another bowl, whip the egg whites until they are stiff.

4. Pour the egg yolk mixture into the flour and stir together briefly. Lumps are okay. Add the grated chocolate and stiffened egg whites and fold together gently until they are just combined. Cook batter in a waffle iron, following the manufacturer's instructions. Serve immediately.

Maple Pecan Waffles

Almond milk adds an extra layer of nuttiness to the flavor of these waffles. If you can't find almond milk in your market, you can make your own (see sidebar) or replace it with regular milk.

INGREDIENTS | YIELDS 8–10 WAFFLES

1½ cups cake flour

2½ teaspoons baking powder

3 tablespoons maple sugar

½ teaspoon kosher salt

½ cup ground pecans

3 eggs, separated

¼ cup (½ stick) unsalted butter, melted

¾ cup milk

¾ cup almond milk

Making Almond Milk

Almond milk is easy to make at home. Chop 1 cup of raw almonds and toast in a 400°F oven for 5 minutes or until fragrant. Add to 2 cups of simmering milk while almonds are still hot, then remove milk from the heat and set aside to steep for at least an hour, or overnight in the fridge. Strain through a cheesecloth before using. Be sure to squeeze out all the nutty goodness. Refrigerate leftovers.

1. Preheat waffle iron according to manufacturer's instructions. Triple-sift flour, baking powder, maple sugar, and salt into a large bowl. Add pecans and set aside.

2. In a separate bowl combine the egg yolks, melted butter, milk, and almond milk. Whisk together thoroughly.

3. In another bowl, whip the egg whites until they are stiff.

4. Pour the egg yolk mixture into the flour and stir together briefly. Lumps are okay. Add the stiffened egg whites to this mixture and fold together gently until they are just combined. Cook batter in a waffle iron, following the manufacturer's instructions. Serve immediately with butter and syrup.

Garlic Herb Waffles

If you're craving a savory waffle treat, try this delectable recipe, and top with a dollop of crème fraiche.

Triple-Sifting

We don't just sift to remove lumps. When the flour goes through the sifter it picks up more air. The more you sift, the lighter the recipe will turn out. This technique helps ensure a light batter.

1. Heat oil in a small saucepan over medium heat. Add garlic and scallions, and cook until tender and slightly golden, about 1 minute. Remove from heat, add thyme and chervil, and set aside to cool.

2. Preheat waffle iron according to manufacturer's instructions. Triple-sift flour, baking powder, sugar, and salt into a large bowl. Set aside.

3. Combine the egg yolks, garlic mixture, and buttermilk. Whisk together thoroughly.

4. In another bowl, whip the egg whites until they are stiff.

5. Pour the egg yolk mixture into the flour and stir together briefly. Lumps are okay. Add the stiffened egg whites to this mixture and fold together gently until they are just combined. Cook batter in a waffle iron, following the manufacturer's instructions. Serve immediately.

Brandied Gingerbread Waffles

Perfect on a cold winter morning, top these waffles as if they were traditional gingerbread, with a spoonful of lemon curd.

INGREDIENTS | YIELDS 8–10 WAFFLES

1 cup golden raisins
½ cup brandy
½ cup boiling water
1 cup cake flour
½ cup whole wheat flour
1 teaspoon ground ginger
½ teaspoon ground cinnamon
½ teaspoon ground nutmeg
¼ teaspoon ground cloves
2½ teaspoons baking powder
3 tablespoons brown sugar
½ teaspoon kosher salt
3 eggs, separated
¼ cup (½ stick) unsalted butter, melted
1½ cups milk
2 tablespoons molasses

1. Combine raisins, brandy, and boiling water. Set aside at room temperature to plump for at least 1 hour, or overnight.

2. Preheat waffle iron according to manufacturer's instructions. Triple-sift cake flour, whole wheat flour, ginger, cinnamon, nutmeg, cloves, baking powder, brown sugar, and salt into a large bowl. Set aside.

3. Combine the egg yolks, melted butter, milk, molasses, and plumped raisins. together thoroughly.

4. In another bowl, whip the egg whites until they are stiff.

5. Pour the egg yolk mixture into the flour and stir together briefly. Lumps are okay. Add the stiffened egg whites to this mixture and fold together gently until they are just combined. Cook batter in a waffle iron, following the manufacturer's instructions. Serve immediately.

Strawberry Buttermilk Waffles

A classic combination, these waffles are given an extra strawberry burst from the addition of jam to the batter. Try the same with raspberry, blackberry, or other fruity jams.

INGREDIENTS | YIELDS 8–10 WAFFLES

4 cups fresh strawberries, washed and halved

2 tablespoons honey

Grated zest of 1 lemon

1½ cups cake flour

2½ teaspoons baking powder

1 tablespoon granulated sugar

½ teaspoon kosher salt

3 eggs, separated

¼ cup (½ stick) unsalted butter, melted

1¼ cups buttermilk

½ cup strawberry jam

1 recipe Crème Chantilly (page 188)

1. Combine berries, honey, and zest in a bowl, and toss to coat. Set aside at room temperature while the waffles are made.

2. Preheat waffle iron according to manufacturer's instructions. Triple-sift flour, baking powder, sugar, and salt into a large bowl. Set aside.

3. In a separate bowl combine the egg yolks, melted butter, buttermilk, and jam. Whisk together thoroughly.

4. In another bowl, whip the egg whites until they are stiff.

5. Pour the egg yolk mixture into the flour and stir together briefly. Lumps are okay. Add the stiffened egg whites to this mixture and fold together gently until they are just combined. Cook batter in a waffle iron, following the manufacturer's instructions. Serve immediately with strawberries and Crème Chantilly.

English Muffins

There is nothing like homemade nooks and crannies. If your griddle is not seasoned, oil it lightly with some vegetable oil or pan spray.

INGREDIENTS | YIELDS 6–8 MUFFINS

1½ cups water

1 tablespoon granulated sugar

1¾ teaspoons active dry yeast (1 package)

1 tablespoon unsalted butter

1 teaspoon kosher salt

2 cups all-purpose flour

Muffin Rings

No more than circles of tin similar to biscuit cutters, muffin rings are available in specialty cookware stores. You can also fashion your own out of empty tuna cans. Remove the top and bottom of the cans, wash them thoroughly, and voila! Instant specialty cookware.

1. In a large bowl, combine water, sugar, and yeast. Mix well and set aside until foamy, about 10 minutes.

2. Add butter, salt, and flour. Beat together 8–10 minutes, until a smooth dough is formed. Cover with plastic wrap and set aside to rise in a warm spot until doubled in volume, about 1 hour.

3. Heat griddle over high heat. Test griddle by sprinkling on a little water. If it sizzles and evaporates, it's ready. Lower heat to medium-low. Place muffin rings on the griddle and fill them halfway with batter. Cover loosely with foil and cook until muffins are browned on the bottom, about 5 minutes. Using a spatula or tongs, flip over each muffin and ring. Cover and cook another 5 minutes. Cool completely before splitting and serving.

Sourdough English Muffins

Sourdough muffins make terrific toast, as well as the perfect base for dishes such as eggs Benedict.

INGREDIENTS | YIELDS 6–8 MUFFINS

¾ cup water

¾ cup Sourdough Starter (page 69)

1 tablespoon granulated sugar

1¾ teaspoons active dry yeast (1 package)

1 tablespoon unsalted butter

1 teaspoon kosher salt

2 cups all-purpose flour

1. In a large bowl, combine water, sourdough starter, sugar, and yeast. Mix well and set aside until foamy, about 10 minutes.

2. Add butter, salt, and flour. Beat together 8–10 minutes, until a smooth dough is formed. Cover with plastic wrap and set aside to rise in a warm spot until doubled in volume, about 1 hour.

3. Heat griddle over high heat. Test griddle by sprinkling on a little water. If it sizzles and evaporates, it's ready. Lower heat to medium-low. Place muffin rings on the griddle and fill them halfway with batter. Cover loosely with foil and cook until muffins are browned on the bottom, about 5 minutes. Using a spatula or tongs, flip over each muffin and ring. Cover and cook another 5 minutes. Cool completely before splitting and serving.

Grilled Leek English Muffins

The subtle onion flavor of leek, the gentle giant of the onion family, makes a superb griddle bread.

INGREDIENTS | YIELDS 6–8 MUFFINS

2 leeks, cleaned and halved lengthwise
2 tablespoons olive oil
1½ cups water
1 tablespoon granulated sugar
1¾ teaspoons active dry yeast
(1 package)
2 teaspoons dried thyme
1 tablespoon unsalted butter
1 teaspoon kosher salt
2 cups all-purpose flour

1. Brush leeks with oil and cook on a hot grill until tender and marked with grill lines. Or, leeks may be cooked under a broiler until browned. Cool, then cut into small dice, and set aside.

2. In a large bowl, combine water, sugar, and yeast. Mix well and set aside until foamy, about 10 minutes.

3. Add leeks, thyme, butter, salt, and flour. Beat together 8–10 minutes, until a smooth dough is formed. Cover with plastic wrap and set aside to rise in a warm spot until doubled in volume, about 1 hour.

4. Heat griddle over high heat. Test griddle by sprinkling on a little water. If it sizzles and evaporates, it's ready. Lower heat to medium-low. Place muffin rings on the griddle and fill them halfway with batter. Cover loosely with foil and cook until muffins are browned on the bottom, about 5 minutes. Using a spatula or tongs, flip over each muffin and ring. Cover and cook another 5 minutes. Cool completely before serving.

Crumpets

*A necessity on your English tea menu, crumpets are delectable smeared
with clotted cream, lemon curd, Nutella, jam, or marmalade.*

INGREDIENTS | **YIELDS 10–12 CRUMPETS**

1½ cups milk

1¾ teaspoons active dry yeast (1 package)

1 egg

2 tablespoons unsalted butter

½ teaspoon kosher salt

1 cup all-purpose flour

Crumpets

A crumpet is similar to an English muffin, but has a more savory flavor, and is never split. It is thought that the English muffin is America's attempt to replicate the crumpet, a staple tea offering in Britain.

1. In a large bowl, combine milk and yeast. Set aside until foamy, about 10 minutes. Mix in egg, 1 tablespoon butter, salt, and flour. Beat together 5 minutes, until a smooth dough is formed. Cover with plastic wrap and rise in a warm spot until doubled in volume, about 1½ hours.

2. Heat griddle over high heat. Test griddle by sprinkling on a little water. If it sizzles and evaporates, it's ready. Lower heat to medium-low. Melt 1 tablespoon of remaining butter on the griddle. Place muffin rings on the griddle and fill them halfway with batter. Cover loosely with foil and cook until crumpets are browned on the bottom, about 5 minutes. Using a spatula or tongs, flip over each crumpet and ring. Cover and cook another 5 minutes. Serve warm.

Lemon Verbena Crumpets

Smear these lemony crumpets with lemon curd and raspberry jam for the perfect pick-me-up.

INGREDIENTS | **YIELDS 10–12 CRUMPETS**

1½ cups warm milk

1 teaspoon granulated sugar

1¾ teaspoons active dry yeast (1 package)

1 egg

¼ teaspoon lemon verbena oil or lemon extract

2 tablespoons unsalted butter

½ teaspoon kosher salt

1 cup all-purpose flour

2 tablespoons dried lemon verbena, crushed

Lemon Verbena

Native to South and Central America, lemon verbena was brought to Europe by Spanish explorers. The leaves are sticky with oil that produces a sweet, lemony scent, much loved in soaps, perfumes, jams, and jellies. It is available in dried form and as an essential oil, and occasionally shows up fresh at farmers' markets. Search for it online, or use lemon thyme or the zest of 2–3 lemons as an acceptable substitute.

1. In a large bowl, combine milk, sugar, and yeast. Set aside until foamy, about 10 minutes. Mix in egg, lemon verbena oil, 1 tablespoon butter, salt, flour, and dried verbena. Beat together 5 minutes, until a smooth dough is formed. Cover with plastic wrap and rise in a warm spot until doubled in volume, about 1½ hours.

2. Heat griddle over high heat. Test griddle by sprinkling on a little water. If it sizzles and evaporates, it's ready. Lower heat to medium-low. Melt 1 tablespoon of remaining butter on the griddle. Place muffin rings on the griddle and fill them halfway with batter. Cover loosely with foil and cook until crumpets are browned on the bottom, about 5 minutes. Using a spatula or tongs, flip over each crumpet and ring. Cover and cook another 5 minutes. Serve warm.

Caramelized Banana Crumpets

Bananas add a touch of the tropics to your high tea or breakfast buffet. Eat these as-is, or try spreading them with peanut butter or Nutella.

INGREDIENTS | **YIELDS 12–16 CRUMPETS**

5–6 tablespoons unsalted butter

¼ cup brown sugar

2 ripe bananas, chopped

1 tablespoon rum

1¼ cups buttermilk

1¾ teaspoons active dry yeast (1 package)

1 egg

1 teaspoon kosher salt

¼ teaspoon ground nutmeg

1¾ cups all-purpose flour

1. Melt 3 tablespoons butter in a large sauté pan over high heat. Add brown sugar, and cook mixture until it sizzles. Add bananas in a single layer and cook, stirring, until golden and caramelized, about 2 minutes. Remove from heat, add rum, and set aside to cool.

2. In a large bowl, combine buttermilk and yeast. Set aside until foamy, about 10 minutes. Add cooled bananas, egg, salt, nutmeg, and flour. Beat together 5 minutes, until a smooth dough is formed. Cover with plastic wrap and set aside to rise in a warm spot until doubled in volume, about 1½ hours.

3. Heat griddle over high heat. Test the griddle by sprinkling on a little water. If it sizzles and evaporates, it's ready. Lower heat to medium. Melt 1 tablespoon of remaining butter on the griddle. Place muffin rings on the griddle and fill them halfway with batter. Cover loosely with foil and cook until crumpets are browned on the bottom, about 5 minutes. Using a spatula or tongs, flip over each crumpet and ring. Cover and cook another 5 minutes. Serve warm.

CHAPTER 13

Scones and Muffins

English Cream Scones

This simple classic makes the very best accompaniment to a pot of Earl Grey.

INGREDIENTS | **YIELDS 6–8 SCONES**

1 egg

1 teaspoon vanilla

⅔ cup heavy cream

1½ cups all-purpose flour

½ teaspoon kosher salt

2 teaspoons baking powder

½ cup granulated sugar

½ cup (1 stick) unsalted butter, diced and well chilled

1 egg yolk

½ cup cream

1 cup crystal sugar

Tea Traditions

English tea is a time-honored tradition, and Cream Tea is a special version in which scones play a major role. Clotted or Devonshire cream, made by heating and thickening unpasteurized milk, is served on top of scones, along with jam and lemon curd. In the States, clotted cream can be found in specialty food stores.

1. Preheat oven to 375°F. Line a baking sheet with parchment. In a small bowl, whisk together the egg, vanilla, and ⅓ cup of cream; set aside. In a large bowl, sift together flour, salt, baking powder, and granulated sugar.

2. Cut the chilled butter into the dry ingredients, breaking it into small, pea-sized pieces with your fingertips or a pastry blender. Be sure not to mix too much. Butter and flour should create a dry, crumbly mixture, not a paste.

3. Make a well in the center of the flour-butter mixture, and pour in the wet ingredients. Stir gently until just moistened. Turn the dough onto a lightly floured work surface and fold it 7 or 8 times, until it holds together. (This is not kneading.) Flatten the dough into a disk 1" thick. Cut the disk into 6–8 wedges and place them on the prepared pan, evenly spaced.

4. Whisk together the yolk and remaining cream and brush generously on the top of each scone. Sprinkle with crystal sugar. Rest 10 minutes before baking until golden brown, about 15 minutes.

Apple Crumb Scones

Take full advantage of the fall apple crop with this scrumptious recipe.

INGREDIENTS | **YIELDS 6–8 SCONES**

For Scones:
2 tablespoons unsalted butter
¾ cup brown sugar
2 Fuji apples, peeled, cored, and diced
½ teaspoon ground cinnamon
½ teaspoon ground nutmeg
1 egg
1 teaspoon vanilla
⅓ cup milk
1½ cups all-purpose flour
½ teaspoon kosher salt
2 teaspoons baking powder
½ cup (1 stick) unsalted butter, diced and well chilled

For Crumb Topping:
1 cup all-purpose flour
½ cup rolled oats (not quick cooking)
½ cup brown sugar
½ cup (1 stick) unsalted butter

1. Melt butter in a large sauté pan over medium heat. Add ¼ cup brown sugar and apples. Cook, stirring, until golden brown and tender, about 5 minutes. Remove from heat, add cinnamon and nutmeg, and set aside to cool.

2. Preheat oven to 375°F. Line a baking sheet with parchment. In a small bowl, whisk together the egg, vanilla, and milk; set aside. In a large bowl, sift together flour, salt, baking powder, and remaining brown sugar.

3. Cut the chilled butter into the dry ingredients, breaking it into small, pea-sized pieces with your fingertips or a pastry blender. Be sure not to mix too much. Butter and flour should create a dry, crumbly mixture, not a paste. Toss in apples.

4. Make a well in the center of the flour-butter mixture, and pour in the wet ingredients. Stir gently until just moistened. Turn the dough onto a lightly floured work surface and fold it 7 or 8 times, until it holds together. (This is not kneading.) Flatten the dough into a disk 1" thick. Cut the disk into 6–8 wedges and place them on the prepared pan, evenly spaced.

5. Rest scones 10 minutes while making the crumb topping. Combine flour, oats, and brown sugar in a large bowl, and cut in the butter until the mixture is moist, but crumbly. Place a generous amount of crumbs on top of each scone, and bake until golden brown, about 15 minutes.

Banana Chip Scones

Make banana chip scones for breakfast, or save them for an afterschool snack for your kids.

INGREDIENTS | **YIELDS 6–8 SCONES**

1 egg

⅓ cup sour cream

1 large ripe banana

1 cup cake flour

½ cup whole wheat flour

½ teaspoon ground cinnamon

½ teaspoon kosher salt

2 teaspoons baking powder

½ cup granulated sugar

1 cup chocolate chips

½ cup (1 stick) unsalted butter, diced and well chilled

½ cup cream

1 cup brown sugar

1. Preheat oven to 375°F. Line a baking sheet with parchment. In a small bowl, combine egg, sour cream, and banana. Stir and mash together with a fork and set aside. In a large bowl, sift together cake flour, whole wheat flour, cinnamon, salt, baking powder, and sugar. Toss in chocolate chips.

2. Cut the chilled butter into the dry ingredients, breaking it into small, pea-sized pieces with your fingertips or a pastry blender. Be sure not to mix too much. Butter and flour should create a dry, crumbly mixture, not a paste.

3. Make a well in the center of the flour-butter mixture, and pour in the wet ingredients. Stir gently until just moistened. Turn the dough onto a lightly floured work surface and fold it 7 or 8 times, until it holds together. (This is not kneading.) Flatten the dough into a disk 1" thick. Cut the disk into 6–8 wedges and place them on the prepared pan, evenly spaced.

4. Brush cream generously on the top of each scone and sprinkle with brown sugar. Rest 10 minutes before baking until golden brown, about 15 minutes.

Blueberry Drop Scones

*Blueberries add a burst of summer sunshine to this flaky recipe.
Try it with raspberries, blackberries, or cherries, too.*

INGREDIENTS | YIELDS 6–8 SCONES

1 egg

½ cup buttermilk

1 tablespoon orange juice concentrate

1½ cups all-purpose flour

½ teaspoon kosher salt

2 teaspoons baking powder

½ cup granulated sugar

Grated zest of 1 large orange

½ cup (1 stick) unsalted butter, diced
and well chilled

1 cup frozen blueberries

½ cup cream

1 cup granulated sugar

Frozen Berries

Folding berries into a batter or dough is a delicate procedure. The fruits are soft, and burst easily. But there is a simple trick to avoiding the blue-green batter that occurs when the mashed berry pigment reacts with the alkaline in the baking powder: use frozen berries. They hold their shape, and defrost quickly during baking. If all you have is fresh blueberries, freeze them hard before adding them.

1. Preheat oven to 375°F. Line a baking sheet with parchment. In a small bowl, whisk together the egg, buttermilk, and orange juice concentrate; set aside. In a separate large bowl, sift together flour, salt, baking powder, and sugar. Toss in zest.

2. Cut the chilled butter into the dry ingredients, breaking it into small, pea-sized pieces with your fingertips or a pastry blender. Be sure not to mix too much. Butter and flour should create a dry, crumbly mixture, not a paste. Toss in blueberries.

3. Make a well in the center of the flour-butter mixture, and pour in the wet ingredients. Stir gently until moistened. Scoop out ¼ cup portions of dough and drop on prepared pan, 2" apart. Brush with cream, sprinkle with sugar, and bake until golden brown, about 15 minutes.

Currant Scones

*This is perhaps the most famous scone of all, which must be
served with its equally famous costar, lemon curd.*

INGREDIENTS | YIELDS 6–8 SCONES

1 egg

⅓ cup milk

1½ cups cake flour

½ teaspoon kosher salt

2 teaspoons baking powder

½ cup granulated sugar

1 cup dried currants

½ cup (1 stick) unsalted butter, diced and well chilled

½ cup cream

1 cup granulated sugar

Lemon Curd

This stovetop custard is easy to make, and can be used for pie and tart filling as well as scone topping. In a large saucepan combine 6 whole eggs, 5 egg yolks, 1¾ cups sugar, zest of 4 lemons, 1⅓ cups lemon juice, and 1 cup (2 sticks) unsalted butter. Place over medium-high heat and cook, stirring constantly, until it becomes thick like sour cream. Strain immediately, cool, and chill before serving.

1. Preheat oven to 375°F. Line a baking sheet with parchment. In a small bowl, whisk together the egg and milk. Set aside. In a large bowl, sift together flour, salt, baking powder, and sugar. Toss in currants.

2. Cut the chilled butter into the dry ingredients, breaking it into small, pea-sized pieces with your fingertips or a pastry blender. Be sure not to mix too much. Butter and flour should create a dry, crumbly mixture, not a paste.

3. Make a well in the center of the flour-butter mixture, and pour in the wet ingredients. Stir gently until just moistened. Turn the dough onto a lightly floured work surface and fold it 7 or 8 times, until it holds together. (This is not kneading.) Flatten the dough into a disk 1" thick. Cut the disk into 6–8 wedges and place them on the prepared pan, evenly spaced.

4. Brush scones generously with cream, and sprinkle with sugar. Rest 10 minutes before baking until golden brown, about 15 minutes.

Maple Sugar Scones

Add nuts or chopped bananas to dress up these scones. Or simply smear them with rich, creamy butter.

INGREDIENTS | **YIELDS 6–8 SCONES**

1 egg

1 cup maple syrup

½ cup milk

1 cup cake flour

½ teaspoon ground cinnamon

½ teaspoon kosher salt

2 teaspoons baking powder

½ cup maple sugar

½ cup (1 stick) unsalted butter, diced and well chilled

1. Preheat oven to 375°F. Line a baking sheet with parchment. In a small bowl, whisk together the egg, 1 tablespoon maple syrup, and milk; set aside. In a large bowl, sift together flour, cinnamon, salt, baking powder, and maple sugar.

2. Cut the chilled butter into the dry ingredients, breaking it into small, pea-sized pieces with your fingertips or a pastry blender. Be sure not to mix too much. Butter and flour should create a dry, crumbly mixture, not a paste.

3. Make a well in the center of the flour-butter mixture, and pour in the wet ingredients. Stir gently until just moistened. Turn the dough onto a lightly floured work surface and fold it 7 or 8 times, until it holds together. (This is not kneading.) Flatten the dough into a disk 1" thick. Cut the disk into 6–8 wedges and place them on the prepared pan, evenly spaced.

4. Brush remaining maple syrup generously on the top of each scone, then rest 10 minutes before baking until golden brown, about 15 minutes.

Scottish Oat Scones

This recipe is an homage to the original scones, which were made from Scottish oats.

INGREDIENTS | **YIELDS 6–8 SCONES**

1 cup Scottish oats

1½ cups milk

1 egg

1 teaspoon vanilla extract

1 cup cake flour

½ cup oat flour

½ teaspoon ground cinnamon

½ teaspoon kosher salt

2 teaspoons baking powder

1½ cups brown sugar

½ cup (1 stick) unsalted butter, diced and well chilled

1 egg yolk

½ cup cream

Traditional Scones

The wedge shape used in these recipes harkens back to the days when baking was about sustenance, not appearance. Today's scones are often cut out of the dough like biscuits or formed into decorative shapes. This results in a bit of wasted dough, which never would have been tolerated in centuries past.

1. Combine oats and 1 cup milk. Refrigerate overnight to soften.

2. Preheat oven to 375°F. Line a baking sheet with parchment. In a small bowl, whisk together the egg, vanilla, and remaining milk; set aside. In a large bowl, sift together cake flour, oat flour, cinnamon, salt, baking powder, and ½ cup brown sugar.

3. Cut the chilled butter into the dry ingredients, breaking it into small, pea-sized pieces with your fingertips or a pastry blender. Be sure not to mix too much. Butter and flour should create a dry, crumbly mixture, not a paste.

4. Make a well in the center of the flour-butter mixture, and add the wet ingredients and the soaked oats. Stir gently until just moistened. Turn the dough onto a lightly floured work surface and fold it 7 or 8 times, until it holds together. (This is not kneading.) Flatten the dough into a disk 1" thick. Cut the disk into 6–8 wedges and place them on the prepared pan, evenly spaced.

5. Whisk together the yolk and cream and brush it generously on the top of each scone. Sprinkle the top with remaining brown sugar. Rest 10 minutes before baking until golden brown, about 15 minutes.

Sour Cream Scones

Sour cream and a small amount of honey combine for a moist and rich crumb. Not too sweet, these scones make the perfect accompaniment to your morning bacon and eggs.

INGREDIENTS | YIELDS 6–8 SCONES

1 egg

⅓ cup sour cream

1 tablespoon honey

1½ cups cake flour

½ teaspoon kosher salt

2 teaspoons baking powder

½ cup (1 stick) unsalted butter, diced and well chilled

½ cup buttermilk

1. Preheat oven to 375°F. Line a baking sheet with parchment. In a small bowl, whisk together the egg, sour cream, and honey; set aside. In a large bowl, sift together flour, salt, baking powder.

2. Cut the chilled butter into the dry ingredients, breaking it into small, pea-sized pieces with your fingertips or a pastry blender. Be sure not to mix too much. Butter and flour should create a dry, crumbly mixture, not a paste.

3. Make a well in the center of the flour-butter mixture, and pour in the wet ingredients. Stir gently until just moistened. Turn the dough onto a lightly floured work surface and fold it 7 or 8 times, until it holds together. (This is not kneading.) Flatten the dough into a disk 1" thick. Cut the disk into 6–8 wedges and place them on the prepared pan, evenly spaced.

4. Brush buttermilk generously on the top of each scone, then rest 10 minutes before baking golden brown, about 15 minutes.

Applesauce Muffins

Add your favorite nut or fruit to personalize this eye-opening recipe.

INGREDIENTS | **YIELDS 10–12 MUFFINS**

⅔ cup whole wheat flour

1½ cups all-purpose flour

½ teaspoon ground cinnamon

½ teaspoon ground nutmeg

1½ teaspoons baking powder

¼ teaspoon baking soda

¼ teaspoon kosher salt

1 cup brown sugar

3 eggs

2 cups applesauce

4 ounces (1 stick) unsalted butter, melted and cooled

1. Preheat oven to 375°F. Coat muffin pan with pan spray. Line with paper muffin cups. In a large bowl stir together whole wheat flour, all-purpose flour, cinnamon, nutmeg, baking powder, baking soda, and salt. Set aside.

2. In another bowl, mix well the brown sugar, eggs, applesauce, and butter. Add wet mixture to dry and stir together until just combined.

3. Fill muffin cups to the rim with batter. Bake until risen and golden brown, about 20 minutes. A pick inserted into the middle muffin should come out clean. Cool muffin pan for 15 minutes before removing muffins.

Cheesy Corn Muffins

Cheesy corn muffins are the perfect accompaniment to a steamy bowl of chili. Spice them up with a can of diced green chilies, or a minced fresh jalapeño, if you dare.

INGREDIENTS | **YIELDS 10–12 MUFFINS**

2 cups all-purpose flour

1 tablespoon baking powder

1 teaspoon kosher salt

2 cups cornmeal

1 cup (2 sticks) unsalted butter

2 tablespoons brown sugar

2 eggs

1½ cups grated Cheddar cheese

2 cups buttermilk

1. Preheat oven to 375°F. Coat muffin pan with pan spray. Line with paper muffin cups. Sift together flour, baking powder, and salt. Stir in cornmeal, and set aside.

2. Beat together butter and brown sugar until creamy. Add eggs one at a time, then stir in cheese. Add dry ingredients to butter mixture alternately with the buttermilk.

3. Fill muffin cups to the rim with batter. Bake until risen and golden brown, about 20 minutes. A pick inserted into the middle muffin should come out clean.

4. Cool pan for 15 minutes before removing muffins.

Bacon and Egg Muffins

Turn these into huevos rancheros *muffins with the addition of a handful of grated cheese and a diced jalapeño or two.*

INGREDIENTS | YIELDS 10–12 MUFFINS

4 slices bacon

2 cups all-purpose flour

1 teaspoon baking powder

½ teaspoon kosher salt

½ teaspoon black pepper

1 tablespoon brown sugar or maple syrup

1 cup milk

2 eggs

1. Preheat oven to 375°F. Cook bacon in a skillet over medium heat until crispy. Drain on paper towels, and reserve rendered fat.

2. Coat muffin pan with pan spray. Line with paper muffin cups. In a large bowl stir together all-purpose flour, baking powder, salt, and pepper; set aside.

3. In another bowl, mix well the brown sugar or syrup, milk, eggs, and reserved bacon drippings. Add wet mixture to dry and stir together until just combined. Crumble cooled bacon and fold into batter.

4. Fill muffin cups to the rim with muffin batter. Bake until risen and golden brown, about 20 minutes. A pick inserted into the middle muffin should come out clean. Cool muffin pan for 15 minutes before removing muffins.

Banana Nut Muffins

This is the classic American quick bread, presented here in a conveniently portable shape.

INGREDIENTS | **YIELDS 12–15 MUFFINS**

3½ cups cake flour
1 teaspoon baking powder
1 teaspoon salt
1 cup buttermilk
1 teaspoon vanilla extract
1 cup (2 sticks) unsalted butter
1 cup brown sugar
2 eggs
2 ripe bananas, chopped
1 cup walnuts, chopped
1 tablespoon cinnamon
½ cup granulated sugar

1. Preheat oven to 375°F. Coat muffin pan with pan spray. Line with paper muffin cups. Sift together cake flour, baking powder, and salt. Set aside. Combine buttermilk and vanilla; set aside.

2. Beat together butter and brown sugar until smooth and creamy. Add eggs one at a time. Add the sifted dry ingredients to the butter mixture alternately with the buttermilk. Fold in bananas and nuts.

3. Fill muffin cups to the rim with muffin batter. Combine cinnamon and sugar, and sprinkle generously on top of muffins. Bake until risen and golden brown, about 20 minutes. A pick inserted into the middle muffin should come out clean. Cool muffin pan for 15 minutes before removing muffins.

Bran Muffins

Sure, bran is healthy. But it can also be delicious, especially when you add sugar, butter, and spices!

INGREDIENTS | YIELDS 12–15 MUFFINS

2 eggs

3 tablespoons canola oil

⅓ cup honey

⅓ cup brown sugar

⅓ cup molasses

1 tablespoon vanilla extract

1½ cups buttermilk

½ cup whole wheat flour

½ cup all-purpose flour

1 cup wheat germ

2¾ cups wheat bran

⅔ cup oat bran

2 teaspoons baking powder

2 teaspoons baking soda

1 teaspoon ground ginger

1 teaspoon ground cinnamon

1 teaspoon ground nutmeg

1. Preheat oven to 375°F. Coat muffin pan with pan spray. Line with paper muffin cups. Combine eggs, oil, honey, brown sugar, molasses, vanilla, and buttermilk. Mix thoroughly. Set aside.

2. In a separate bowl, combine all remaining ingredients; stir to mix. Pour the wet mixture into the dry and stir together until just blended.

3. Fill muffin cups to the rim with muffin batter. Bake until risen and golden brown, about 20 minutes. A pick inserted into the middle muffin should come out clean. Cool muffin pan for 15 minutes before removing muffins.

Cinnamon Date Streusel Muffins

The rich, juicy date has been a sweet treat since ancient times.
It's updated here with the crispy crunch of streusel.

INGREDIENTS | **YIELDS 12–15 MUFFINS**

½ cup brown sugar

1 cup all-purpose flour

½ cup chopped almonds

1½ cups (3 sticks) unsalted butter

3½ cups cake flour

1 teaspoon baking powder

2 teaspoons ground cinnamon

1 teaspoon kosher salt

1 cup date sugar

2 eggs

½ cup pitted dates, chopped

1 cup milk

1. To make streusel, combine brown sugar, all-purpose flour, and almonds in a large bowl. Cut in 1 stick butter until the mixture resembles moist crumbs. Set aside in the refrigerator.

2. Preheat oven to 375°F. Coat muffin pan with pan spray. Line with paper muffin cups. Sift together cake flour, baking powder, cinnamon, and salt. Set aside.

3. Beat together remaining butter with date sugar until smooth and creamy. Add eggs one at a time. Add the sifted dry ingredients to the butter mixture alternately with the milk. Fold in dates.

4. Fill muffin cups to the rim with muffin batter. Top each generously with streusel. Bake at 375°F until risen and golden brown, about 20 minutes. A pick inserted into the middle muffin should come out clean. Cool muffin pan for 15 minutes before removing muffins.

Hearty Granola Muffins

Here's a breakfast treat that even the most finicky eater will enjoy.

INGREDIENTS | YIELDS 15–20 MUFFINS

2 cups all-purpose flour

2 teaspoons baking powder

1½ teaspoons baking soda

1 teaspoon kosher salt

2 teaspoons cinnamon

1 cup honey

1½ cups vegetable oil

4 eggs

3 cups granola cereal

1 cup chopped walnuts

1 cup brown sugar

1. Preheat oven to 375°F. Coat muffin pan with pan spray. Line with paper muffin cups. Sift together flour, baking powder, baking soda, salt, and cinnamon; set aside. In a large bowl, mix together honey, oil, eggs, granola, and walnuts. Slowly add the sifted ingredients, combine thoroughly, and fold in nuts.

2. Fill muffin cups to the rim with muffin batter and sprinkle brown sugar generously on top of each muffin. Bake until risen and golden brown, about 20 minutes. A pick inserted into the middle muffin should come out clean. Cool muffin pan for 15 minutes before removing muffins.

Mocha Chip Muffins

Here's a muffin that will satisfy you and wake you up in one step.

INGREDIENTS | YIELDS 10–12 MUFFINS

3¼ cups cake flour

¼ cup cocoa powder

1 teaspoon baking powder

1 teaspoon kosher salt

1 cup (2 sticks) unsalted butter

2 tablespoons instant espresso powder or instant coffee

1 cup granulated sugar

2 eggs

1 cup sour cream

1½ cups chocolate chips

1 cup turbinado sugar

1. Preheat oven to 375°F. Coat muffin pan with pan spray. Line with paper muffin cups. Sift together cake flour, cocoa powder, baking powder, and salt. Set aside.

2. Combine butter, espresso powder, and sugar; beat until creamy. Add eggs one at a time. Add the sifted dry ingredients to the butter mixture alternately with the sour cream. Fold in chocolate chips.

3. Fill muffin cups to the rim with muffin batter, and sprinkle the tops with turbinado sugar. Bake until risen and golden brown, about 20 minutes. A pick inserted into the middle muffin should come out clean. Cool muffin pan for 15 minutes before removing muffins.

Pumpkin Spice Muffins

This comforting muffin can be easily enhanced with the addition of dried fruits or nuts. Try adding up to 1½ cups of cranberries, dates, figs, walnuts, pecans, pumpkin seeds, or hazelnuts.

INGREDIENTS | **YIELDS 10–12 MUFFINS**

1 cup all-purpose flour

½ cup brown sugar

1 cup walnuts, chopped

1½ cups (3 sticks) unsalted butter

3½ cups cake flour

½ teaspoon ground cinnamon

½ teaspoon ground nutmeg

½ teaspoon ground ginger

¼ teaspoon ground cloves

1 teaspoon baking powder

1 teaspoon kosher salt

1 cup sour cream

1 tablespoon molasses

1 cup granulated sugar

2 eggs

Ground Spices

Once ground, spices immediately begin to lose their flavor. For the most pungent spice mix, buy spices whole and grind them yourself. Cinnamon and cloves are easily crushed in a mortar, or ground in a coffee grinder. Nutmeg graters, available in most cookware stores, allow you to add delicious fresh nutmeg to all your favorite dishes.

1. In a large bowl combine all-purpose flour, brown sugar, and walnuts. Cut in 4 ounces (1 stick) of butter until the mixture resembles moist crumbs. Set aside in the refrigerator.

2. Preheat oven to 375°F. Coat muffin pan with pan spray. Line with paper muffin cups. Sift together cake flour, cinnamon, nutmeg, ginger, cloves, baking powder, and salt. Set aside. Combine sour cream and molasses, and set aside.

3. Combine remaining butter and the sugar; beat until creamy. Add eggs one at a time. Add the sifted dry ingredients to the butter mixture alternately with the sour cream mixture.

4. Fill muffin cups to the rim with muffin batter. Top with streusel. Bake until risen and golden brown, about 20 minutes. A pick inserted into the middle muffin should come out clean. Cool muffin pan for 15 minutes before removing muffins.

CHAPTER 14

Biscuits

Baking Powder Biscuits

This basic biscuit is the perfect accompaniment to your chicken dinner.
Or, douse with gravy for a hearty breakfast.

INGREDIENTS | **YIELDS 12–15 BISCUITS**

2 cups cake flour

1 tablespoon baking powder

1 teaspoon granulated sugar

½ teaspoon plus 1 pinch kosher salt

6 tablespoons (¾ stick) unsalted butter, cold

1 cup cold milk

1 egg

1 tablespoon water

Resting

Double-acting baking powder works in two stages, once when it is moistened, and again when it is heated. To get the full benefit (and the fluffiest biscuits), allow the dough to rest for a short time before baking.

1. Line a baking sheet with parchment. In a large bowl, sift together cake flour, baking powder, sugar, and ½ teaspoon salt. Cut in butter until mixture resembles coarse meal.

2. Make a well in the center of the flour mixture, and pour in milk. Using a fork, blend the flour and milk until the dough just comes together.

3. Turn onto a floured surface and fold dough over onto itself 6–8 times. (Be careful not to knead or overwork.) Pat into 1" thickness. Cut into circles using a floured round cutter. Place biscuits 2" apart on prepared pan and set aside to rest 10–15 minutes. Preheat oven to 425°F.

4. Mix the egg with a pinch of salt and 1 tablespoon water. Brush lightly onto biscuits, then bake 15–20 minutes, until golden brown. Turn pan halfway through baking to promote even browning.

Big Daddy Biscuits

These biscuits rise high and flaky, like down-home puff pastry.

INGREDIENTS | YIELDS 15–20 BISCUITS

3 cups cake flour
4 teaspoons baking powder
1 tablespoon granulated sugar
½ teaspoon kosher salt
1 cup (2 sticks) unsalted butter, cold
1 egg
1 cup cold milk
1 cup heavy cream

Flakiness

The size of the butter bits is directly related to the flakiness of the biscuit. In the heat of the oven, the water inside the butter is turned into steam. The steam rises, and pushes up the dough around it. This creates pockets of air in the finished product. Those pockets are what we call flakiness. The bigger the butter bits, the flakier the biscuit.

1. Line a baking sheet with parchment. In a large bowl, sift together cake flour, baking powder, sugar, and salt. Cut in butter until it is broken down into pea-sized pieces.

2. Whisk together egg and milk. Make a well in the center of the flour mixture, and pour in wet ingredients. Using a fork, blend until the dough just comes together.

3. Turn onto a floured surface and fold dough over onto itself 6–8 times. (Be careful not to knead or overwork.) Pat into 1" thickness. Cut into circles using a floured round cutter. Place biscuits 2" apart on prepared pan and set aside to rest 10–15 minutes. Preheat oven to 425°F.

4. Brush cream generously onto biscuits, then bake 15–20 minutes, until golden brown. Turn pan halfway through baking to promote even browning.

Curry Spice Biscuits

*These exotic morsels make perfect appetizers when filled with
a spicy cucumber salad or your favorite chutney.*

INGREDIENTS | YIELDS 12–15 BISCUITS

2 cups cake flour

3 teaspoons baking powder

2 tablespoons curry powder

1 teaspoon granulated sugar

1 teaspoon kosher salt

5 tablespoons unsalted butter, cold

½ cup cold milk

1 cup heavy cream

1 teaspoon paprika

Curry

If you'd like to make your own curry powder, combine the following ingredients in a coffee grinder or mortar: ¼ cup each coriander seed, cumin seed, and brown mustard seed; 3 tablespoons each turmeric, fenugreek, and black peppercorns; 2 tablespoons each ground ginger and cardamom seeds; 1 tablespoon dried chilies; and 2 cinnamon sticks.

1. Line a baking sheet with parchment. In a large bowl, sift together cake flour, baking powder, curry powder, sugar, and salt. Cut in butter until it is broken down into pea-sized pieces.

2. Make a well in the center of the flour mixture, and pour in milk. Using a fork, blend the flour and milk until the dough just comes together.

3. Turn onto a floured surface and fold dough over onto itself 6–8 times. (Be careful not to knead or overwork.) Pat into 1" thickness. Cut into circles using a floured round cutter. Place biscuits 2" apart on prepared pan and set aside to rest 10–15 minutes. Preheat oven to 425°F.

4. Brush cream generously onto biscuits, sprinkle with paprika, then bake 15–20 minutes, until golden brown. Turn pan halfway through baking to promote even browning.

Drop Biscuits

These free-form biscuits are crispy on the outside, light on the inside, and are quick and easy to make.

INGREDIENTS | **YIELDS 8–10 BISCUITS**

1¾ cups cake flour
2 teaspoons baking powder
½ teaspoon kosher salt
6 tablespoons (¾ stick) unsalted butter, cold
1½ cups cold milk

1. Line a baking sheet with parchment. In a large bowl, sift together cake flour, baking powder, and salt. Cut in butter until it is broken down into pea-sized pieces.

2. Make a well in the center of the flour mixture, and pour in 1 cup milk. Using a fork, blend the flour and milk until the dough just comes together.

3. Drop biscuits by heaping spoonfuls (about ¼ cup) 2" apart on prepared pan. Set aside to rest 10–15 minutes. Preheat oven to 425°F.

4. Brush remaining milk generously onto biscuits, then bake 15–20 minutes, until golden brown. Turn pan halfway through baking to promote even browning.

Dumplings

Nothing will cure your ills faster than a raft of fluffy dumplings floating in pot of homemade chicken soup.

INGREDIENTS | **YIELDS 8–10 DUMPLINGS**

1 cup all-purpose flour
2 teaspoons baking powder
½ teaspoon kosher salt
1 egg
⅔ cup milk
1 quart simmering broth, or a simmering pot of your favorite soup

1. In a large bowl, sift together all-purpose flour, baking powder, and salt. Mix together egg and milk.

2. Make a well in the center of the flour mixture, and pour in milk mixture. Blend together just until a dough is formed.

3. Drop dough by heaping spoonfuls (about ¼ cup) into simmering broth or soup. Cover and simmer 10–15 minutes. Serve immediately.

Gorgonzola Fig Biscuits

Sweet and salty, these biscuits have a distinctive Mediterranean flavor. They are especially nice served with roasted lamb, duck, or your favorite red meat.

INGREDIENTS | YIELDS 15–20 BISCUITS

3 cups cake flour

4 teaspoons baking powder

1 teaspoon granulated sugar

½ teaspoon kosher salt

½ teaspoon crushed black pepper

1 cup (2 sticks) unsalted butter, cold

4 ounces Gorgonzola

1 cup dried black mission figs, chopped

1 egg

1 cup cold milk

1 cup heavy cream

Pepper

Pepper is always a bit spicy, but when it's freshly ground, the amount of heat it adds to a recipe is more substantial. In this recipe, the heat helps to balance the sweet fruit and rich cheese.

1. Line a baking sheet with parchment. In a large bowl, sift together cake flour, baking powder, sugar, salt, and pepper. Cut in butter and Gorgonzola until they are broken down into pea-sized pieces. Toss in figs.

2. Whisk together egg and milk. Make a well in the center of the flour mixture, and pour in wet ingredients. Using a fork, blend until the dough just comes together.

3. Turn onto a floured surface and fold dough over onto itself 6–8 times. (Be careful not to knead or overwork.) Pat into 1" thickness. Cut into circles using a floured round cutter. Place biscuits 2" apart on prepared pan and set aside to rest 10–15 minutes. Preheat oven to 425°F.

4. Brush cream generously onto biscuits, then bake 15–20 minutes, until golden brown. Turn pan halfway through baking to promote even browning.

Herbs de Provence Biscuits

The sweet flavors of rosemary, lavender, and thyme will whisk you to the south of France.

INGREDIENTS | YIELDS 8–10 BISCUITS

2 cups cake flour

1 tablespoon herbes de Provence

1 tablespoon baking powder

1 teaspoon granulated sugar

1 teaspoon plus 1 pinch kosher salt

6 tablespoons (¾ stick) unsalted butter, cold

1 cup cold milk

1 egg

1 tablespoon water

1. Line a baking sheet with parchment. In a large bowl, sift together cake flour, herbs, baking powder, sugar, and 1 teaspoon salt. Cut in butter until mixture resembles coarse meal.

2. Make a well in the center of the flour mixture, and pour in milk. Using a fork, blend the flour and milk until the dough just comes together.

3. Turn onto a floured surface and fold dough over onto itself 6–8 times. (Be careful not to knead or overwork.) Pat into 1" thickness. Cut into circles using a floured round cutter. Place biscuits 2" apart on prepared pan and set aside to rest 10–15 minutes. Preheat oven to 425°F.

4. Mix egg with a pinch of salt and 1 tablespoon water. Brush lightly onto biscuits, then bake 15–20 minutes, until golden brown. Turn pan halfway through baking to promote even browning.

Jalapeño Corn Biscuits

Serve these Southwestern biscuits with your next pot of chili. Make the corn bread jealous.

INGREDIENTS | **YIELDS 8–10 BISCUITS**

½ cup cornmeal

1 cup milk

1½ cups all-purpose flour

1 tablespoon baking powder

2 teaspoons granulated sugar

1 teaspoon plus 1 pinch kosher salt

1 cup (2 sticks) unsalted butter, cold

1 cup pepper jack cheese, grated

1 chopped jalapeño

1 egg

1 tablespoon water

Working with Chilies

The white membrane inside a chili contains the capsaicin, which is the compound that creates the sensation of heat on the tongue. This stuff can create some discomfort, especially on tender, sensitive skin. To be safe, wear gloves when chopping chilies, and keep your hands away from your eyes. If you'd like less heat, remove the membrane and the seeds that attach to it.

1. Stir together cornmeal and ¾ cup milk. Set aside in the refrigerator for 30 minutes to soften.

2. Line a baking sheet with parchment. In a large bowl, sift together all-purpose flour, baking powder, sugar, and 1 teaspoon salt. Cut in butter until mixture resembles coarse meal. Toss in cheese and jalapeño.

3. Make a well in the center of the flour mixture, and pour in cornmeal mixture and remaining milk. Using a fork, blend until the dough just comes together.

4. Turn onto a floured surface and fold dough over onto itself 6–8 times. (Be careful not to knead or overwork.) Pat into 1" thickness. Cut into circles using a floured round cutter. Place biscuits 2" apart on prepared pan and set aside to rest 10–15 minutes. Preheat oven to 425°F.

5. Mix egg with a pinch of salt and 1 tablespoon water. Brush lightly onto biscuits, then bake 15–20 minutes, until golden brown.

Overnight Biscuits

This recipe combines the best of flaky biscuits with the goodness of yeast breads.

INGREDIENTS | YIELDS 10–12 BISCUITS

1¼ cups buttermilk

1¾ teaspoons active dry yeast
(1 package)

2½ cups all-purpose flour

2 teaspoons baking powder

2 teaspoons granulated sugar

1 teaspoon kosher salt

½ cup (1 stick) unsalted butter, cold

1. In a small bowl, stir together buttermilk and yeast. Set aside until foamy, about 10 minutes.

2. Line a baking sheet with parchment. In a large bowl, sift together all-purpose flour, baking powder, sugar, and salt. Cut in butter until mixture resembles coarse meal.

3. Make a well in the center of the flour mixture, and pour in buttermilk-yeast mixture. Using a fork, blend until the dough just comes together. Turn onto a floured surface and fold dough over onto itself 6–8 times. (Be careful not to knead or overwork.) Place in a large bowl, cover tightly, and refrigerate overnight (no longer than 48 hours).

4. Turn risen dough onto a floured surface. Using a rolling pin, roll to 1" thick. Cut out circles of dough using a floured round cutter. Place biscuits 2" apart on prepared pan and set aside to rest 10–15 minutes. Preheat oven to 425°F.

5. Dust the biscuits lightly with flour, then bake 15–20 minutes, until golden brown.

Parmesan and Chive Biscuits

These crispy, savory nuggets make a nice accompaniment to a fresh green salad, or make mini versions and serve them as an hors d'oeuvre at your next cocktail party.

INGREDIENTS | **YIELDS 10–12 BISCUITS**

1¾ cups all-purpose flour

¼ cup semolina flour

2 teaspoons baking powder

1 teaspoon baking soda

½ teaspoon kosher salt

¼ cup (½ stick) unsalted butter, cold

1½ cups grated Parmesan

¼ cup chopped fresh chives

¼ cup buttermilk

⅓ cup olive oil

Parmesan Cheese

This hard, salty, aged, granular cheese is made all over the world. But the good stuff comes from the regions of Mantua, Bologna, Modena, and Parma, in Italy. Buy a hunk and grate it as needed. It will last for weeks if wrapped properly and kept cool and dry.

1. Line a baking sheet with parchment. In a large bowl, sift together all-purpose flour, semolina flour, baking powder, baking soda, and salt. Cut in butter until mixture resembles coarse meal, then add Parmesan and chives.

2. Make a well in the center of the flour mixture, and pour in buttermilk and olive oil. Using a fork, blend until the dough just comes together.

3. Drop heaping spoonfuls of dough (about ¼ cup) onto prepared pan, 2" apart. Set aside to rest 10 minutes. Preheat oven to 425°F.

4. Bake 15–20 minutes, until golden brown. Turn pan halfway through baking to promote even browning.

Bacon and Cheddar Biscuits

Serve these savory biscuits instead of toast alongside your next omelet.

INGREDIENTS | YIELDS 8–10 BISCUITS

2 cups cake flour

1 tablespoon baking powder

1 teaspoon granulated sugar

1 teaspoon plus 1 pinch kosher salt

6 tablespoons (¾ stick) unsalted butter, cold

3 strips crisp, cooked bacon, crumbled

1 cup Cheddar cheese, grated

1 cup cold milk

1 egg

1 tablespoon water

1. Line a baking sheet with parchment. In a large bowl, sift together cake flour, baking powder, sugar, and 1 teaspoon salt. Cut in butter until mixture resembles coarse meal, then add bacon and cheese.

2. Make a well in the center of the flour mixture, and pour in milk. Using a fork, blend the flour and milk until the dough just comes together.

3. Turn onto a floured surface and fold dough over onto itself 6–8 times. (Be careful not to knead or overwork.) Pat into 1" thickness. Cut into circles using a floured round cutter. Place biscuits 2" apart on prepared pan and set aside to rest 10–15 minutes. Preheat oven to 425°F.

4. Mix egg with a pinch of salt and 1 tablespoon water. Brush lightly onto biscuits, then bake 15–20 minutes, until golden brown. Turn pan halfway through baking to promote even browning.

Buttermilk Biscuits

Buttermilk adds a distinct flavor, but it also mixes with the baking soda for an extra puff of gas in the oven, creating a light and airy texture.

INGREDIENTS | YIELDS 12–15 BISCUITS

2 cups all-purpose flour

4 teaspoons baking powder

¼ teaspoon baking soda

¾ teaspoon plus 1 pinch kosher salt

¼ cup (½ stick) unsalted butter

1 cup cold buttermilk

1 egg

1 tablespoon water

1. Line a baking sheet with parchment. In a large bowl, sift together flour, baking powder, baking soda, and ¾ teaspoon salt. Cut in butter until it is broken down into pea-sized pieces.

2. Make a well in the center of the flour mixture, and pour in buttermilk. Using a fork, blend the flour and buttermilk until the dough just comes together.

3. Turn onto a floured surface and fold dough over onto itself 6–8 times. (Be careful not to knead or overwork.) Pat into 1" thickness. Cut into circles using a floured round cutter. Place biscuits 2" apart on prepared pan and set aside to rest 10–15 minutes. Preheat oven to 425°F.

4. Mix egg with a pinch of salt and 1 tablespoon water. Brush lightly onto biscuits, then bake 15–20 minutes, until golden brown. Turn pan halfway through baking to promote even browning.

Sesame Scallion Biscuits

Biscuits are not a very Asian recipe, but they lend themselves nicely to these traditional Asian flavors. Try serving them alongside your best teriyaki chicken.

INGREDIENTS | YIELDS 10–12 BISCUITS

2 cups cake flour

1 teaspoon ground ginger

1 tablespoon baking powder

6 tablespoons (¾ stick) unsalted butter, cold

4 scallions, finely chopped

¾ cup milk

2 tablespoons soy sauce

½ teaspoon sesame oil

1 egg

1 pinch salt

1 tablespoon water

¼ cup raw sesame seeds

1. Line a baking sheet with parchment. In a large bowl, sift together cake flour, ginger, and baking powder. Cut in butter until mixture resembles coarse meal, then add scallions.

2. Mix together milk, soy sauce, and sesame oil. Make a well in the center of the flour mixture, pour in the wet ingredients, and mix with a fork until the dough just comes together.

3. Turn dough onto a floured surface and fold over onto itself 6–8 times. (Be careful not to knead or overwork.) Pat into 1" thickness. Cut into circles using a floured round cutter. Place biscuits 2" apart on prepared pan and set aside to rest 10–15 minutes. Preheat oven to 425°F.

4. Mix egg with a pinch of salt and 1 tablespoon water. Brush lightly onto biscuits; sprinkle generously with sesame seeds. Bake 15–20 minutes, until golden brown. Turn pan halfway through baking to promote even browning.

Sweet Potato Biscuits

This is the perfect addition to your holiday table.

INGREDIENTS | YIELDS 15–20 BISCUITS

3 cups cake flour

½ teaspoon ground allspice

4 teaspoons baking powder

3 tablespoons brown sugar

½ teaspoon kosher salt

½ cup (1 stick) unsalted butter, cold

1 cup mashed sweet potatoes

½ cup cold milk

1 cup heavy cream

Sweet Potatoes or Yams?

They're similar, but are actually two different plant species. Unfortunately, markets often don't make that distinction. (Canned "yams" are frequently sweet potatoes.) They can be used interchangeably in most recipes, and can be replaced outright by pumpkin or squash purée.

1. Line a baking sheet with parchment. In a large bowl, sift together flour, allspice, baking powder, brown sugar, and salt. Cut in butter until it resembles coarse meal.

2. Stir together sweet potatoes and milk, then add to dry ingredients. Use a fork and blend until the dough just comes together.

3. Turn onto a floured surface and fold dough over onto itself 6–8 times. (Be careful not to knead or overwork.) Pat into 1" thickness. Cut into circles using a floured round cutter. Place biscuits 2" apart on prepared pan and set aside to rest 10–15 minutes. Preheat oven to 425°F.

4. Brush cream generously onto biscuits, then bake 15–20 minutes, until golden brown. Turn pan halfway through baking to promote even browning.

Virginia Ham Biscuits

Nothing accompanies a plate of scrambled eggs better than these hammy biscuits. Add a handful of cheese if you're feeling really decadent.

INGREDIENTS | YIELDS 15–20 BISCUITS

3 cups cake flour

½ teaspoon ground nutmeg

4 teaspoons baking powder

1 tablespoon brown sugar

1 teaspoon kosher salt

1 cup (2 sticks) unsalted butter, cold

1½ cups diced ham

1 egg

1 cup cold milk

2 tablespoons Dijon mustard

1 cup heavy cream

1. Line a baking sheet with parchment. In a large bowl, sift together flour, nutmeg, baking powder, brown sugar, and salt. Cut in butter until it is broken down into pea-sized pieces, then add ham.

2. Whisk together egg and milk. Make a well in the center of the flour mixture, and pour in wet ingredients. Using a fork, blend until the dough just comes together.

3. Turn out onto a floured surface and fold dough over onto itself 6–8 times. (Be careful not to knead or overwork.) Pat into 1" thickness. Cut into circles using a floured round cutter. Place biscuits 2" apart on prepared pan and set aside to rest 10–15 minutes. Preheat oven to 425°F.

4. Mix together mustard and cream, and brush generously onto biscuits. Bake 15–20 minutes, until golden brown. Turn pan halfway through baking to promote even browning.

Pull-Apart Biscuits

This is a fun and easy preparation for any biscuit recipe. If you'd like something sweeter, used cinnamon sugar instead of the garlic and herbs.

INGREDIENTS | **YIELDS 12–15 BISCUITS**

Dough from 1 recipe Baking Powder Biscuits (page 220)
¼ cup (½ stick) unsalted butter, melted
1 teaspoon dried thyme
½teaspoon dried rosemary
½ teaspoon dried oregano
2 cloves garlic, minced

1. Coat an 8" cake pan with pan spray. Place a circle of parchment in the bottom of the pan, and coat with more spray. Prepare biscuit dough as directed. Mix together melted butter, dried herbs, and garlic; set aside.

2. Preheat oven to 375°F. Turn dough onto a floured surface, and flatten to 1" thick. Using a floured knife, cut into 1" cubes. Roll each in melted butter mixture and place in prepared pan, overlapping slightly, until the pan is filled.

3. Bake 15–20 minutes, until golden brown. The center of the loaf should be firm to the touch. Cool in pan 10 minutes before unmolding onto a serving platter.

CHAPTER 15

The Bread Machine

Wonder White Bread

This is the perfect comfort food, slathered with creamy peanut butter and Concord grape jam.

INGREDIENTS | **YIELDS 1 1½-POUND LOAF**

1¼ cups milk

1½ tablespoons unsalted butter

3 cups bread flour

4 teaspoons granulated sugar

¾ teaspoon kosher salt

1 teaspoon active dry yeast

Place ingredients into the bread machine according to the manufacturer's instructions. (Order of ingredients may vary.) Use the regular or basic white bread setting, and choose a medium crust. Check the dough during the first few minutes of kneading, and adjust as necessary with more water or flour, 1 tablespoon at a time.

Machine Capacity

Recipes in this chapter are based in the average bread machine capacity of 1½ pounds. For a 2-pound capacity machine, increase ingredients by ⅓.

Sesame Wheat Bread

Toasty sesame adds an extra layer of flavor to this heart-healthy bread.

INGREDIENTS | **YIELDS 1 1½-POUND LOAF**

1¼ cups milk

1 tablespoon honey

1 tablespoon tahini

1½ cups bread flour

1½ cups whole wheat flour

1 tablespoon toasted sesame seeds

¾ teaspoon kosher salt

1 teaspoon active dry yeast

Place ingredients into the bread machine according to the manufacturer's instructions. (Order of ingredients may vary.) Use the whole grain cycle if available, or the regular basic white setting, and a medium crust. Check the dough during the first few minutes of kneading, and adjust as necessary with more water or flour, 1 tablespoon at a time.

Bread Machine Pizza

Set your inner Italian free with a homemade pizza. This dough is as easy as the push of a button.

INGREDIENTS | YIELDS 1 1½-POUND LOAF (1 PIZZA CRUST)

1 cup water
4 teaspoons olive oil
3 cups bread flour
1 teaspoon honey
¾ teaspoon kosher salt
1 teaspoon active dry yeast
¼ cup cornmeal
2 cups tomato sauce
8 ounces buffalo mozzarella
Up to 1½ cups any additional toppings
3 tablespoons extra-virgin olive oil
½ cup fresh basil, chopped

Pizza Stones

A stone is not a necessity, but it makes the best pizza. A preheated cookie sheet will work, but a better substitute is an outdoor grill. Preheat the grill on high, brush it lightly with olive oil, and cook the dough on one side until golden and marked by the grill (about 5 minutes). Flip dough over, add sauce and toppings, then close the grill cover and cook until bubbly, about 2–5 more minutes.

1. Place water, olive oil, bread flour, honey, kosher salt, and yeast into the bread machine according to the manufacturer's instructions. (Order of ingredients may vary.) Set the machine on dough cycle. Check the dough during the first few minutes of kneading, and adjust as necessary with more water or flour, 1 tablespoon at a time.

2. When dough cycle is complete, transfer dough to a large bowl, cover, and set aside to rest 15 minutes.

3. Place a ceramic pizza stone or terracotta tiles on the oven rack. Preheat oven to 500°F. Sprinkle the peel surface generously with the cornmeal. Working on a floured surface, with floured fingers, pat and pull dough out into a large, flat disk as far as it will go. When dough starts to spring back, rest 5 minutes, then continue until it reaches the desired size. Place circle of dough on the cornmeal-lined peel.

4. Assemble the pizza on a peel or the back of a cookie sheet. Ladle up to 2 cups of tomato sauce onto dough, and spread it to the edges. Do not put too much sauce on, as it will make the crust soggy. Arrange slices of mozzarella and any toppings evenly across the surface of the pizza, all the way out to the edge. Carry peel to the oven, and slide pizza out onto hot tile. (Hold the peel 2"–3" directly above the stone, tilt downward, and pull the peel out, leaving the pizza behind.)

5. Cook 10 minutes, and then rotate pizza so it browns evenly. Cook another 5–10 minutes, until crust is golden brown on the bottom and top. Grab the pizza with tongs and slide out onto a platter. Top with a drizzle of olive oil and fresh chopped basil.

Bread Machine Calzone

A calzone may look like nothing more than a pizza turnover, but when made correctly, it's a work of art unto itself. Keep filling ingredients to a minimum to maximize their effect.

INGREDIENTS | YIELDS 1 1½-POUND LOAF (2 CALZONES)

1 recipe Bread Machine Pizza crust (page 237)

¼ cup cornmeal

2 cups tomato or pesto sauce

8 ounces buffalo mozzarella

Up to 1 cup additional ingredients, such as sautéed mushrooms, artichoke hearts, olives, or cooked sausage

3 tablespoons extra-virgin olive oil

Ingredient Order

Bread machine instructions are very specific about the order in which the ingredients are added. If you are planning on mixing and baking right away, it really isn't that important. If, however, you are using the delay setting to make your bread, the order becomes very important. Ingredients must remain inert until the machine turns itself on. This means liquid and yeast have to remain separate until the mixing and kneading begins. Be careful to keep yeast out of direct contact with salt and sugar.

1. Follow recipe for Bread Machine Pizza crust. When dough cycle is complete, transfer dough to a large bowl, cover, and set aside to rest for 15 minutes.

2. Place a ceramic pizza stone or terracotta tiles on the oven rack. Preheat oven to 450°F. Form the calzone on a peel or the back of a cookie sheet. Sprinkle the peel surface generously with cornmeal. Turn dough onto a floured surface, and divide into 2 equal portions. Working with floured fingers, pat and pull dough out into two large, flat disks as far as it will go. When dough starts to spring back, rest 5 minutes, then continue until it reaches the desired size.

3. On each disk spread half the dough with sauce, keeping it to within 1" of the edge. Top each with cheese and filling ingredients, then fold over plain half of dough to create a half-moon shape. Crimp edges together well, and transfer carefully to prepared peel. Brush the top with olive oil, then carry peel to the oven and slide calzone out onto hot tile. (Hold the peel 2"–3" directly above the stone, tilt downward, and pull the peel out, leaving the calzone behind.)

4. Cook 15 minutes, and then rotate calzone so it browns evenly. Cook another 5–10 minutes, until crust is golden brown on the bottom and top. Slide the calzone out of the oven with tongs and onto a platter. Cool slightly before serving.

Almond Oatmeal Bread

Almonds and oatmeal are a delicious match made in healthy heaven.

INGREDIENTS | **YIELDS 1 1½-POUND LOAF**

1 cup quick-cooking oats

1 cup milk

1 tablespoon unsalted butter

2½ cups bread flour

2 tablespoons honey

¾ teaspoon kosher salt

1 teaspoon active dry yeast·

½ cup sliced skin-on almonds, lightly toasted

Place ingredients into the bread machine according to the manufacturer's instructions. (Order of ingredients may vary.) Use the whole grain cycle if available. Check the dough during the first few minutes of kneading, and adjust as necessary with more water or flour, 1 tablespoon at a time.

Chili Cheese Bread

Green chilies add a touch of the West to this rich loaf. If you'd prefer, you can use fresh jalapeños, or even mild sweet bell peppers.

INGREDIENTS | **YIELDS 1 1½-POUND LOAF**

¾ cup shredded Cheddar cheese

¾ cup milk

2 tablespoons olive oil

1 4-ounce can diced green chilies

3 cups bread flour

1 teaspoon honey

¾ teaspoon kosher salt

1 teaspoon active dry yeast

Place ingredients into the bread machine according to the manufacturer's instructions. (Order of ingredients may vary.) Use the white bread cycle, and the light crust setting if available. Check the dough during the first few minutes of kneading, and adjust as necessary with more water or flour, 1 tablespoon at a time.

Cheese and Onion Bread

INGREDIENTS | YIELDS 1 1½-POUND LOAF

¾ cup shredded Swiss cheese

1¼ cups milk

1 egg

3¼ cups bread flour

1 tablespoon granulated sugar

¾ teaspoon kosher salt

1 teaspoon active dry yeast

½ cup finely chopped scallions

Place ingredients into the bread machine according to the manufacturer's instructions. (Order of ingredients may vary.) Use the white bread cycle, and the light crust setting if available. Check the dough during the first few minutes of kneading, and adjust as necessary with more water or flour, 1 tablespoon at a time.

Salt-Free Whole Wheat

This bread offers a burst of flavor from orange zest and dried herbs. Use it for your favorite heart-healthy sandwiches.

INGREDIENTS | YIELDS 1 1½-POUND LOAF

1 cup water

2 teaspoons olive oil

2 teaspoons honey

2 cups whole wheat flour

1 cup bread flour

½ teaspoon dried thyme

Grated zest of 1 orange

¾ teaspoon active dry yeast

Place ingredients into the bread machine according to the manufacturer's instructions. (Order of ingredients may vary.) Use the white bread cycle, and the light crust setting if available. Check the dough during the first few minutes of kneading, and adjust as necessary with more water or flour, 1 tablespoon at a time.

Rum Raisin Bread

This bread makes excellent toast smeared with soft cream cheese.
Or try it as French toast for a twist on a favorite brunch dish.

INGREDIENTS | YIELDS 1 1½-POUND LOAF

½ cup raisins
¼ cup dark rum
¾ cup buttermilk
1 egg
2 teaspoons unsalted butter
3 cups bread flour
3 tablespoons brown sugar
¾ teaspoon kosher salt
1 teaspoon active dry yeast

1. Combine raisins and rum in a small bowl, and set aside at room temperature to plump for 1 hour, or overnight if possible.

2. Place ingredients into the bread machine according to the manufacturer's instructions. (Order of ingredients may vary.) Use the white bread cycle and a light crust setting. Check the dough during the first few minutes of kneading, and adjust as necessary with more water or flour, 1 tablespoon at a time.

Cherry Nut Bread

Cherries and almonds are in the same botanical family, which is why they are the perfect pair.

INGREDIENTS | YIELDS 1 1½-POUND LOAF

½ cup dried cherries
½ cup apple juice
1 cup milk
2 tablespoons unsalted butter
3 cups bread flour
¼ cup honey
¾ teaspoon kosher salt
1 teaspoon active dry yeast
¾ cup sliced skin-on almonds

1. Combine cherries and apple juice in a small bowl, and set aside at room temperature to plump for 1 hour, or overnight if possible.

2. Place ingredients into the bread machine according to the manufacturer's instructions. (Order of ingredients may vary.) Use the white bread cycle and a light crust setting. Check the dough during the first few minutes of kneading, and adjust as necessary with more water or flour, 1 tablespoon at a time.

Pull-Apart Cardamom Buns

Cardamom is used heavily in Eastern curries, but in Scandinavia it is favored for baking.

INGREDIENTS | **YIELDS 1 1½-POUND PULL-APART LOAF**

1 cup milk

1 egg

2 tablespoons plus ½ cup (1 stick) unsalted butter

3 cups bread flour

¼ cup honey

¾ teaspoon kosher salt

¾ teaspoon ground cardamom

1 teaspoon active dry yeast

Adapting Your Favorite Recipes to the Bread Machine

Most recipes can be adapted to the bread machine. For a 1½ pound loaf, reduce or increase the total amount of flour to 3 cups, then reduce or increase the remaining ingredients according to the percentage the flour quantity was changed. For example, if the original recipe called for 4–5 cups of flour, choose the lower amount, 4, and decrease it by one-fourth to 3 cups. Next, decrease everything else by one-fourth. For items like eggs, use the closest whole egg quantity.

1. Place all ingredients, except ½ cup butter, into the bread machine according to the manufacturer's instructions. (Order of ingredients may vary.) Use the dough cycle. Check the dough during the first few minutes of kneading, and adjust as necessary with more water or flour, 1 tablespoon at a time.

2. Coat a round 9" (2" deep) cake pan with pan spray. Cut a circle of parchment to fit in the bottom, then coat the parchment with pan spray. Melt ½ cup butter. When the dough cycle is complete, turn dough onto floured surface, and with a rolling pin, roll to ½" thickness. Using a 1" diameter biscuit cutter, cut dough into as many circles as possible. Re-roll scraps, and continue cutting until all dough is used.

3. Dip each circle of dough into melted butter, and arrange in concentric circles, overlapping as needed, in prepared cake pan. Cover loosely and allow to rise 30 minutes. Preheat oven to 375˚F.

4. Bake until golden brown, about 35–45 minutes. Remove from oven and brush again with melted butter while still hot. Cool 15–20 minutes before inverting bread onto a serving platter. To serve, allow guests to pull pieces apart.

Blueberry Muffin Bread

Buttermilk and sour cream give this yeast bread the richness of a breakfast quick bread.

INGREDIENTS | YIELDS 1 1½-POUND LOAF

⅔ cup buttermilk

½ cup sour cream

1 egg

1 tablespoon unsalted butter

3 cups bread flour

3 tablespoons brown sugar

¾ teaspoon kosher salt

¼ teaspoon ground cinnamon

1 teaspoon active dry yeast

⅓ cup dried blueberries

Place all ingredients into the bread machine according to the manufacturer's instructions. (Order of ingredients may vary.) Use the white bread cycle, and the light crust setting if available. Check the dough during the first few minutes of kneading, and adjust as necessary with more water or flour, 1 tablespoon at a time.

Chocolate Marshmallow Bread

This is the perfect bread to use for a fun peanut butter sandwich, or perhaps a fluffernutter!

INGREDIENTS | YIELDS 1 1½-POUND LOAF

1 cup milk

3 tablespoons granulated sugar

1 teaspoon vanilla extract

1 egg

4 teaspoons unsalted butter

2¾ cups bread flour

¼ teaspoon cocoa powder

¾ teaspoon kosher salt

1 teaspoon active dry yeast

⅓ cup chocolate chips

⅓ cup mini marshmallows

Place all ingredients into the bread machine according to the manufacturer's instructions. (Order of ingredients may vary.) Use the white bread cycle, and the light crust setting if available. Check the dough during the first few minutes of kneading, and adjust as necessary with more water or flour, 1 tablespoon at a time.

Sour Lemon Bread

Bring the sunshine indoors with this bread, which is bursting with lemony goodness.

INGREDIENTS | YIELDS 1 1½-POUND LOAF

3 tablespoons granulated sugar

Grated zest of 2 lemons

½ cup buttermilk

⅓ cup sour cream

1 egg

3 tablespoons unsalted butter

3 cups bread flour

¾ teaspoon kosher salt

1 teaspoon active dry yeast

2 cups powdered sugar

1 cup lemon juice

1. Combine sugar and lemon zest in a small coffee grinder or food processor and blend until the sugar is bright yellow and moist.

2. Place all ingredients, except the powdered sugar and lemon juice, into the bread machine according to the manufacturer's instructions. (Order of ingredients may vary.) Use the white bread cycle, and the light crust setting if available. Check the dough during the first few minutes of kneading, and adjust as necessary with more water or flour, 1 tablespoon at a time.

3. Mix together powdered sugar and lemon juice, and when the dough is removed from the machine, brush it generously across the crust. Let it soak in, and repeat until all the glaze is absorbed.

CHAPTER 16

Quick Breads

Banana Walnut Bread

Banana Walnut is the king of all quick breads, and this version is particularly regal.

INGREDIENTS | YIELDS 1 LOAF

¼ cup (½ stick) unsalted butter

¾ cup granulated sugar

3 ripe bananas

1 egg

¼ cup sour cream

1 teaspoon vanilla extract

2 cups all-purpose flour

1½ teaspoons baking powder

½ teaspoon kosher salt

1 cup chopped walnuts

Quick Baking

Quick breads are so-named because they are leavened with baking powder and/or baking soda, which do not require the prolonged fermentation time that yeast does. However, quick breads are not necessarily quick to bake. Batters baked in a loaf pan require time to allow heat to penetrate to the center. Regardless of the indicated baking time, the skewer test is the only true measure of doneness. When inserted, it must come out clean.

1. Preheat oven to 350°F. Coat a 9" × 5" loaf pan with pan spray, and line the bottom and short sides with a strip of parchment.

2. In a large bowl, beat together butter and sugar until creamy and smooth. Add bananas and egg, and beat until creamy. Stir in sour cream and vanilla. Sift together all-purpose flour, baking powder, and salt; slowly stir into batter. Fold in walnuts.

3. Transfer batter to prepared pan, and smooth the top. Bake 30 minutes Reduce oven temperature to 325°F and bake 30 minutes longer, or until a pick inserted in the center comes out clean. Tent with foil if loaf browns too quickly.

4. Remove from oven and cool 10 minutes before removing from pan. Continue cooling on a rack.

Black Bean Corn Bread

With beans and corn, this spicy bread packs a punch of protein and flavor.

INGREDIENTS | YIELDS 1 LOAF

½ cup (1 stick) unsalted butter

¼ cup granulated sugar

1 egg

1 cup all-purpose flour

1 cup yellow cornmeal

1 tablespoon baking powder

1 teaspoon kosher salt

1 cup sour cream

1 15-ounce can black beans, rinsed and drained

½ cup corn kernels

2 scallions, chopped

1 jalapeño, diced

½ cup grated jack cheese

Black Out

To prevent canned black beans from turning the entire batter black, rinse them under cold water until the water runs clear. This removes the starchy, salty liquid they are packed in, which, if added with the beans, would not only color the batter, but also drastically alter the flavor and consistency of the finished quick bread. After rinsing, drain them well before folding into the batter.

1. Preheat oven to 350°F. Coat a 9" × 5" loaf pan with pan spray, and line the bottom and short sides with a strip of parchment.

2. In a large bowl, beat together butter and sugar until creamy and smooth. Add egg, and beat until creamy. Sift together all-purpose flour, cornmeal, baking powder, and salt, then add to butter mixture alternately with sour cream. Fold in beans, corn, scallions, jalapeño, and cheese.

3. Transfer batter to prepared pan; smooth the top. Bake 30 minutes. Reduce oven temperature to 325°F and bake 30 minutes longer, or until a pick inserted in the center comes out clean. Tent with foil if loaf browns too quickly.

4. Remove from oven and cool 10 minutes before removing from pan. Continue cooling on a rack.

Blackberry Bread

If you find luscious fresh berries, freeze them in a single layer until solid before adding them to this batter. It's the best way to prevent creating a loaf of purple bread.

INGREDIENTS | YIELDS 1 LOAF

3½ cups cake flour
1 teaspoon baking powder
1 teaspoon kosher salt
1 cup sour cream
1 tablespoon vanilla extract
Grated zest of 1 orange
1 cup (2 sticks) unsalted butter
1 cup granulated sugar
2 eggs
2 cups frozen blackberries

1. Preheat oven to 350°F. Coat a 9" × 5" loaf pan with pan spray, and line the bottom and short sides with a strip of parchment.

2. Sift together cake flour, baking powder, and salt. Set aside. Combine sour cream, vanilla, and orange zest. Set aside.

3. Beat together butter and sugar until smooth and creamy. Add eggs one at a time. Add the sifted dry ingredients alternately with the sour cream. Fold in blackberries.

4. Transfer batter to prepared pan; smooth the top. Bake 30 minutes. Reduce oven temperature to 325°F and bake 30 minutes longer, or until a pick inserted in the center comes out clean. Tent with foil if loaf browns too quickly.

5. Remove from oven and cool 10 minutes before removing from pan. Continue cooling on a rack.

Brazil Nut Bread

Big, buttery Brazil nuts are a welcome surprise in this sweet, dense loaf.

INGREDIENTS | YIELDS 1 LOAF

2 cups all-purpose flour

½ teaspoon ground allspice

½ teaspoon baking powder

½ teaspoon baking soda

½ teaspoon kosher salt

1 egg

1 cup brown sugar

1 teaspoon vanilla extract

1 cup buttermilk

1½ cups Brazil nuts, chopped

The Brazil Nut

Brazil nuts are seeds from an Amazon rain forest tree. They are commonly sold during the holidays, still encased in their hard, triangular shell. Inside, their creamy white center is mild and crunchy. Brazil nuts can also be found shelled in several good food stores (see Appendix B).

1. Preheat oven to 350°F. Coat a 9" × 5" loaf pan with pan spray, and line the bottom and short sides with a strip of parchment.

2. Sift together all-purpose flour, allspice, baking powder, baking soda, and salt. Set aside. Combine egg, brown sugar, and vanilla. Add the sifted dry ingredients to the egg mixture alternately with the buttermilk. Fold in nuts.

3. Transfer batter to prepared pan; smooth the top. Bake 30 minutes, until risen. Reduce oven temperature to 325°F and bake 30 minutes longer, or until a pick inserted in the center comes out clean. Tent with foil if loaf browns too quickly.

4. Remove from oven and cool 10 minutes before removing from pan. Continue cooling on a rack.

Brown Sugar Apple Bread

*Try this recipe with sweet and firm pears instead of apples for
a slightly different take on a classic combination.*

INGREDIENTS | YIELDS 1 LOAF

¾ cup (1½ sticks) unsalted butter
3 large apples, peeled, cored, and diced
1½ cups brown sugar
2 cups cake flour
1 teaspoon ground nutmeg
1 tablespoon baking powder
½ teaspoon kosher salt
2 eggs
⅔ cup buttermilk

1. Melt ¼ cup (½ stick) butter in a large sauté pan over medium heat. Add apples and ½ cup brown sugar. Cook, stirring, until apples are caramelized and tender, about 10 minutes. Set aside to cool.

2. Preheat oven to 350°F. Coat a 9" × 5" loaf pan with pan spray, and line the bottom and short sides with a strip of parchment.

3. Sift together cake flour, remaining brown sugar, nutmeg, baking powder, and salt. Cut in remaining stick of butter until the mixture resembles coarse meal. Whisk together eggs and buttermilk; add to flour mixture along with cooled apples. Mix until the batter just comes together.

4. Transfer batter to prepared pan; smooth the top. Bake 30 minutes, until risen. Reduce oven temperature to 325°F and bake 30 minutes longer, or until a pick inserted in the center comes out clean. Tent with foil if loaf browns too quickly.

5. Remove from oven and cool 10 minutes before removing from pan. Continue cooling on a rack.

Chocolate Fig Bread

Dark chocolate and figs are especially complementary in this bread when it is served warm.

INGREDIENTS | YIELDS 1 LOAF

2 cups all-purpose flour
¼ cup cocoa powder
1 cup granulated sugar
1½ teaspoons baking soda
½ teaspoon baking powder
¼ teaspoon kosher salt
½ cup (1 stick) unsalted butter, melted
1 egg
¾ cup milk
½ cup chocolate syrup
1 cup bittersweet chocolate chips
1½ cup dried figs, chopped

Figs

First brought to the American West by Spanish missionaries, the fig has an ancient past. There are many varieties, including the California Black Mission, Smyrna or Calimyrna, Adriatic, and Brunswick, to name a few. Dried figs should be plump and moist, but if they're not, plump them in water, juice, tea, or alcohol. Set them aside for a few hours to soak up the moisture, or do it quickly by boiling the liquid.

1. Preheat oven to 350°F. Coat a 9" × 5" loaf pan with pan spray, and line the bottom and short sides with a strip of parchment.

2. Sift together all-purpose flour, cocoa powder, sugar, baking soda, baking powder, and salt. Set aside. Whisk together melted butter, egg, milk, and chocolate syrup. Stir wet ingredients into dry, and mix until batter just comes together. Fold in chocolate chips and figs.

3. Transfer batter to prepared pan; smooth the top. Bake 30 minutes, until risen. Reduce oven temperature to 325°F and bake 30 minutes longer, or until a pick inserted in the center comes out clean. Tent with foil if loaf browns too quickly.

4. Remove from oven and cool 10 minutes before removing from pan. Continue cooling on a rack.

Coconut Lime Bread

The tropical essence of lime zest pairs perfectly with rich coconut in this exotic bread. Get creative and embellish it with a cup of chopped macadamia nuts or dried pineapple chunks.

INGREDIENTS | **YIELDS 1 LOAF**

½ cup (1 stick) unsalted butter

1¼ cups granulated sugar

Grated zest and juice of 4 limes, reserved separately

2 eggs

1½ cups cake flour

1 teaspoon baking powder

½ teaspoon kosher salt

½ cup sour cream

1½ cups shredded unsweetened coconut, lightly toasted

½ cup water

1. Preheat oven to 350°F. Coat a 9" × 5" loaf pan with pan spray, and line the bottom and short sides with a strip of parchment.

2. Beat butter and ¾ cup granulated sugar together until smooth and creamy. Add lime zest and eggs. Sift together cake flour, baking powder, and salt; add to butter mixture alternately with sour cream. Fold in coconut.

3. Transfer batter to prepared pan; smooth the top. Bake 30 minutes, until risen. Reduce oven temperature to 325°F and bake 30 minutes longer, or until a pick inserted in the center comes out clean. Tent with foil if loaf browns too quickly.

4. As the bread bakes, combine remaining ½ cup sugar, lime juice, and ½ cup water in a small saucepan, and bring to a boil over high heat. At the boil, remove from heat and set aside.

5. Remove finished bread from oven and cool 10 minutes before removing from pan. Drizzle with lime syrup and continue cooling on a rack.

Date Nut Bread

*This classic bread is perfect for breakfast, teatime, as an afterschool snack,
or in the middle of the night . . . which means it's perfect anytime.*

INGREDIENTS | YIELDS 1 LOAF

2 cups dried dates

1 tablespoon vanilla extract

1 cup boiling water

2 cups all-purpose flour

1 teaspoon freshly grated nutmeg

½ teaspoon cardamom

1 teaspoon baking powder

½ teaspoon kosher salt

1 egg, beaten

½ cup walnuts, chopped

½ cup pecans, chopped

½ cup almonds, chopped

¼ cup powdered sugar

1. Preheat oven to 350°F. Coat a 9" × 5" loaf pan with pan spray, and line the bottom and short sides with a strip of parchment. Combine dates and vanilla in a small bowl, add boiling water, and set aside for 30 minutes.

2. Sift together all-purpose flour, nutmeg, cardamom, baking powder, and salt. Make a well in the center and add egg, soaked dates, and all nuts. Mix together, transfer to prepared pan, and smooth the top. Bake 30 minutes, until risen. Reduce oven temperature to 325°F and bake 30 minutes longer, or until a pick inserted in the center comes out clean. Tent with foil if loaf browns too quickly.

3. Remove from oven and cool 10 minutes before removing from pan. Immediately dust the top generously with powdered sugar, and continue cooling on a rack.

Honey Rose Bread

Rose water, brought back to Europe from colonial India, was a hugely popular flavoring during the Victorian era. Today it can be found in any Indian or Middle Eastern market.

INGREDIENTS | YIELDS 1 LOAF

1 cup (2 sticks) unsalted butter

1 cup granulated sugar

4 eggs

1 tablespoon rose water

2 cups all-purpose flour

½ cup whole wheat flour

1 teaspoon baking powder

¼ teaspoon kosher salt

2 tablespoons milk

½ cup honey

Rose Sugar

You can use your own rose petals to make rose sugar. Gently wash petals and air dry, then stack in a glass jar between layers of granulated sugar. Be sure all petals are buried, then cover jar loosely with cheesecloth. Set aside at room temperature for 2 weeks, until petals release their moisture and oil into sugar. Remove petals and use rose sugar for tea, simple syrup, or baking.

1. Preheat oven to 350°F. Coat a 9" × 5" loaf pan with pan spray, and line the bottom and short sides with a strip of parchment.

2. Beat butter and sugar together until smooth and creamy. Add eggs one at a time, then rose water. Combine all-purpose flour, whole wheat flour, baking powder, and salt; add to butter mixture alternately with milk.

3. Transfer batter to prepared pan; smooth the top. Bake 30 minutes, until risen. Reduce oven temperature to 325°F and bake 30 minutes longer, or until a pick inserted in the center comes out clean. Tent with foil if loaf browns too quickly.

4. Remove from oven and cool 10 minutes before removing from pan. Gently warm honey and drizzle it over bread while still warm. Continue cooling on a rack.

Kuchen with Apricots

Moist and tender, this kuchen has a sweet, brown sugar surprise in the center.

INGREDIENTS | YIELDS 1 LOAF

1 cup dried apricots, chopped

½ cup orange liqueur

2½ cups cake flour

½ teaspoon ground cinnamon

¾ cup granulated sugar

1 teaspoon baking powder

½ teaspoon kosher salt

6 tablespoons (¾ stick) unsalted butter, cold

1 egg

¼ cup milk

½ cup sour cream

¼ cup (½ stick) unsalted butter, melted

⅔ cup brown sugar

Kuchen

Kuchen means "cake" in German, and there are an infinite number of variations for this recipe. In the United States, kuchen typically refers to a cake that is made by the cut-in method. This method, used also for biscuits, scones, and pie crusts, produces a crumb more tender than can be achieved by the creaming method. Frequently, the kuchen has a sweet filling or a streusel topping.

1. Combine apricots and orange liqueur; set aside to plump for at least 30 minutes. Preheat oven to 350°F. Coat a 9" × 5" loaf pan with pan spray, and line the bottom and short sides with a strip of parchment.

2. Sift together cake flour, cinnamon, granulated sugar, baking powder, and salt. Cut in cold butter until the mixture resembles coarse meal. Toss in apricots, and then make a well in the center of the mixture.

3. Whisk together egg, milk, and sour cream. Add to the flour mixture, and mix until a batter just comes together.

4. Transfer half the batter to prepared pan. Pour melted butter onto batter, sprinkle brown sugar evenly on top, then add remaining batter. Bake 20 minutes, until risen. Reduce oven temperature to 325°F and bake 30 minutes longer, or until a pick inserted in the center comes out clean. Tent with foil if loaf browns too quickly.

5. Remove from oven and cool 10 minutes before removing from pan. Cool on a rack.

Marmalade Bread

Typically made with orange marmalade, this recipe works equally well with lemon, tangerine, blood orange, or grapefruit varieties.

INGREDIENTS | YIELDS 1 LOAF

½ cup (1 stick) unsalted butter

1 cup granulated sugar

Grated zest and juice of 3 oranges, reserved separately

2 eggs

2 cups cake flour

1 teaspoon baking soda

½ teaspoon kosher salt

⅔ cup sour cream

1 teaspoon vanilla extract

1 cup orange marmalade

Making Marmalade

Marmalade is nothing more than citrus jam, and is easy to make. Combine the zest from 6–8 oranges or lemons with their juice and sugar to taste. (The amount of sugar will vary from ¼ cup to 3 or 4 cups depending on the fruit.) Boil, stirring, until the liquid is reduced and thick. (Be careful not to burn the jam.) Cool citrus jam completely, and store in the refrigerator. Now you can have a taste of sunshine whenever you want.

1. Preheat oven to 350°F. Coat a 9" × 5" loaf pan with pan spray, and line the bottom and short sides with a strip of parchment.

2. In a large bowl, beat together butter, sugar, and orange zest until creamy and smooth. Add eggs one by one. Sift together cake flour, baking soda, and salt; add to butter mixture alternately with sour cream. Stir in vanilla.

3. Transfer half the batter to prepared pan. Spread ¾ cup marmalade onto batter, top with remaining batter, and swirl briefly with a spoon. Bake 20 minutes, until risen. Reduce oven temperature to 325°F and bake 30 minutes longer, or until a pick inserted in the center comes out clean. Tent with foil if loaf browns too quickly.

4. Remove from oven and cool 10 minutes before removing from pan. Brush remaining marmalade across the warm crust, then continue cooling on a rack.

Oatmeal Raisin Bread

*Personalize this loaf to fit your mood with a variety of other
dried fruits or the addition of up to 1 cup of nuts.*

INGREDIENTS | YIELDS 1 LOAF

1¼ cups rolled oats (not quick cooking)

1 cup raisins

1 cup milk

1 teaspoon vanilla extract

2 eggs, beaten

6 tablespoons (¾ stick) unsalted butter, melted

2 cups all-purpose flour

1 teaspoon ground cinnamon

¼ cup brown sugar

2¼ teaspoons baking powder

½ teaspoon kosher salt

3 tablespoons granulated sugar

1. Combine 1 cup oats and raisins in a large bowl, add milk and vanilla, and soak for 30 minutes. Preheat oven to 350°F. Coat a 9" × 5" loaf pan with pan spray, and line the bottom and short sides with a strip of parchment.

2. Stir eggs and butter into the soaked oatmeal, and mix well. Sift together flour, cinnamon, brown sugar, baking powder, and salt; stir thoroughly into oats.

3. Transfer batter to prepared pan, top with remaining oats and granulated sugar, and bake 20 minutes, until risen. Reduce oven temperature to 325°F and bake 30 minutes, or until a pick inserted in the center comes out clean. Tent with foil if loaf browns too quickly.

4. Remove from oven and cool 10 minutes before removing from pan. Cool on a rack.

Pumpkin Nut Bread

A staple of fall, this bread is sure to keep out the autumn chill.

INGREDIENTS | YIELDS 1 LOAF

1 cup (2 sticks) unsalted butter

1½ cups brown sugar

4 large eggs

3 cups all-purpose flour

2 teaspoon baking powder

1 teaspoon ground cinnamon

1 teaspoon ground nutmeg

½ teaspoon ground ginger

¼ teaspoon ground cloves

½ teaspoon kosher salt

1 cup solid-pack pumpkin purée

½ cup milk

1 cup walnuts, toasted and chopped

⅓ cup granulated sugar

Pumpkin Purée

Any thick purée can be used to make this bread. Canned pumpkin is the most prevalent, but why not make your own? Peel and dice 2–3 cups of pumpkin, butternut squash, acorn squash, sweet potatoes, or yams. Toss in 1 tablespoon vegetable oil, then spread on a baking sheet in a single layer and roast at 450°F until tender and just golden, about 30 minutes. Purée in a food processor, then bake to your heart's content.

1. Preheat oven to 350°F. Coat a 9" × 5" loaf pan with pan spray, and line the bottom and short sides with a strip of parchment.

2. Beat butter and brown sugar together until smooth and creamy. Add eggs one at a time. Combine all-purpose flour, baking powder, cinnamon, nutmeg, ginger, cloves, and salt. Set aside. Stir together pumpkin and milk and add to creamed mixture alternately with flour mixture. Fold in walnuts.

3. Transfer batter to prepared pan. Sprinkle the top evenly with granulated sugar and bake 20 minutes, until risen. Reduce oven temperature to 325°F and bake 30 minutes longer, or until a pick inserted in the center comes out clean. Tent with foil if loaf browns too quickly.

4. Remove from oven and cool 10 minutes before removing from pan. Cool on a rack.

Pumpkin Seed Bread

The distinct flavor of pumpkin seeds sets this nutty bread apart.

INGREDIENTS | YIELDS 1 LOAF

2 cups pumpkin seeds (pepitos)

1¼ cups all-purpose flour

½ cup whole wheat flour

1 teaspoon baking powder

½ teaspoon baking soda

1 teaspoon kosher salt

4 eggs

½ cup sour cream

2 teaspoons vanilla extract

6 tablespoons (¾ stick) unsalted butter, melted

3 tablespoons brown sugar

1. Preheat oven to 350°F. Spread pumpkin seeds on a baking sheet in a single layer, and toast until lightly golden and fragrant, about 5 minutes. Seeds will plump and pop. Set aside to cool. Coat a 9" × 5" loaf pan with pan spray, and line the bottom and short sides with a strip of parchment.

2. Sift together all-purpose flour, whole wheat flour, baking powder, baking soda, and salt. Set aside. Beat together eggs, sour cream, vanilla, and butter, then add dry ingredients and mix in thoroughly. Fold in pumpkin seeds.

3. Transfer batter to prepared pan. Sprinkle the top evenly with brown sugar, and bake 20 minutes, until risen. Reduce oven temperature to 325°F and bake 30 minutes longer, or until a pick inserted in the center comes out clean. Tent with foil if loaf browns too quickly.

4. Remove from oven and cool 10 minutes before removing from pan. Cool on a rack.

Zucchini Bread

Use this recipe to unload your surplus zucchini harvest on unsuspecting neighbors.

INGREDIENTS | YIELDS 2 LOAVES

2 cups all-purpose flour

1 cup whole wheat flour

1 teaspoon ground cinnamon

¼ teaspoon baking powder

1 teaspoon baking soda

1 teaspoon kosher salt

3 eggs

1 cup canola oil

2 cups granulated sugar

2 cups grated zucchini

1 teaspoon vanilla extract

Veggie Breads

Like most recipes, zucchini bread can be embellished with additional ingredients. Dried fruits and nuts are nice, and add a touch of sweetness and a pleasant crunch. This bread also stands up well to a variety of vegetable additions. Try grating in a mixture of carrots, yellow squash, and red bell peppers, for a bread that looks like a slice of confetti. You can add up to an additional 1½ cups of extra ingredients.

1. Preheat oven to 350°F. Coat two 9" × 5" loaf pans with pan spray, and line the bottom and short sides with a strip of parchment.

2. Sift together all-purpose flour, whole wheat flour, cinnamon, baking powder, baking soda, and salt. Set aside. Beat together eggs, oil, sugar, zucchini, and vanilla. Mix dry ingredients thoroughly into wet.

3. Transfer batter to prepared pans, and bake 20 minutes, until risen. Reduce oven temperature to 325°F and bake 30 minutes longer, or until a pick inserted in the center comes out clean. Tent with foil if loaves brown too quickly.

4. Remove finished bread from oven and cool 10 minutes before removing from pans. Cool on a rack.

CHAPTER 17

Holiday Breads

Christmas Star

This is a big loaf, and will require your largest baking sheet, or your standard-sized sheet flipped upside down to avoid the pesky pan edges.

INGREDIENTS | YIELDS 1 LARGE LOAF, SERVES 8–10

2 cups warm water

3½ teaspoons active dry yeast (2 packages)

2 cups all-purpose flour

2 tablespoons grated nutmeg

¼ cup honey

1 tablespoon vanilla extract

1 cup milk

3 teaspoons plus 1 pinch kosher salt

¼ cup (½ stick) unsalted butter, softened

6–8 cups bread flour

1 egg

1 tablespoon water

Rich Holiday Breads

Celebrations take many forms around the world, but one universal element is the desire to bring out and share the best ingredients. This is why the fruit cake is the international celebration food. Before airplanes, preservatives, and Cryovac, fruits were a treat, available fresh only once or twice a year, then carefully preserved. Similarly, precious animal products were never wasted. And unless you were rich, expensive spices and nuts were reserved for special occasions.

1. To make the sponge, combine water and yeast, stir to dissolve, and set aside until foamy, about 10 minutes. Add all-purpose flour and beat 1 minute. Cover and let stand at room temperature 8–12 hours.

2. Add to the sponge the nutmeg, honey, vanilla, milk, 3 teaspoons salt, butter, and enough bread flour to make a soft dough. Turn onto a floured work surface and knead 8–10 minutes. Add flour only to reduce stickiness. Return to bowl, dust with flour, cover with plastic, and rise at room temperature until doubled in volume, about 1½ hours.

3. Line a large baking sheet with parchment. Turn risen dough onto a floured surface and divide into 9 equal portions. Shape each into a tight rope, no longer than 12", and lay each on the floured surface in a U shape. Arrange the Us in a circle on the prepared pan, with the curved middle of each strand facing the center, and the open ends facing out. Next, overlap the right arm of each U so that it is crossed over or under the strand next to it. Finally, take any 3 arms and form a tight, 3-strand braid (see Chapter 5). Repeat with remaining arms until the loaf resembles a six-pointed star. Cover loosely with plastic wrap and proof 30 minutes. Preheat oven to 375°F.

4. Whisk egg with 1 pinch salt and 1 tablespoon water; brush gently onto the top of the risen loaf. Bake until golden brown and hollow sounding, about 30–40 minutes. Cool completely on a rack before serving.

Christopsomo

This Greek Christmas bread is a sacred tradition in orthodox homes,
shaped with curled ends in an early form of the Holy Cross.

INGREDIENTS | YIELDS 2 LOAVES

Grated zest and juice of 4 oranges
¼ cup ouzo
1 cup golden raisins
1 cup dried figs, chopped
½ cup water
¾ cup granulated sugar
1¾ teaspoons active dry yeast
(1 package)
2–3 small pieces mastic gum
⅓ cup olive oil
1 tablespoon cinnamon
1 tablespoon ground anise seeds
¼ teaspoon ground cloves
¼ cup pine nuts, toasted
1 teaspoon plus 1 pinch kosher salt
3–4 cups bread flour
1 egg
1 tablespoon water

Mastic

Made from the dried sap (resin) of a tree, these "golden tears" are ground to a powder and added to impart a deliciously unique cedar-like essence. Mastic is common throughout the Middle East and Balkans in pastries and confectionary, including the original Turkish Delight, but is relatively unknown in the United States. It is also a popular breath freshener. (See Appendix B for sources.)

1. Combine orange zest and juice, ouzo, raisins, and figs. Set aside to plump overnight.

2. Combine water, 1 tablespoon sugar, and yeast. Stir to dissolve and let stand until foamy, about 10 minutes. Combine mastic gum with 1 teaspoon sugar; grind to a powder and add to yeast. Add soaked fruits and liquid, remaining sugar, oil, cinnamon, anise, cloves, pine nuts, 1 teaspoon salt, and enough bread flour to make a soft dough. Turn onto a floured work surface and knead 8–10 minutes. Add flour only to reduce stickiness. Return to bowl, dust with flour, cover with plastic, and rise at room temperature until doubled in volume, about 1½ hours.

3. Line a baking sheet with parchment. Turn risen dough onto a floured surface, divide into 2 equal pieces, and form into 2 ropes, each about 15" long. Place onto prepared pan in a cross (a Greek cross, like a plus sign), and curl each end into a clockwise spiral. Cover lightly with plastic and proof 30 minutes. Preheat oven to 350°F.

4. Whisk egg with 1 tablespoon water and 1 pinch salt; brush lightly onto the surface of the risen loaf. Bake until golden brown and hollow sounding, about 30–40 minutes. Cool on a rack.

Cranberry Eggnog Bread

There are few flavor combinations as evocative of the holidays as rum and nutmeg. Studded with winter rubies, this is a loaf fit for family and friends.

INGREDIENTS | **YIELDS 1 LOAF**

½ cup dark rum

1 cup orange juice

1½ cups dried cranberries

½ cup (1 stick) unsalted butter, melted

1 cup granulated sugar

2 eggs

1 vanilla bean, scraped

2 teaspoons rum extract

1½ cups all-purpose flour

2 teaspoons freshly grated nutmeg

2 teaspoons baking powder

½ teaspoon kosher salt

1 cup prepared eggnog

1. Combine rum, orange juice, and cranberries. Set aside to plump overnight.

2. Preheat oven to 350°F. Coat a 9" × 5" loaf pan with pan spray, and line the bottom and short sides with a strip of parchment.

3. In a large bowl, beat together butter and sugar until creamy and smooth. Add eggs one by one. Add vanilla bean and rum extract. Sift together all-purpose flour, nutmeg, baking powder, and salt; add alternately to butter mixture with eggnog. Fold in plumped cranberries and juice.

4. Transfer batter to prepared pan; smooth the top. Bake 30 minutes, until risen. Reduce oven temperature to 325°F and bake 30 minutes longer, or until a pick inserted in the center comes out clean. Tent with foil if loaf browns too quickly.

5. Remove from oven and cool 10 minutes before removing from pan. Continue cooling on a rack.

Danish Kringle

Shaped like a wreath, this loaf, made with both yeast bread and cut-in methods, makes a stunning holiday presentation.

Christmas Kringle

In Denmark, the kringle is a sweet or salty knotted bread, like a pretzel, available at bakeries all year long. In the United States, Danish-American communities have helped evolve the kringle into a sweet loaf stuffed with nuts or fruit that makes a special appearance during the Christmas season. Kringles can be filled with a variety of fruits or nuts, but pecan is the most popular in America.

1. Combine milk, sugar, and yeast. Stir to dissolve and let stand until foamy, about 10 minutes.

2. In a large bowl sift together all-purpose flour and ½ teaspoon salt. Cut in ½ cup (1 stick) cold butter until the mixture resembles coarse meal. Make a well in the center, add 1 egg and yeast mixture, and stir until the dough just comes together. Cover and set aside in the refrigerator to rise overnight (8–12 hours).

3. Beat pecans, brown sugar, and room temperature butter into a paste-like filling. Set aside.

4. Preheat oven to 375°F and line a baking sheet with parchment. Remove the risen dough from the refrigerator. Working on a floured surface, roll dough into a long rectangle, approximately 9" × 30", and about ½" thick. Spread pecan mixture down the center, then fold over the side edges to conceal the filling, overlapping the edges a bit and pinching to seal. Transfer to prepared pan, seam-side down, and form into a circle, connecting the two open ends. Cover loosely with plastic and rise 30 minutes.

5. Whisk together 1 egg, 1 pinch salt, and 1 tablespoon water. Brush gently onto the top of risen loaf. Bake until golden brown and hollow sounding, about 45–60 minutes. Cool completely on a rack before serving.

Easter Kulich

This Russian Easter bread is tall and regal, and is commonly served with pashka, a molded sweet cheese studded with more fruits. If you are short on #10 cans, bake this dough in two traditional loaf pans.

INGREDIENTS | **YIELDS 1 LARGE CYLINDRICAL LOAF, OR 2 TRADITIONAL LOAVES**

¼ cup golden raisins

¼ cup dark raisins

½ cup dark rum

1 cup milk, warmed

2–3 threads saffron

½ teaspoon granulated sugar

3½ teaspoons active dry yeast (2 packages)

4 egg yolks

1 cup (2 sticks) unsalted butter, softened

1 teaspoon plus 1 pinch kosher salt

1 vanilla bean, scraped

¼ cup skin-on almonds, toasted and chopped

¼ cup candied citrus zest

Grated zest and juice of 2 lemons, reserved separately

4–6 cups bread flour

2 cups powdered sugar, sifted

1. Combine raisins and rum and set aside to plump overnight.

2. Combine warmed milk and saffron; set aside for 10 minutes. Add sugar and yeast, stir to dissolve, and let stand until foamy, about 10 minutes.

3. Add soaked raisins and liquid, egg yolks, butter, 1 teaspoon salt, vanilla bean, almonds, candied zest, grated zest (reserve juice), and enough bread flour to make a soft dough. Turn onto a floured work surface and knead 8–10 minutes. Add flour only to reduce stickiness. Return to bowl, dust with flour, cover with plastic, and rise at room temperature until doubled in volume, about 1½ hours.

4. Use a church-key can opener to make three holes in the bottom of a #10 can. Coat the can with pan spray, and line the sides with a cylinder of parchment. Turn risen dough onto a floured surface and shape into an oblong loaf. Place end-first into prepared can, cover loosely with plastic, and proof 30 minutes. Preheat oven to 350°F.

5. Bake until golden brown and hollow sounding, about 45–60 minutes. Cool 10 minutes, remove loaf from the can, and cool completely on a rack.

6. Combine powdered sugar with lemon juice and 1 pinch salt; beat until smooth and creamy. Add more sugar or a touch of water as needed. Drizzle icing onto the top of cooling loaf, and let it drip down the sides. Decorate the top of the iced loaf with candied fruits.

Figgy Pudding Bread

Real figgy pudding is a more of a steamed cake than a quick bread, but this easy version is no less festive.

INGREDIENTS | YIELDS 1 LOAF

1½ cups dried figs, chopped
1 cup brandy
1 cup (2 sticks) unsalted butter
1 cup brown sugar
2 eggs
Grated zest of 2 lemons
2 cups cake flour
1 teaspoon ground nutmeg
½ teaspoon ground cinnamon
1 tablespoon baking powder
½ teaspoon kosher salt
⅔ cup buttermilk
1 cup walnuts, toasted and chopped

1. Combine figs and brandy. Set aside to plump overnight.

2. Preheat oven to 350°F. Coat a 9" × 5" loaf pan with pan spray, and line the bottom and short sides with a strip of parchment.

3. Beat together butter and brown sugar until creamy and lump-free. Add eggs, one by one, and lemon zest. Sift together cake flour, nutmeg, cinnamon, baking powder, and salt; add to butter mixture alternately with buttermilk. Fold in walnuts and plumped figs.

4. Transfer batter to prepared pan; smooth the top. Bake 30 minutes until risen. Reduce oven temperature to 325°F and bake 30 minutes longer, or until a pick inserted in the center comes out clean. Tent with foil if loaf browns too quickly.

5. Remove from oven and cool 10 minutes before removing from pan. Continue cooling on a rack.

German Stollen

This German Christmas bread is said to be formed in the shape of the baby Jesus wrapped in swaddling clothes.

INGREDIENTS | YIELDS 1 LOAF

¼ cup dried apricots

¼ cup dried dates

¼ cup dried figs

¼ cup golden raisins

¼ cup dried pineapple

1 cup brandy

Water, as needed

¼ cup milk

1¼ cups granulated sugar

1¾ teaspoons active dry yeast (1 package)

2 eggs

1 cup (2 sticks) unsalted butter, softened

¼ cup almond paste

Grated zest and juice of 1 lemon, reserved separately

Grated zest of 1 orange

1 vanilla bean, scraped

1 teaspoon plus 1 pinch kosher salt

1 teaspoon ground cardamom

1 teaspoon ground nutmeg

1 cup sliced almonds

3–5 cups bread flour

1 tablespoon water

½ cup powdered sugar, plus more as needed

Stollen

Thought to have originated in Dresden in the 1400s, this holiday staple was originally made without butter. Saxony aristocracy petitioned the pope to lift the traditional Advent ban on butter and milk, which he did, but only in Dresden. Ever since, stollen, also known as Dresden stollen, struzel, striezel, stutenbrot, and christstollen, has been a beloved holiday tradition.

1. Combine apricots, dates, figs, raisins, pineapple, and brandy. Add enough water to cover fruit, then set aside to plump overnight.

2. Combine milk, ¼ cup sugar, and yeast. Stir to dissolve and let stand until foamy, about 10 minutes. Add 1 egg, soaked fruit and liquid, ½ cup (1 stick) butter, almond paste, lemon zest, orange zest, vanilla bean, 1 teaspoon salt, cardamom, nutmeg, almonds, and enough bread flour to make a soft dough. Turn onto a floured work surface and knead 8–10 minutes. Add flour only to reduce stickiness. Return to bowl, dust with flour, cover with plastic, and rise at room temperature until doubled in volume, about 2 hours.

3. Line a baking sheet with parchment. Turn risen dough onto a floured surface and shape into a round loaf. Cover loosely with plastic wrap and rest 10 minutes. Flatten rested loaf into a disk about 2" thick, then fold in half so that the top edge stops 2" short of meeting the bottom edge. Place onto prepared pan, cover loosely, and proof 10 minutes. Preheat oven to 350°F.

4. Whisk remaining egg with 1 tablespoon water and 1 pinch salt; brush lightly onto the surface of the risen loaf. Bake until golden brown and hollow sounding, about 30–40 minutes. Cool on a rack.

5. Melt remaining butter and beat together with remaining granulated sugar, powdered sugar, and lemon juice. Brush all over cooled loaf. When hardened and dry, brush on another layer. Repeat sequence with remaining icing. Dust with powdered sugar before serving. Wrap and store at room temperature for 2 weeks, or freeze for 2 months.

Gingerbread

The holidays aren't complete without the smell of this bread wafting through the air. Lemon icing is the perfect accompaniment, setting off this rich, spicy bread with a pleasant tartness.

INGREDIENTS | SERVES 8–12

6 ounces (1½ sticks) butter, softened
¼ cup brown sugar
1 egg
1 cup molasses
1 cup hot water
2⅓ cups all-purpose flour
1½ teaspoons baking soda
½ teaspoon salt
1 teaspoon ground ginger
1 teaspoon cinnamon
1 teaspoon ground nutmeg
½ teaspoon ground cloves
2 1-pound boxes powdered sugar, sifted
Grated zest of 1 lemon
¼ cup lemon juice
1 tablespoon milk

1. Preheat oven to 350°F. Coat a 9" × 13" rectangular pan with pan spray. Beat together 4 ounces (1 stick) butter and brown sugar until smooth and creamy. Add egg and mix well. Combine the molasses and water; set aside. Sift together all-purpose flour, baking soda, salt, ginger, cinnamon, nutmeg, and cloves; add to butter mixture alternately with mixed molasses and water. Blend until smooth.

2. Transfer to prepared pan and bake at 350°F 30–40 minutes, until a pick inserted at the center comes out clean. Cool completely.

3. Cream together remaining butter and half the powdered sugar until smooth and lump-free. Slowly add lemon zest, juice, and milk. Blend until smooth. Add remaining sugar and beat until fluffy. Adjust consistency with more sugar or milk as needed. Spread frosting evenly onto gingerbread. To serve, slice in squares.

Hot Cross Buns

Thought to have originated in Tudor times, these sweet, spicy buns were only allowed by law to be sold on Good Friday and Christmas.

INGREDIENTS | **YIELDS 15–20 BUNS**

Grated zest and juice of 3 oranges

1 teaspoon vanilla extract

1½ cups dried currants

1¾ cups milk

1¾ teaspoons active dry yeast (1 package)

1 cup granulated sugar

4 eggs

½ cup (1 stick) unsalted butter

1 teaspoon ground mace

1 teaspoon plus 1 pinch kosher salt

3–6 cups bread flour

1 tablespoon water

Grated zest and juice of 1 lemon

1 tablespoon cream

3–4 cups powdered sugar, sifted

1. Combine orange zest and juice, vanilla, and currants. Set aside to plump overnight.

2. Combine milk, yeast, and 1 tablespoon sugar. Stir to dissolve and let stand until foamy, about 10 minutes.

3. Add soaked currants and liquid, remaining sugar, 3 eggs, butter, mace, 1 teaspoon salt, and enough bread flour to make a soft dough. Turn onto a floured work surface and knead 8–10 minutes. Add flour only to reduce stickiness. Return to bowl, dust with flour, cover with plastic, and rise at room temperature until doubled in volume, about 2 hours.

4. Line a baking sheet with parchment. Turn risen dough onto a floured surface. Shape into a rope, about 3" thick. Slice 2" pieces off the rope, then roll each into a tight ball. Place balls on the prepared pan, seam-side down. Dust with flour, cover loosely with plastic wrap, and proof 30 minutes. Preheat oven to 375°F.

5. Whisk together 1 egg, 1 pinch salt, and 1 tablespoon water; brush gently onto the top of the risen buns. With a serrated knife, slash a cross or X on the top of each roll. Bake until golden brown, about 20–30 minutes. Cool completely.

6. Beat together lemon zest and juice, cream, and enough powdered sugar to make a smooth, thick icing. Pipe or drizzle icing into the cross cut in the top of each bun.

King's Cake

Justice, faith, and power are symbolized by the purple, green, and gold sugars atop this famous New Orleans Mardi Gras loaf.

INGREDIENTS | YIELDS 1 LARGE LOAF TO SERVE 12–15 PEOPLE

1 cup milk

½ cup granulated sugar

3½ teaspoons active dry yeast (2 packages)

4 whole eggs

4 egg yolks

½ cup (1 stick) unsalted butter, softened

1 teaspoon grated nutmeg

Grated zest and juice of 2 lemons, reserved separately

1 teaspoon plus 1 pinch kosher salt

4–6 cups bread flour

1 small ovenproof toy, china doll, coin, or dried bean

1 tablespoon water

1 tablespoon milk

1 teaspoon vanilla

3–4 cups powdered sugar, sifted

Purple, green, and gold (or yellow) colored sugars

King's Cake

Traditionally prepared between Twelfth Night and Ash Wednesday, King's Cake is the center of every Mardi Gras celebration. A prize is baked into the cake for one lucky partygoer to find. In the 1800s, rich plantation owners would bake in a precious jewel. More commonly, the surprise is a small toy baby. The recipient is crowned king or queen, and is then obligated to host next year's party (not unlike the Mexican Rosca des Reyes tradition; see page 274).

1. Combine milk, 1 tablespoon sugar, and yeast. Stir to dissolve and let stand until foamy, about 10 minutes.

2. Add 3 eggs and yolks, remaining sugar, butter, nutmeg, lemon zest, 1 teaspoon salt, and enough bread flour to make a soft dough. Turn out onto a floured work surface and knead 8–10 minutes. Add flour only to reduce stickiness. Return to bowl, dust with flour, cover with plastic, and rise at room temperature until doubled in volume, about 2 hours.

3. Preheat oven to 325°F, and line a baking sheet with parchment. Working on a floured surface, roll into a 2-foot-long rope. Form the rope into a circle on the prepared pan, carefully pinching ends together. Gently press the toy into the dough. Cover loosely with plastic and rise again 45–60 minutes.

4. Whisk together 1 egg, 1 pinch salt, and 1 tablespoon water; brush gently onto the top of the risen loaf. Bake until golden brown and hollow sounding, about 45–60 minutes. Cool completely on a rack.

5. Beat together reserved lemon juice, milk, vanilla, and powdered sugar until thick and smooth. Spread icing on loaf, then divide the surface into thirds, and each with a different colored sugar. Slice and serve.

Anise Kugelhopf

Although this loaf originated in Austria, it has become synonymous with the Alsace region of France. Some say it was brought to France by the Austrian-born Marie Antoinette.

INGREDIENTS | **YIELDS 1 LARGE LOAF TO SERVE 8–12**

½ cup raisins

¼ cup Pernod

¼ cup water

2 cups milk

1 cup granulated sugar

3½ teaspoons active dry yeast (2 packages)

2 eggs

¼ cup (½ stick) unsalted butter, melted

¾ cup skin-on almonds, toasted and chopped

Grated zest of 2 lemons

2 tablespoons anise seed, toasted and crushed

1 teaspoon kosher salt

6 cups all-purpose flour

½ cup powdered sugar

The Kugelhopf Pan

Considered to be the inspiration for the bundt pan, the kugelhopf is often called turban-shaped, which is thought to be a reference to the Ottoman siege of Vienna in the sixteenth century. The shape of the pan has practical applications as well as symbolism. The center tube and decorative fluted indentations around the sides focus heat and promote even baking.

1. Combine raisins, Pernod, and water. Set aside to plump overnight.

2. Combine milk, 1 tablespoon sugar, and yeast. Stir to dissolve and let stand until foamy, about 10 minutes. Add soaked raisins and liquid, remaining sugar, eggs, butter, almonds, lemon zest, anise, salt, and enough flour to make a soft dough. Turn onto a floured surface and knead 8–10 minutes. Add flour only to reduce stickiness. Return to bowl, dust with flour, cover with plastic, and rise at room temperature until doubled in volume, about 2 hours.

3. Coat a kugelhopf, bundt, or angel food pan with pan spray, and dust with flour. Give the batter a stir, and turn it into prepared pan. Cover loosely with plastic and set aside to rise again 45–60 minutes. Preheat oven to 350°F.

4. Bake until golden brown and hollow sounding, about 30–40 minutes. Cool 10 minutes, remove loaf from pan, and cool completely on a rack. Dust with sifted powdered sugar before serving.

Panettone

This Italian bread hails from Milan, and has become a holiday favorite throughout the world, especially in Latin America, where it is a Christmas dinner staple. It also makes super French toast on Boxing Day.

INGREDIENTS | YIELDS 1 LARGE LOAF TO SERVE 12–15

1 cup golden raisins

½ cup dried currants

½ cup dried apricots, chopped

1 cup amaretto liqueur

1 cup milk

⅓ cup sugar

3½ teaspoons active dry yeast (2 packages)

5 eggs

1 cup (2 sticks) unsalted butter, softened

¼ cup candied orange peel, chopped

¼ cup candied lemon peel

Grated zest of 1 lemon

1 teaspoon plus 1 pinch kosher salt

4–6 cups bread flour

1 tablespoon water

1. Combine raisins, currants, apricots, and amaretto. Set aside to plump overnight.

2. Combine milk, 1 tablespoon sugar, and yeast. Stir to dissolve and let stand until foamy, about 10 minutes.

3. Add soaked fruits and liquid, remaining sugar, 4 eggs, butter, orange peel, lemon peel, lemon zest, 1 teaspoon salt, and enough bread flour to make a soft dough. Turn onto a floured surface and knead 8–10 minutes. Add flour only to reduce stickiness. Return to bowl, dust with flour, cover with plastic, and rise at room temperature until doubled, about 2 hours.

4. Coat a panettone pan or tall-sided cake pan (10" × 4") with pan spray, and line the bottom and sides with parchment. Turn risen dough onto a floured surface and shape into a large round loaf. Place bottom-first into prepared pan, cover loosely with plastic, and proof 45–60 minutes. Preheat oven to 325°F.

5. Whisk remaining egg with 1 tablespoon water and a pinch of salt; brush lightly onto the surface of the risen loaf. Bake until golden brown and hollow sounding, about 60–90 minutes. Cool 10 minutes, remove loaf from pan, and cool completely on a rack.

Rosca des Reyes

Rosca des Reyes means "spiral of kings," and it is meant to form a crown, like those worn by the Magi.

INGREDIENTS | **YIELDS 1 LARGE LOAF TO SERVE 12–15**

⅓ cup water

1½ cups sugar

1¾ teaspoons active dry yeast (1 package)

5 eggs

¾ cup (1½ sticks) unsalted butter

1½ teaspoons ground cinnamon

½ teaspoon anise seed, toasted and crushed

1 vanilla bean, scraped

½ cup dried mango, chopped

½ cup dried pineapple, chopped

½ cup dried papaya, chopped

½ cup candied cherries, chopped

Grated zest and juice of 1 lemon

½ teaspoon plus 1 pinch kosher salt

4–6 cups bread flour

1 small baby figurine

1 tablespoon water

Celebrating The Kings

The similarities between King's Cake and Rosca de Reyes are no coincidence. They are both consumed during the season between Epiphany and Mardi Gras. Also known as Twelfth Night, Epiphany commemorates the Magi's discovery of the baby Jesus after twelve nights of travel. This notable event in Christianity is symbolized not just by the crown shape of the bread, but by the figure baked into it, which must be "found" by eating.

1. Combine water, 1 tablespoon sugar, and yeast. Stir to dissolve and let stand until foamy, about 10 minutes.

2. Add 4 eggs, 1 cup sugar, butter, cinnamon, anise, and vanilla. In a separate bowl, mix together the mango, pineapple, papaya, cherries, and citrus zest and juice. Set aside ½ cup of this mixture to decorate the loaf, then add the remainder to the dough. Add salt and enough bread flour to make a soft dough. Turn onto a floured work surface and knead 8–10 minutes. Add flour only to reduce stickiness. Return to bowl, dust with flour, cover with plastic, and rise at room temperature until doubled, about 2 hours.

3. Preheat oven to 325°F, and line a baking sheet with parchment. Turn risen dough onto a floured surface, divide into 3 equal portions, and roll each into a rope, about 2 feet long. Form the ropes into a 3-strand braid (see Chapter 5) and place on prepared pan. Shape braid into a circle, carefully pinching the ends together. Gently press the figurine into the dough. Arrange the reserved fruits decoratively on top and press in gently. Cover loosely with plastic and rise again for 45–60 minutes.

4. Whisk together remaining egg, 1 pinch salt, and 1 tablespoon water. Brush gently onto the top of the risen loaf; dust with remaining sugar. Bake until golden brown and hollow sounding, about 45–60 minutes. Cool completely on a rack.

St. Lucia Bread

Celebrated throughout Scandinavia, the Feast of Saint Lucy celebrates light on what was, in the Julian calendar, the longest night of the year, December 13.

INGREDIENTS | YIELDS 1 LOAF

4–5 strands saffron

⅔ cup sugar

2 cups milk

3½ teaspoons active dry yeast (2 packages)

2 eggs

¾ cup (1½ sticks) unsalted butter

1 teaspoon ground cardamom

½ teaspoon plus 1 pinch kosher salt

1 cup raisins

4–6 cups bread flour

1 tablespoon water

Santa Lucia

A Sicilian martyr, Saint Lucy represents light, partly because she lost her sight in a particularly nasty episode with the Romans, yet was still able to see. On Saint Lucy's day, young girls dress in white and offer sweets while wearing a wreath of candles on their heads. For that reason, Saint Lucy's bread takes the form of a braided wreath, or crown.

1. Combine saffron and ½ teaspoon sugar in a mortar, and grind to a fine powder. Combine this saffron sugar with milk in a small saucepan and bring to a simmer over medium heat. Remove from heat and cool to room temperature. Then add yeast, stir to dissolve, and let stand until foamy, about 10 minutes.

2. Add 1 egg, butter, cardamom, ½ teaspoon salt, raisins, and enough bread flour to make a soft dough. Turn onto a floured work surface and knead 8–10 minutes. Add flour only to reduce stickiness. Return to bowl, dust with flour, cover with plastic, and rise at room temperature until doubled in volume, about 2 hours.

3. Preheat oven to 325°F, and line a baking sheet with parchment. Turn risen dough onto a floured surface, divide into three equal portions, and roll each into a rope, about 1"–2" thick. Form the ropes into a 3-strand braid (see Chapter 5) and place on prepared pan. Shape the braid into a wreath, carefully pinching ends together. Cover loosely with plastic and rise again 45–60 minutes.

4. Whisk together remaining egg, 1 pinch salt, and 1 tablespoon water. Brush gently onto the top of the risen loaf. Bake until golden brown and hollow sounding, about 35–45 minutes. Cool completely on a rack.

Tsoureki

Like many Greek and Middle Eastern recipes, this Easter bread is flavored with mastic and mahlab (or malhepi), which can be found in Greek and Middle Eastern markets or on the Internet (see Appendix B). Both may be replaced by orange zest, though with different effect.

INGREDIENTS | YIELDS 1 LOAF

½ cup milk

½ cup granulated sugar

1¾ teaspoon active dry yeast (1 package)

2 teaspoons mahlab (malhepi)

2–3 small pieces mastic (about 1 teaspoon)

4 eggs

¼ cup (1 stick) unsalted butter, softened

½ teaspoon plus 1 pinch kosher salt

4–6 cups bread flour

3 hard-boiled eggs, dyed red

1 tablespoon water

¼ cup raw sesame seeds

1. Combine milk, 1 tablespoon sugar, and yeast. Stir to dissolve and let stand until foamy, about 10 minutes.

2. Combine mahlab, mastic, and 1 teaspoon sugar in a mortar, grind to a fine powder, and add to yeast. Add 3 eggs, butter, ½ teaspoon salt, and enough bread flour to make a soft dough. Turn out onto a floured surface and knead 8–10 minutes. Add flour only to reduce stickiness. Return to bowl, dust with flour, cover with plastic, and rise at room temperature until doubled, about 2 hours.

3. Preheat oven to 325°F, and line a baking sheet with parchment. Turn risen dough onto a floured surface, divide into 3 equal portions, and roll each into a rope, about 1"–2" thick. Form the ropes into a 3-strand braid (see Chapter 5) and set on prepared pan. Tuck hard-boiled eggs into the braid, cover loosely with plastic, and rise again for 30 minutes.

4. Whisk together remaining egg, 1 pinch salt, and 1 tablespoon water. Brush gently onto the top of the risen loaf; sprinkle with sesame seeds. Bake until golden brown and hollow sounding, about 35–45 minutes. Cool completely on a rack.

CHAPTER 18

Breads in a Hurry

Banana Beer Bread

It may sound like a weird combination, but the yeastiness of the beer is complimented nicely by the sweet bananas.

INGREDIENTS | **YIELDS 1 LOAF**

1½ cups all-purpose flour

1 teaspoon ground allspice

1 cup brown sugar

½ teaspoon kosher salt

2 mashed bananas

4 tablespoons melted butter

1 12-ounce can or bottle of dark beer

Baking with Bananas

The best bananas for baking are overripe and black. Their starch has completely converted to sugar, which makes them awful to eat fresh, but perfectly moist and sweet for baking. If your bananas are headed in that direction but you don't have time to bake, remove them from their skin, place them in a plastic zipper bag, smash them up a little, and store in the freezer. They'll be ready at a moment's notice for your next banana bake-off.

1. Preheat oven to 350°F. Coat a 9" × 5" loaf pan with pan spray, and line the bottom and short sides with a strip of parchment.

2. In a large bowl, mix together flour, allspice, brown sugar, and salt; set aside. In another bowl combine mashed bananas, melted butter, and beer. Add wet ingredients to dry, and mix until just blended.

3. Transfer batter to prepared pan; smooth the top. Bake 30 minutes until risen. Reduce oven temperature to 325°F and bake 30 minutes longer, or until a pick inserted in the center comes out clean. Tent with foil if loaf browns too quickly.

4. Remove from oven and cool 10 minutes before removing from pan. Continue cooling on a rack.

Beer Bread

*Despite the speed with which it is made, this easy bread is quite delicious,
and is the perfect accompaniment to soups, stews, and meatloaf.*

INGREDIENTS | **YIELDS 1 LOAF**

3 cups self-rising flour

3 tablespoons granulated sugar

1 12-ounce can or bottle of beer

Self-Rising Flour

Because it already contains leaveners, self-rising flour is perfect for quick bread baking. You can also make your own self-rising flour by combining 3 cups flour with 4½ teaspoons baking powder and 1½ teaspoons kosher salt. Blend this mixture well before measuring. Self-rising flour is not a substitute for yeast.

1. Preheat oven to 350°F. Coat a 9" × 5" loaf pan with pan spray, and line the bottom and short sides with a strip of parchment.

2. In a large bowl, mix together flour, sugar, and beer until just blended. Transfer batter to prepared pan; smooth the top.

3. Bake 30 minutes, until risen. Reduce oven temperature to 325°F and bake 15 minutes longer. Tent with foil if loaf browns too quickly.

4. Remove from oven and cool 10 minutes before removing from pan. Continue cooling on a rack.

Pop-Up Bread

*For this recipe, recycle your coffee cans and their plastic lids. The "pop-up" refers
to the lid of the can, which is how you'll know the dough is finished rising.*

INGREDIENTS | **YIELDS 2 LOAVES**

1¾ teaspoons rapid rise yeast
(1 package)

½ cup powdered milk

¼ cup granulated sugar

1 cup water

¼ cup canola oil

½ teaspoon kosher salt

3½ cups bread flour

1. Using a church-key can opener, make 3 holes on the bottom of two 1-pound coffee cans. Coat with pan spray, and line with a cylinder of parchment.

2. In a large bowl combine all ingredients except flour. Stir until just combined. In a separate bowl, add flour, make a well in the center, and add yeast mixture. Stir to combine. Divide between two cans, replace lids, and set aside to rise until the lids pop off, about 2 hours. Preheat oven to 350°F.

3. Remove lids and bake until golden brown, about 30–40 minutes. Cool 10 minutes before removing loaves from cans, then cool completely on a rack.

Biscuit Dough Empanadas

*Made quick and easy by the use of refrigerated dough, these are just as good
if made using homemade biscuit, pie, or white bread dough.*

INGREDIENTS | **YIELDS 8 EMPANADAS**

2 tablespoons olive oil

1 small yellow onion, chopped

1 teaspoon honey

Grated zest and juice of 1 orange

Grated zest and juice of 1 lime

1 teaspoon chili powder

2 cups shredded turkey, chicken, or pork

1 teaspoon plus

1 pinch kosher salt

1 package refrigerated biscuit dough

1 egg

1 tablespoon water

4–6 cups canola oil

Empanadas

From the Spanish and Portuguese word *empanar*, which means roughly "to wrap," these tasty fried turnovers can be found wherever the Spanish and Portuguese languages have taken hold. The pastries often are savory, filled with local meat and produce, but they also can be filled with sweets and enjoyed for breakfast or dessert.

1. Heat oil in a large sauté pan over high heat. Add onions, reduce heat to medium, and cook until tender and golden, about 5 minutes. Add honey, orange and lime zest and juice, chili powder, turkey, and teaspoon of salt. Cook, stirring, 5 minutes, until liquids are reduced. Transfer from sauté pan to a baking sheet and set aside to cool.

2. Separate refrigerated dough into 8 sections. Working on a floured surface, press or roll each piece of dough into a disk ¼" thick.

3. Whisk egg with a pinch of salt and a tablespoon of water; brush around the edges of dough circles. Place a tablespoon of cooled turkey filling in the center of each circle, fold dough in half over filling, and seal edges by pinching firmly. Score edges with a fork or crimp decoratively. Place in freezer until firm, about 15 minutes.

4. In a sturdy, high-sided skillet, heat oil over high heat to 375°F. (Test oil's readiness by sticking in a skewer and watching for sizzling bubbles.) Add two or three empanadas to oil, being careful not to crowd. Cook until golden brown, about 2 minutes per side. Drain on paper towels before serving warm.

Boston Brown Bread Muffins

This bread is classically steamed in a can, which takes a while to cook. This quicker baked version has the same delicious flavor in half the time.

INGREDIENTS | YIELDS 12–15 MUFFINS

1 egg
⅓ cup canola oil
¼ cup brown sugar
⅓ cup molasses
¾ cup sour cream
¾ cup whole wheat flour
¾ cup all-purpose flour
½ cup cornmeal
1 teaspoon baking soda
½ teaspoon kosher salt
1 cup raisins

1. Preheat oven to 375°F. Coat a muffin pan with pan spray. Line with paper muffin cups. Combine egg, oil, brown sugar, molasses, and sour cream; mix thoroughly. Set aside.

2. Combine remaining ingredients in a large bowl. Stir to mix. Make a well in the center, pour the wet mixture into the dry, and stir together until just blended.

3. Fill muffin cups to the rim with muffin batter. Bake until risen and golden brown, about 20 minutes. A pick inserted into the middle muffin should come out clean. Cool in pan for 15 minutes before removing muffins.

Coffee Can Bread

This is a fun and easy bread to make with kids, or someone who just enjoys acting like a kid.

INGREDIENTS | YIELDS 1 LOAF

½ cup all-purpose flour
½ cup whole wheat flour
¼ cup wheat germ
¼ cup oatmeal
1 tablespoon baking powder
¼ teaspoon baking soda
½ teaspoon kosher salt
1 cup buttermilk

1. Coat a 1-pound coffee can with pan spray, and line it with a cylinder of parchment.

2. In a large bowl, mix together all ingredients except buttermilk. Make a well in the center, pour in buttermilk, and mix until just blended.

3. Transfer batter to prepared can, cover with can lid, and set aside to rest for 30 minutes. Preheat oven to 350°F.

4. Remove lid and bake 20 minutes. Reduce oven temperature to 325°F and bake 30 minutes longer. Tent with foil if loaf browns too quickly.

5. Remove from oven and cool 10 minutes before removing from can. Continue cooling on a rack.

Freezer Bread Sticks

Once these sticks are formed they will keep, unbaked and frozen, for several weeks. Break out 4–6 each night and bake them to order.

INGREDIENTS | **YIELDS 10–15 STICKS**

2–3 cups all-purpose flour

¼ teaspoon sugar

1¾ teaspoons rapid rise yeast (1 package)

1 tablespoon unsalted butter, melted

½ cup water

¾ teaspoon kosher salt

Olive oil, as needed

1. In a large bowl, combine 1 cup all-purpose flour, sugar, and yeast. Make a well in the center, add melted butter and water, and beat for 2 minutes. Add salt and enough remaining flour to make a soft dough.

2. Coat a baking sheet with pan spray. Turn dough onto a floured surface and cut into 10–15 equal pieces. Roll each into a thin rope. Place on prepared sheet and freeze until firm. When firm, transfer to a plastic zipper bag for prolonged freezer storage.

3. To bake, preheat oven to 350°F. Place sticks on a baking sheet lined with parchment. Brush with olive oil and bake until golden brown, about 5 minutes.

Garlic Toast

This is the easiest and best-loved way to jazz up an ordinary loaf of bread.

INGREDIENTS | **YIELDS 8–10 PIECES**

1 large loaf French or Italian bread

¼ cup extra-virgin olive oil or butter

1 clove garlic, minced

2 tablespoons fresh chives, chopped

1 teaspoon dried oregano

¼ cup Parmesan cheese, freshly grated

1. Preheat oven to 350°F, and coat a baking sheet with pan spray. Slice bread into 1" slices.

2. Heat oil in a small saucepan over low heat. Add garlic, chives, and oregano; simmer 2–3 minutes to blend flavors. Brush the flavored oil onto both sides of sliced bread, place on baking sheet, and sprinkle with Parmesan cheese. Bake for 5–10 minutes until well toasted, and serve hot.

Garlic Bread Americano
This beloved accompaniment to spaghetti and meatballs is thought to be derived from Italian bruschetta. Bruschetta today is typically made of toasted bread topped with olive oil, tomatoes, and herbs.

Ice Cream Scones

This improbable recipe is surprisingly delicious. Personalize the scone by adding frozen berries, nuts, zest, dried fruit, or chocolate chips.

INGREDIENTS | **YIELDS 6–8 SCONES**

3 cups self-rising flour
2½ cups melted vanilla ice cream
¼ cup granulated sugar

1. Preheat oven to 375°F. Line a baking sheet with parchment. Sift self-rising flour into a large bowl, and make a well in the center. Add melted ice cream and stir until just combined.

2. Turn the dough onto a lightly floured work surface and fold it 7 or 8 times, until it holds together. (This is not kneading.) Flatten the dough into a disk 1" thick. Cut the disk into 6–8 wedges, and place wedges on the prepared pan, evenly spaced.

3. Sprinkle the top of scones generously with sugar, then bake until golden brown, about 15 minutes.

Mayonnaise Biscuits

Rich and moist, these biscuits excel because of the mayonnaise. Once you try them, you may never make old-fashioned biscuits again.

INGREDIENTS | **YIELDS 8–10 BISCUITS**

2 cups self-rising flour
½ teaspoon granulated sugar
1¼ cups milk
¼ cup mayonnaise

1. Preheat oven to 375°F. Line a baking sheet with parchment. Sift self-rising flour and sugar into a large bowl, and make a well in the center. Mix 1 cup milk with mayonnaise, add to the dry ingredients, and stir until just combined.

2. Drop heaping spoonfuls (about ¼ cup) into the prepared pan, evenly spaced. Brush with remaining milk, then bake until golden brown, about 15 minutes. Serve warm.

Pita Chips

*These chips are great for dipping, but they also stand alone as a
terrific snack and a healthy alternative to potato chips.*

INGREDIENTS | SERVES 6–8

½ cup olive oil

2 cloves garlic, minced

½ teaspoon dried oregano

½ teaspoon dried basil

½ teaspoon dried rosemary

½ teaspoon black pepper

8 pita pocket bread rounds

½ cup grated Parmesan cheese

1. In a small bowl combine olive oil, garlic, oregano, basil, rosemary, and black pepper. Stir to combine and set aside to infuse flavors at least 30 minutes, or overnight.

2. Preheat oven to 400°F. Coat two or three baking sheets with pan spray. Cut each pita round into 8 triangles. Separate into individual triangles and spread on baking sheets in 1 layer. Brush oil mixture lightly onto each triangle and sprinkle with Parmesan cheese. Bake 5–7 minutes, until golden brown and crisp.

Quick Croutons

This is terrific way to use up leftover hamburger buns and the heels from sandwich loaves.

INGREDIENTS | YIELDS 2–4 CUPS

3 tablespoons olive oil

1 teaspoon garlic salt

1 tablespoon Italian herb blend

2–4 cups cubed day-old bread

Preheat oven to 350°F. In a large bowl mix together oil, garlic salt, and herbs. Add bread and toss quickly to coat. Spread onto dry baking sheet and toast until golden brown, about 5 minutes. Stir once or twice to promote even browning. Cool completely before serving.

Soda Pop Bread

Experiment with flavor by using any soda pop you like, except diet. The yeast needs real sugar to work quickly.

INGREDIENTS | YIELDS 1 LOAF

3 cups bread flour

1¾ teaspoons rapid rise yeast (1 package)

1 12-ounce can room-temperature soda pop

1. Preheat oven to 375°F. Coat a 9" × 5" loaf pan with pan spray, and line the bottoms and short sides with a strip of parchment.

2. Combine flour and yeast in a large bowl, and mix thoroughly. Slowly stir in soda pop; mix well. Transfer to prepared pan and bake until golden brown and hollow sounding, about 30–40 minutes. Cool 10 minutes before removing loaf from pan, and cool completely on a rack.

Spoon Bread

Spoon bread is more closely related to soufflés than it is to bread. It is delightfully light and flavorful, and makes a terrific change of pace from the usual dinner roll.

INGREDIENTS | SERVES 4–6

1 cup cornmeal

1 teaspoon kosher salt

2 cups water

1 egg yolk

1¾ cups milk

1 tablespoon unsalted butter, melted

2 egg whites

1. Preheat oven to 350°F. Coat a 9" × 5" loaf pan with pan spray.

2. Combine cornmeal, salt, and water in a medium saucepan. Bring to a boil, stirring frequently. At the boil, reduce heat to low and cook, stirring continuously, 3–5 minutes until very thick. Remove from heat.

3. In a separate bowl whisk together yolk, milk, and melted butter, then stir into cooling cornmeal. Whip whites until stiff and gently fold in.

4. Transfer to prepared pan and bake 30 minutes, until golden brown. Serve warm.

Wampus Bread

Fried like fritters, this bread stands out with the savory addition of potato and onion.

INGREDIENTS	YIELDS 1 LOAF

2–3 cups canola oil

2 cups cornmeal

1 cup all-purpose flour

1 teaspoon granulated sugar

1 teaspoon kosher salt

1 tablespoon baking powder

1 cup milk

1 small yellow onion, chopped

1 medium russet potato, peeled and grated

1. In a large, high-sided, heavy skillet, heat oil to 375°F.

2. In a large bowl, mix together cornmeal, all-purpose flour, sugar, salt, and baking powder. Make a well in the center. Add milk, onion, and potato to the dry ingredients; mix until just combined.

3. Drop batter by heaping spoonfuls (about ¼ cup) into hot oil, and cook until golden brown, about 1–2 minutes per side. Drain on paper towels and serve hot.

Wampus History

A wampus is a half wildcat, half woman creature from Cherokee mythology, and the tale is well known throughout the Appalachians, eastern Tennessee, Kentucky, and Virginia. Wildcats run very fast, with their legs askew, a fact that gave rise to the term "caddy," "kitty," or "catty wampus," meaning crooked or out of alignment. How this translated to fried dough is open to speculation, although these fried dough balls are anything but straight.

Glossary

Add-ins: A term referring to garnishes folded into dough and batter, such as chocolate chips, nuts, or raisins.

Adding alternately: A mixing technique in which dry and wet ingredients are divided into 3 or 4 portions each and added to a batter, a little at a time, alternating first dry, then wet. The purpose is even and thorough incorporation.

Amaretti: Crunchy Italian macaroon cookies flavored with bitter almonds.

Amaretto: An Italian liqueur with the distinctive flavor of bitter almonds.

Angel food pan: A round cake pan with a hollow interior tube that allows heat to penetrate the batter from the middle. The resulting cake has a hole in the center, like a giant doughnut.

Anise: An annual flowering herb, related to parsley. The seeds have a distinctive licorice flavor, which is used in liqueurs, candies, sauces, and cosmetics.

Annatto: Derived from the seed of the achiote tree, this red spice is used as a coloring for butter, cheese, candies, oils, stocks, and sauces throughout Central American, Mexican, and Philippine cuisines.

Antioxidants: Molecules that slow oxidation of other molecules. Oxidation can produce free radicals, which trigger chain reactions that damage cells. In addition to preventing these reactions, antioxidants can inhibit them, once begun.

Balsamic: An Italian vinegar made since the Middle Ages from the Trebbiano grape, and aged for as long as 25 years.

Blanch: To boil briefly, then submerge in ice water to halt cooking. The process is used to loosen the skin and intensify the color of vegetables and fruits. Also referred to as parboiling.

Bread flour: Flour containing less starch and more protein than all-purpose flour, perfect for bread making, when a strong elastic dough structure is needed.

Buckle: Similar to a coffee cake, with fruit added to the batter, and streusel added to the top.

Buckwheat: The seed from a plant in the rhubarb family, ground into flour or cooked the same way as rice, in which case it is called "kasha."

Cajun seasoning: A blend of herbs and spices that typically includes garlic, onions, chilies, pepper, and mustard.

Cake flour: A soft flour containing less protein and more starch than all-purpose flour, perfect for cakes and other delicate baked goods that don't need a strong, elastic dough structure.

Candied ginger: Gingerroot, cooked in sugar syrup and coated in sugar; used in baked goods.

Capsaicin: The compound found in chilies that gives them their fiery heat.

Caramelized: To cook food until the sugar, naturally occurring or added, darkens to an amber "caramel" color. Caramelization brings out the food's deep, sweet, rich flavors.

Cassis: A black currant berry used to make syrup and liqueur.

Cheesecloth: A fine linen mesh cloth, traditionally used in cheese making to strain whey from curds. Used by chefs for fine straining of all foods, as well as covering, wrapping, or steeping foods.

Chutney: A chunky condiment from Southern Asia and India, sometimes cooked and jam-like, made with fruits or vegetables and often spiced with chilies.

Citron: A large citrus fruit use mainly for its thick peel, which is utilized for its oil as well as candied for use in baked goods.

Clarified butter: Pure butterfat, made by melting butter and removing the solids and salts. The lack of salts and solids allows the fat to withstand higher temperature.

Clarify: The term means "to clear," and refers to removing cloudy sediment.

Clotted cream: Thick cream from unpasteurized milk. Also known as Devonshire cream.

Cognac: A fine, double-distilled brandy from the town Cognac and its surrounding region on the southwest coast of France.

Cointreau: An orange-flavored brandy made in France.

Confectioners' sugar: Another name for powdered sugar.

Creaming: A term used to describe the blending of two ingredients into a creamy, smooth, paste-like texture.

Crumble: A dessert also known as a crisp, consisting of fruit with a streusel topping.

Currants: Tiny raisins made from the miniature zante grape. Do not confuse them with red, white or black currants, which are small berries used for preserves, pastries, and the liqueur cassis. Also known as zante currants.

Curry powder: A spice blend originated by the British during their colonial rule of India, so they could bring home the flavor of the regional curry dishes. The flavor of the powder found in supermarkets is fairly generic, but throughout India and other parts of Asia, there are dozens of unique curry sauce variations.

Cut in: A method of incorporating fat into dry ingredients by breaking it into small pieces. With heat, moisture is released from the fat, creating a flaky texture. Used in recipes such as biscuits and pie dough.

Durum: A strain of wheat, very high in protein, used to make semolina flour.

Egg wash: A glaze made from egg, sometimes with added water, milk, or cream, used to promote browning of pastry and bread crust.

Emulsified: The blending of two ingredients by suspension of small globules of one inside the other, so that the resulting blend becomes one homogenous substance.

Fennel: The edible bulb, leaves, and seeds from an aromatic vegetable with a subtle licorice flavor. Known as "finnocio" in Italian, fennel is sometimes misnamed "sweet anise" in American markets, even though anise is a completely different plant species.

Feta: Fresh Greek cheese made from sheep's or goat's milk. It is white and crumbly, and stored in a salty brine.

Foam: A culinary term for anything with air whipped into it; usually refers to eggs, egg yolks, or egg whites.

Folding: A mixing method used to combine two substances of different texture, usually a dense batter and a foam of eggs or cream. The gentle motion of folding, as apposed to beating or stirring, is mean to prevent light airy mixtures from deflating, which would inhibit leavening or reduce the airy quality of the finished product.

Food mill: A tool used to grind and press cooked food through small holes in preparation for purée.

Fuji: A crisp, sweet Japanese apple variety introduced in the 1960s, popularized in the United States in the 1980s.

Gala: A New Zealand apple variety, developed in the 1920s.

Garam masala: The most common spice blend from Northern India. The word *garam* means "warm" or "hot." While the blend can be spicy, the name denotes the toasting of the spices prior to grinding.

Ghee: A clarified butter used in Indian cuisine. All the moisture is evaporated, and the fat browns and takes on a nutty flavor.

Giandujia: Milk chocolate flavored with hazelnuts.

Gluten: The protein in wheat endosperm that promotes elasticity in bread dough. When moistened and agitated, gluten proteins tighten, creating a smooth, firm dough that can stretch to hold the gas of fermentation.

Gluten flour: High protein, hard-wheat flour in which most of the starch has been extracted, leaving a very high gluten content. Used to increase gluten content in bread recipes. Also known as vital wheat gluten.

Gorgonzola: Commonly referred to as a blue-vein cheese, this Italian cow's-milk cheese has veins that appear more green than blue. Made since the Middle Ages, Gorgonzola can be creamy, crumbly, or firm. Its piquant flavor comes from the addition of bacteria, added and allowed to germinate into mold.

Grana: Hard, grainy cheese, such as Parmesan or Romano, used for grating.

Gruyère: A nutty, semi-firm cow's-milk cheese from Switzerland.

Herbes de Provence: A blend of herbs commonly used in Mediterranean cuisine, including lavender, thyme, sage, marjoram, basil, rosemary, fennel, and savory.

Hors d'oeuvre: A dish served outside the main meal as an appetizer.

Horseradish: A spicy root used as a condiment, grated fresh and mixed with cream or preserved in vinegar.

Infuse: To steep two foods or flavors together.

Instant-read: A thermometer designed to determine the internal temperatures of food.

Italian seasoning: A spice and herb blend commonly used in Italian recipes, including fennel, rosemary, basil, and oregano.

Julienne: A classic knife-cut that looks like long, thick matchsticks.

Kalamata: Greek black olives marinated in wine and olive oil.

Kamut: An ancient strain of wheat, thought the be one of the original strains of grain. Found in Egyptian tombs, kernels of this grain were brought to the United States, where it is currently cultivated. It is high in protein, and much larger in size than modern wheat.

Kasha: See Buckwheat.

Kosher: Food that conforms to strict Jewish law, prepared under the supervision of a rabbi, and given the kosher seal.

Legumes: Dried beans from seed pods that split open along the side when ripe. Legume varieties include soybeans, peas, garbanzo beans, and peanuts.

Lemon curd: A tart lemon custard used as a spread or a filling.

Macerate: To soak food, usually fruit, in liquid to infuse flavor.

Masa harina: Flour made from dried hominy corn, used for corn tortillas and tamales.

Mascarpone: An Italian triple cream cheese, soft like clotted or sour cream, and mild in flavor.

Millet: Known mainly as bird seed in the United States, this tiny, high-protein grain is popular throughout Asia and Africa, and used for breads, pilaf, and porridge.

Mortar: A bowl, usually made of ceramic or stone, into which spices, herbs, vegetables, and pharmaceuticals are put to be crushed by a pestle, a hard instrument shaped like a small baseball bat.

Microplane: A fine grater used for citrus zest and grana cheeses. The tool was originally a carpenter's rasp used for sanding wood.

Millet: A tiny, bland grain packed with protein, which can be boiled like rice or ground into a flour.

Nigella: A smoky, peppery spice used in Indian cuisine, often referred to as black cumin or black onion seeds, although unrelated to both.

Nutella: A sweet spread from Italy made from ground hazelnuts and milk chocolate. The product was first developed in World War II as a way to extend rationed chocolate.

Oat: Available as groats, rolled, quick cooking, and steel cut, oats are known as one of the most nutritious grains. High in soluble fiber, vitamins B1, B2, and E, oat bran is generally believed to reduce cholesterol.

Old Bay: A spice blend from Chesapeake Bay, used to season seafood, consisting of celery seeds, bay, mustard, cinnamon, and ginger.

Organic: Foods raised, grown, and manufactured without artificial ingredients, preservatives, hormones, antibiotics, pesticides, fertilizers, radiation, or food additives.

Panella: A fresh, unaged Mexican cheese, fairly bland and firm, similar to paneer.

Pain de mie: A dense white sandwich bread from France.

Parchment: Heavy paper that withstands heat, water, and grease; used to line pans and wrap foods.

Pastry blender: A U-shaped tool consisting of several wires with a handle, used to cut fat into dry ingredients. (See Cut in.)

Pimentos: Sweet red peppers, available fresh in limited areas in late summer, readily available peeled and preserved in a brine. Pimento peppers are the basis for paprika, and are stuffed into green Spanish olives.

Pink peppercorns: Unrelated to white and black peppercorns, these dried berries come from ornamental trees native to Brazil.

Purée: Any food pulverized to a smooth paste of varying consistencies.

Quinoa: An ancient grain of the Incas, and one of the few vegetable sources of complete protein.

Rancidity: Oxidation of oil that results in foul flavor and odor.

Reduce: A culinary term meaning to cook the water out of a dish, reducing its volume, intensifying its flavor, and thickening its sauce.

Romano: An Italian grana cheese from Rome. Pecorino Romano is made from sheep's milk, while others can be made from goat's or cow's milk.

Roquefort: A French blue cheese made specifically from sheep's milk, exposed to *Penicillium roqueforti* mold spores, and aged in limestone caves in southwestern France.

Roux: A thickening agent made with equal parts melted fat (usually butter) and flour.

Rye: This sturdy grass was historically given to the lower classes, while wheat, with much higher gluten content, was reserved for the rich. Closely related to barley and wheat, rye is also available rolled and as rye berries, in which the grain is whole with the bran removed.

Sauté: To cook food quickly, over high heat, constantly stirring for even browning. The term means "to jump"; sauté pans are designed with a curved lip, making constant motion as easy as a flick of the wrist.

Semolina: Made from protein-rich durum wheat, this coarse flour is traditionally used for pasta. It resembles, and is often mistaken for, cornmeal.

Shallots: A milder cousin of the onion consisting of a few small bulbs that grow together, with a brown, papery skin.

Simple syrup: A pastry staple ingredient, made by boiling equal parts sugar and water. Used for moistening cakes, sweetening sauces and fruit purées, and as a recipe ingredient.

Sofrito: A blend of herbs, spices, chilies, onions, and garlic, used to season various dishes in the cuisines of Spain, Italy, Mexico, Cuba, and Puerto Rico. Recipes are similar, but vary from region to region, with regionally specific ingredients.

Spelt: This ancient strain of wheat, native to Southern Europe, is protein-rich and suitable for use as flour, pilaf, and porridge.

Sponge: A thin pre-dough or yeast batter that is made prior to making bread in order to prolong fermentation for improved flavor and texture.

Star anise: A potent anise-flavored spice from the star-shaped fruit of an Asian evergreen tree.

Stone fruit: A tree fruit that contains a pit, or stone, such as peaches, apricots, cherries, and plums.

Sweet anise: Another name for fennel, though true anise is unrelated.

Tabasco: A small red pepper from the Mexican state of Tabasco, grown in Louisiana specifically for use in the pepper sauce of the same name.

Tahini: A paste made of ground sesame seeds.

Tandoor: Used in Indian cuisine, this cylindrical clay charcoal oven cooks food at extremely high temperatures, retaining moisture, flavor, and nutritional benefits.

Teff: This tiny grain from Africa is high in protein, calcium, and iron, and is cooked similar to rice, as well as ground into flour for breads.

Triple sec: A clear orange-flavored liqueur.

Turbinado: Light brown coarse sugar, also known as raw sugar.

Turmeric: A spice derived from the root of a plant in the ginger family, used for its bitter flavor and bright yellow color.

Vanilla: The seed pod of a climbing orchid (*vanilla planifolia*), vanilla has been treasured for centuries. Look for beans that are thick and tough but pliable. To use vanilla beans, pound them first before splitting them lengthwise to crush the millions of inner mini-seeds and activate as much oil as possible. Once scraped, spent pods can be stored in sugar or steeped in rum to harness as much of the oil as possible.

White pepper: The same berry as the black peppercorn, allowed to ripen and dry, resulting in a slightly hotter flavor.

Zante currants: Tiny raisins made from dried miniature seedless grapes.

Zest: The colorful outermost rind of a citrus fruit, containing a high concentration of the essential oils and flavor compounds that flavor the fruit itself.

Zester: A small tool designed to strip the aromatic, colorful, oil-rich skin from citrus fruit.

Internet Resources

Bakeware

KitchenEmporium.com
Offers a large selection of mini pans, including bundt, muffin, pie, tart, and popover pans, all available in several materials. In addition, this site offers appliances, cookbooks, coffee, tea, and wine products.

Kitchenu.com
Offers paper pans, silicone pans, and fantastically shaped specialty pans.

KingArthurFlour.com
Offers a huge selection of bakeware, including mini pans of all kinds, seasonal pans, as well as bake-and-give paper pans.

Pans.com
Offers cookware, utensils, small appliances, and bakeware made from several materials, including silicone, aluminum, nonstick, cast iron, and glass.

Ingredients

BarryFarm.com
Provides candied lemon and citron, as well as more unusual candied tropical fruits.

Bulkfood.net
A fantastic assortment of extracts, including strawberry, black walnut, and maple.

GourmetShopper.com.au
Offers lots of spices and flavors, including malhab and sumac.

GreekInternetMarket.com
A wonderful source for Mediterranean ingredients, including mastic gum.

HomeGrownHarvest.com
Provides a variety of grains, seeds, nuts, beans, and even bread machines and grain mills.

KingArthurFlour.com
Not just bakeware, King Arthur carries a wide selection of baking ingredients, including flours, chocolate baton (also called chocolate sticks), and candied lemon and orange peel.

OliveNation.com
Offers some of the finest olive oils, coffee, sea salts, and other pantry items from traditional farmers in Italy and around the world.

TheSpiceHouse.com
Offers a great variety of spices, plus extracts including coffee, almond, chocolate, and vanilla.

Index

Note: Page numbers in **bold** indicate recipe category lists.

We Have EVERYTHING® on Anything!

With more than 19 million copies sold, the Everything® series has become one of America's favorite resources for solving problems, learning new skills, and organizing lives. Our brand is not only recognizable—it's also welcomed.

The series is a hand-in-hand partner for people who are ready to tackle new subjects—like you!

For more information on the Everything® series, please visit *www.adamsmedia.com*

The Everything® list spans a wide range of subjects, with more than 500 titles covering 25 different categories:

Business	History	Reference
Careers	Home Improvement	Religion
Children's Storybooks	Everything Kids	Self-Help
Computers	Languages	Sports & Fitness
Cooking	Music	Travel
Crafts and Hobbies	New Age	Wedding
Education/Schools	Parenting	Writing
Games and Puzzles	Personal Finance	
Health	Pets	